Passing the Award in
Education and Training

About the authors

Andrea McMahon has been training teachers since 1996 and is based at Newham College of Further Education where she teaches and manages the portfolio of teacher training courses and is co-ordinator of the Professional Development Centre. She holds an MA in Teaching English as a Foreign Language, a PGCE and ESOL specific teacher training qualifications.

Clare Tyrer is based at Newham College of Further Education, where she delivers the CELTA/PTLLS and Level 3 Award in English for Language and Literacy Teaching. She has QTLS status and holds an MA in English Language Teaching, a PGCE and ESOL specific teacher training qualifications.

Passing the Award in
Education and Training

Andrea McMahon
Clare Tyrer

NIACE The National Voice for Lifelong Learning

Published by the National Institute of Adult Continuing Education
(England and Wales)
21 De Montfort Street
Leicester LE1 7GE

Company registration no. 2603322
Charity registration no. 1002775

NIACE is the National Institute of Adult Continuing Education, the national voice for lifelong
learning. We are an internationally respected development organisation and think-tank,
working on issues central to the economic renewal of the UK, particularly in the political
economy, education and learning, public policy and regeneration fields.

www.niace.org.uk

For details of all our publications, visit http://shop.niace.org.uk

Follow NIACE on Twitter: @NIACEhq
@NIACECymru (Wales)
@NIACEbooks (Publications)

Cataloguing in Publications Data
A CIP record for this title is available from the British Library

978-1-86201-836-5 (Print)
978-1-86201-837-2 (PDF)
978-1-86201-838-9 (ePub)
978-1-86201-839-6 (Kindle)

All websites referenced in this book were correct and accessible at the time of going to press.

The views expressed in this publication are not necessarily endorsed by the publisher.

Printed in the UK by Charlesworth Press.
Designed and typeset by Patrick Armstrong Book Production Services.

Contents

Acknowledgements

We would like to thank David Shaw at NIACE for giving us the opportunity to write this book. We would especially like to thank the following people for their understanding and support:

Rashida Adam
Beatrice Adusei
Farah Akhtar
Ivy Anderson
Clive Ansell
Joanne Bailey
Shahnaz Begum
Patrick Burke
Martin Compton
Vidjea Gaikwad
Wendy Gibson
Richard Harris
Nuvit Hussein
Tonia Irving
Keith Layfield
Ruby Manku
Ross Morrison McGill
Jo Newland
Rebeka Rangelov
Stephen Roberts
John Sutter
Jo Swindells
Sindu Vijayan
Mark Vivian
Benita Volney
Jeanette Whyman
Shaun Wilden

Introduction

The aims of this chapter are to:

❭ clarify the features of this book

❭ explain the main components of the Level 3 Award in Education and Training

❭ outline possible future development routes

WHO IS THIS BOOK FOR?

This book is designed for those who are, or who have an interest in, working in the further education and skills sector. You do not need to be currently teaching but may wish to gain an insight into the different skills and knowledge required to become an effective practitioner. This book covers:

❭ the roles and responsibilities of a teacher
❭ key legislation relating to the further education and skills sector
❭ motivating and managing learning
❭ identifying and catering for individual needs
❭ how to plan effectively
❭ teaching and learning strategies, including working with ICT
❭ assessment and evaluation methods
❭ planning, delivering and evaluating a microteaching session
❭ how to support learners
❭ the importance of functional skills
❭ teaching with technology
❭ some teaching and learning ideas

THE LEVEL 3 AWARD IN EDUCATION AND TRAINING

The Level 3 Award in Education and Training is not a full teaching qualification; it provides an introduction to teaching. It replaces the Level 3/4 award Preparing to Teach in the Lifelong Learning Sector (PTLLS) and is worth 12 credits.

There are six units: three Education and Training units and three Learning and Development units. Unit 301: Understanding roles, responsibilities and training, worth three credits, is the only mandatory unit.

The different units are outlined overleaf.

Education and Training units

	Unit	Title	Credit
Group A	301	Understanding roles, responsibilities and relationships in education and training	3
Group B	302	Understanding and using inclusive teaching and learning approaches in education and training	6
Group C	305	Understanding assessment in education and training	3

Learning and Development units

	Unit	Title	Credit
Group B	303	Facilitate learning and development for individuals	6
Group B	304	Facilitate learning and development in groups	6
Group C	306	Understanding the principles and practices of assessment	3

It is possible to do both the units from the Education and Training module or mix and match if the learning provider allows this. For example, you can opt for units 302 and 306. Alternatively, you can select two additional units from the Learning and Development units to make 12 credits depending on the context in which you are working. However, you must do the mandatory unit 301, a unit from group B and a unit from group C to be eligible for the Award.

If you have already achieved some Learning and Development units, you should be able to carry them forward: check with the learning provider for further clarification. The learning outcomes of each chapter are mapped to the units of the Award in Education and Training which will help you when you come to writing your assignments.

FEATURES OF THE BOOK

This book is written with new teachers in mind. We appreciate that if you are new to the further education and skills sector, the amount of jargon you will come across can make it seem daunting. We have, therefore, tried to make this book as accessible as possible. At the back of the book we have provided a glossary of terms and a list of common acronyms that you may come across in your teaching, assessing or learning support role.

For clarity, we have generally used the word *teacher*, although we recognise that there are terms which describe a similar role: instructor, trainer and facilitator, for example. We have also used the word *learner* to describe the individual studying on a learning programme, to provide a consistent point of reference.

Each chapter of the book follows a similar pattern. As teacher trainers currently working in the sector, we wanted to keep the content as practical as possible. There is some reference to theory but it is always related to practice; in each chapter there are tasks for you to complete. These are to get you thinking about the topic and considering how they relate to your own context. At the end of each chapter there is a 'talking point' to encourage you to reflect on what you have read. Some of these are personal development activities, such as completing self-audits, and others are for you to consider issues from different perspectives. We do not always provide suggested answers to these reflective tasks as there is not necessarily a solution. It is important to adopt a critical stance to current practice and issues in education to help you to formulate your own opinions. You may find, as we do, that your views change as you gain experience, discuss issues with other professionals and read around the subject.

At the end of the book we have included some teaching ideas to help you apply what you have read to practice. This is by no means an exhaustive list but we hope that you and your learners find them beneficial. If you are not currently teaching, you may be able to use some of the ideas in your microteaching session (see chapter 8).

WHAT MAKES A GOOD TEACHER?

Is there a recipe for good teaching: a sprinkle of resilience, a kilo of flexibility, a gallon of enthusiasm? It is not always easy to quantify learning, but it is safe to say that there are certain qualities and habits that effective teachers have. Throughout the book we look at the principles of effective teaching and learning and the different roles that a teacher will need to undertake to ensure that individual learners are achieving their full potential and gaining the most they can from the learning experience.

WHAT NEXT?

Once you have completed the Level 3 Award in Education and Training, you may decide you want or need to undertake an additional teaching qualification; this may be a requirement of your employer. You can choose to go on to study for the Level 4 Certificate or the Level 5 Diploma; you do not need to achieve these qualifications in succession. It is possible to progress straight to the Level 5 Diploma after completing the Level 3 Award.

If you wish to teach or are currently teaching literacy, ESOL, numeracy or individuals with additional learning needs, you should consider taking a specialist Level 5 qualification. Again, you will need to check with your employer and consider which qualification is most appropriate for you.

SUMMARY

In this chapter you have read about the different features of the book and how to use them, the units that make up the Level 3 Award in Education and Training and possible future development routes.

Understanding the further education and skills sector

LEARNING AIMS

By the end of this chapter, the reader will have a better understanding of:

❭ the current landscape of the further education and skills sector

❭ the different roles and responsibilities in education and training

❭ key aspects of legislation, regulatory requirements and codes of practice relating to roles and responsibilities

❭ ways to promote equality and value diversity

❭ how the teaching role involves working with other professionals

❭ the boundaries between the teaching role and other professional roles

❭ points of referral to meet the individual needs of learners

THE CURRENT LANDSCAPE

The further education and skills sector has undergone a number of changes over the past three decades. It is currently facing new challenges and striving to find its own identity. It feels like we just get a handle on the qualifications framework and funding stipulations, only for everything to change. So what do we mean by the term 'the further education and skills sector'? The name itself has evolved. Post-compulsory education has been referred to as further education, lifelong learning, the learning and skills sector and currently the further education and skills sector, the latter reflecting more accurately its focus on attainment of skills as well as achievement of academic qualifications.

TASK 1.1

What do you think the further education and skills sector comprises? Make a list of the different institutions, bodies and agencies that could be included.

The sector itself is vast and incredibly diverse, encompassing a range of agencies and catering for learners over a very wide age span: from 14 upwards. Your list may include:

- further education (FE) colleges including tertiary education
- sixth-form colleges
- work-based learning
- private or charitable training providers
- voluntary organisations
- higher education (HE) institutions offering FE courses
- adult community settings
- the armed services
- offender learning
- library, archive and information services

The diverse and complex nature of the further education and skills sector has made it difficult to regulate, and it has also been difficult to implement a national framework of qualifications. In the past, it has been referred to as the 'Cinderella' sector because of its lower profile in comparison with the schools sector; it also lacks a clear and specific professional identity. Attempts have been made to professionalise the sector via government legislation. The most recent reforms were implemented in 2007 with the establishment of the sector skills council for the further education sector, Lifelong Learning UK, and its subsidiary, Standards Verification UK. These bodies were responsible for producing a new set of professional standards for teachers in the sector and endorsing mandatory teacher training qualifications. It became a requirement for those wishing to practise in the profession to obtain a minimum of a Level 3 initial teaching training qualification before taking additional qualifications to become fully qualified as a teacher in the sector. The ultimate aims were to raise standards in teaching, to obtain a fully qualified workforce and for the sector to respond better to employers' needs. In addition, it was mandatory for all teachers to become members of the Institute for Learning (IfL) , a regulatory body responsible for monitoring professional standards. From 2007, all teachers and trainers were required to complete an annual continuing professional development (CPD) requirement of 30 hours for full-time staff, pro rata for part-time. In addition, they had to conform to a new professional code of practice and its disciplinary procedures.

☑ TASK 1.2

The term 'diverse' is often used to describe post-compulsory education. What do you think makes the sector so diverse? How is it different from the more traditional school sectors? Consider a) the learners receiving provision, b) the types of subjects taught and c) the individuals working in the sector.

One of the key differences between the post-compulsory sector and the other sectors is found in the name itself. Individuals attend courses in further education voluntarily or are sent on work placements by their employers who have made a decision to do this. There is also a range of learners attending courses in the sector on a flexible basis. If we think back to the different bodies that constitute the further education and skills sector, we can see that learners will attend courses for a variety of reasons; they will have different educational backgrounds, skills and experience, and needs. For example, there will be learners aged between 14 and 16, perhaps who have been previously disadvantaged in education and want to develop their life skills in a further education setting. There will also be individuals studying on higher education courses and those studying A Levels or retaking their GCSEs in sixth-form colleges. ESOL learners may attend classes in further education colleges or in a community setting and adults with additional learning needs may require support in life skills to make themselves more employable. Individuals can be referred by Jobcentre Plus as they need further training, often in ESOL, to enable them to get back into work. Finally, there will be individuals attending courses on day release from their work, perhaps to obtain a vocational qualification, and inmates receiving support in literacy and numeracy.

In addition, we can see a distinction between the types of subject taught. Historically, education in the schools sector has focused on 'academic' subjects such as history and science, rather than on providing training in vocational areas. However, in the further education and skills sector, particularly within the 14 to 19 age group, it is essential that teachers have the necessary experience and proficiency to teach the vocational curricula, for example BTEC qualifications, National Vocational Qualifications (NVQs) and Apprenticeships.

> "We suggest that the vocational role of FE (at both the further and higher educational levels) should be regarded as having primacy." (BIS, 2012)

A final distinction is the different teaching qualification pathways into the schools and further education and skills sectors. The entry qualifications for individuals wishing to become school teachers is specific. Despite some variations in how they obtain their 'graduate status', they are generally required to have degrees followed by a teacher training qualification. In the further education and skills sector, however, there are a number of different vocational entry routes. Those teaching in the sector will have experience working in a trade or profession such as hairdressing, plumbing, etc. and they are not required to be graduates. Teachers are seen as being 'dual professionals'; in other words, they are specialists in both their subject and/or vocational area as well as in teaching and learning.

WHY THE NEED FOR CHANGE?

Despite the reforms put in place to support professional values in further education, it was felt that the sector was too diverse to impose a one-size-fits-all policy. In 2012, the Department for Business, Innovation and Skills (BIS) instigated a review of the legislative requirements for further education teachers which had been introduced in 2007 aimed at professionalising the sector. The review considered the mandatory initial teaching qualifications, the teaching standards, QTLS (qualified teacher learning and skills), the code of practice, mandatory CPD requirements and the role of the IfL as the representative professional body for teachers in the lifelong learning sector. The published report from the independent review panel, chaired by Lord Lingfield, concluded that a mandatory set of teaching qualifications had proven to be ineffectual and a rethink of the national framework was needed. It was in the sector's own interest to become self-regulating and for organisations and employers to make their own judgements as to which qualifications and training should be offered to their staff.

"Our conclusions, then, are intended to help create an environment in which the professionalism of further education lecturers, instructors, workplace supervisors and assessors might naturally flourish, without interference." (BIS, 2012)

TALKING POINT

What is your view on teaching qualifications? Is it essential for teachers to be fully qualified in whichever sector they are working? Are fully qualified teachers better teachers? Are you more likely to have a greater sense of professional identity if you are more qualified? Could those working in vocational areas be deterred from entering the teaching profession if they were made to complete mandatory teaching qualifications?

ROLES, RESPONSIBILITIES AND RELATIONSHIPS

There are many different roles in the further education and skills sector, not only teachers but also assessors, support workers, learning managers, work-based supervisors, librarians, and so on. All of these individuals will be expected to take on a range of roles and carry out different responsibilities. If you are teaching in the sector, you may be referred to in different ways: as a lecturer, tutor, curriculum team leader, trainer or instructor, for example. Nevertheless, whether you are working in a more traditional educational setting or in a vocational environment, you will share a common goal: to ensure that your learners have sufficient opportunities to progress in their learning.

So, what do we mean exactly by roles and responsibilities? The Oxford English dictionary defines 'role' as 'the function assumed or part played by a person or thing in a particular situation'. Attached to this is the idea that we expect somebody to act in a certain way because of social conventions and our knowledge of the position. For example, we expect teachers to be able to control the group of learners they are teaching, thus assuming the role of a classroom manager or manager of the learning environment. We expect them to devise resources, accommodating their learners' needs; here, we could say teachers are also resource developers or creators. Therefore, in an educational setting, teachers will adopt a number of roles in the learning process. The term 'responsibilities' refers to the duties which teachers are expected to carry out within each role.

✔ TASK 1.3

Look at the list of responsibilities below taken from a sample job description for a lecturer in a further education college. Which different roles would you expect to adopt in each case?

1. Stimulate and promote effective, student-centred, independent learning strategies for students of all levels of ability
2. Undertake continuous (formative) and summative assessments of students
3. Contribute to the development and design of course and course modules
4. Advise on the development of new business services and solutions, and new market opportunities
5. Undertake regular and systematic monitoring of all targets set for your area of work
6. Collect, organise and maintain information and other records as required by college policies and systems
7. Undertake a proactive role in the maintenance of student discipline

You may have used different language to describe them but possible roles are the following:

❱ Facilitator, trainer and educator, enabler, implementer, motivator
❱ Assessor, helper and supporter
❱ Course designer, curriculum organiser
❱ Promoter, advocate, innovator, collaborator, communicator
❱ Monitor, fact finder
❱ Administrator, record keeper
❱ Classroom manager, manager of the learning environment, disciplinarian (possibly a bit strong!)

We can see that teachers are expected to take on a multitude of roles. The diagram opposite provides a list of 12 key roles that a teacher is expected to adopt.

You can add to this list depending on your own role in the sector. For example, you may find that there are people in your workplace who monitor attendance or draw up personal learning plans so the responsibility does not lie with you. You may have fewer roles because of your level or experience or because you are working part time or as a lecturer paid hourly. It is worth remembering that these roles are not static. They will evolve as you are provided with more or different responsibilities and your own perception of your role develops through your personal values, experience and your interactions with your colleagues and learners. We do not mean to imply that teaching is an easy job. It can be a turbulent journey: you may sometimes find the number of roles you are expected to adopt overwhelming and you may not always be sure of what to do in different situations. Everybody faces such dilemmas and, although throughout this book we will offer suggestions and provide techniques on how to deal with different situations, nobody can claim to be an expert on teaching. There will always be a certain amount of 'muddling through' (Brookfield, 2006).

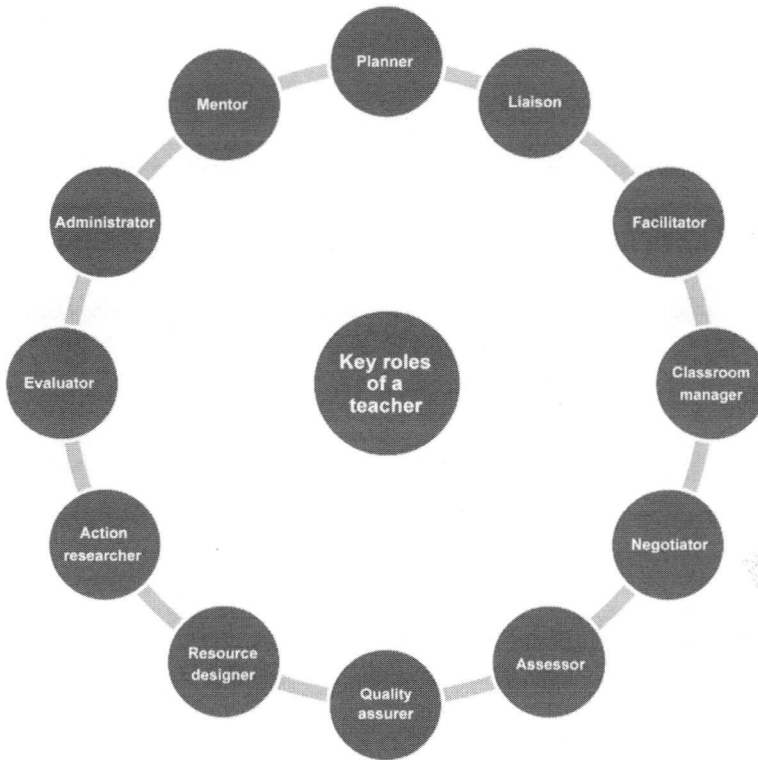

PROFESSIONAL STANDARDS

In April 2013, new Education and Training qualifications were introduced – the Level 3 Award in Education and Training being one of them. In the same year the Education and Training Foundation was launched with a view to professionalising the sector and ensuring continuous development of the workforce. Although teachers are now working in a deregulated context, no longer required to obtain QTLS, it was felt that a new set of professional standards for teachers and trainers was necessary to provide support, to improve learner outcomes and standards of teaching, and to highlight the values to which everyone should aspire. In other words, these standards are not to be seen as a checklist, a list of competences that individuals can tick off once they feel they have been met. They are more about the ethos and values that underpin a teacher's professional practice.

> "The values and attributes described in the Professional Standards are not 'nice to haves'. Rather, they are fundamental, integral and essential to excellent teaching and learning, and supporting learners to be able to reach their full potential." (Initial Guidance for users of the Professional Standards for Teachers and Trainers in Education and Training – England, May 2014)

The new standards, launched in May 2014, are divided into three interrelated areas of equal importance to which teachers and trainers should commit in their professional practice:

❭ Professional values and attributes
❭ Professional knowledge and understanding
❭ Professional skills

One of the key features of the standards is the importance of continuous professional development, for individuals to acknowledge their dual professionalism. They need to be able to identify their personal development needs and continue to update their subject and/or vocational knowledge and teaching skills.

One final point to make about the standards is how they will be used to assess performance in initial teacher education. One of the aims of the standards is to support initial teacher education. In the new Ofsted inspection handbook for initial teacher education provision for the schools and further education and skills sector, it is made clear that they will be used to assess how well trainee teachers are meeting the minimum level of practice (Ofsted, 2014).

The full standards can be found in Appendix B.

RELATIONSHIPS WITH OTHER PROFESSIONALS

One key role of a teacher is the need to liaise with others. There may be times when life as a teacher can feel quite solitary, particularly when you're planning a lesson or a scheme of work, wading through paperwork or marking assignments. You may be unsure of how much support you should give learners, not knowing what the boundaries with regard to your teaching role are. However, as part of your role, you will need to liaise with other professionals on a regular basis: with colleagues, line managers, mentors, support teams, and so on. There should be a range of advice and support facilities at your institution to which you can refer your students. That does not, of course, mean shirking your responsibilities and, as a teacher, you are required to accommodate your learners' needs as best you can. However, there will be instances when something is not within your remit and you need to be aware of both internal and external organisations which provide appropriate support.

✔ TASK 1.4

Read the examples below of learners who have particular support needs. Decide which points of referral would be appropriate for them.

1. A learner who is hard of hearing having difficulty picking up key information.
2. A student who is having difficulty with reading and organising her written work. Her spelling is poor and she has mentioned that she finds it difficult to manage and organise her time effectively.
3. A second language English speaker on a childcare course who is having difficulties with written assignments and following the course content.
4. A young adult who has had a change in his financial circumstances. Although he does not have to pay the fees of the course, he is expected to pay other costs such as travel, stationery and resources.
5. A learner who has recently suffered a bereavement and is struggling to cope with the demands of the course.

may have come up with something that includes:

- sensory support, for example providing support workers, assistive technology and so on
  blind, visually impaired, deaf and hard of hearing learners
- lexia support
- L, literacy and numeracy support
- ncial support
- selling services

I support services within your place of work would include:

- rs or study coaches to support learners and teachers
- technicians
- e-learning advisers
- additional learning needs support
- support in employability skills
- security staff
- litigation services

External support might include:

- social services
- careers advice
- emergency services
- mental health and counselling services
- family support services
- health centres, GPs, Samaritans
- legal and financial services

It is important that you are sensitive and open to the learner's support needs. In many cases you will need to signpost the learner to a specific internal or external institution rather than following it up yourself. Personal details should not be revealed (Data Protection Act, 1998); only in exceptional circumstances should you break the learner's confidentiality (see the section on safeguarding, p.17). If you are not sure how to deal with any of your learners' support needs, it is worth talking to a colleague or your line manager without revealing any personal details.

TALKING POINT

Remembering your school days, what was the primary role of a teacher and students in the classroom? Traditionally, the teacher was viewed as an imparter of knowledge, an expert in his or her field and the students in the classroom were passive recipients. Over the years there has been a shift in the role of the teacher. Referring to the professional standards, you will notice key phrases such as 'enable learners to share responsibility for their own learning and assessment' and 'inspire, motivate and raise aspirations of learners'.

We can see that a key role of a teacher is a facilitator, encouraging learners to develop their own strategies for learning and building on their experience and prior knowledge. Some teachers, perhaps because of their educational backgrounds or simply because of how they perceive the role of the teacher, find it difficult to implement a more student-centred approach in the classroom and resort to what they know best. What do you consider your role as a teacher to be? Which factors does it depend on? Do you think that teachers might feel devalued or experience a loss of control if they hand over the responsibility of learning to their students?

EQUALITY AND DIVERSITY

We have decided to look at the terms equality and diversity early on in the book because whatever your role working in education – teacher, assessor, cleaner, technician and so on – you are required to understand these terms and ensure that you are actively promoting them. The concepts are complex and we need to be constantly looking at our own practice to ensure that we are engaging with them. We have to make sure that we are not making snap judgements about people and imposing our own beliefs and opinions on individuals.

☑ TASK 1.5

What do you understand by the terms equality and diversity? Write a definition for each.

Did you include the word 'equal' in the definition? Equality refers to treating people fairly rather than equally. We should all have an equal shot at education but it is often fairer to treat people differently to ensure they have the same opportunities as everyone else. For example, if you have a learner who has difficulty reading a handout because of the size of the typeface, in order for them to have an equal chance of understanding the material, it would be fairer to enlarge the typeface.

Diversity means valuing individuals and their differences in age, gender, academic background, sexuality, ethnicity, knowledge, skills and experience. It is important that we actively promote diversity so that learners feel their contributions and skills are being recognised. If learners feel they are valued, they will feel more comfortable in the learning environment and there will be more opportunities for them to learn and fulfil their potential.

Ensuring that all learners are able to access education and be given appropriate support is one of the key components of the inspection framework outlined by the Office for Standards in Education, Children's Services and Skills. Ofsted is the body responsible for inspecting and regulating provision in the further education and skills sector.

- learners with disabilities and those with additional learning needs
- learners from low-income backgrounds

As practitioners, we need to ensure that we are removing barriers pertaining to these social groups so that learners are more likely to benefit from their learning experiences and have better employment opportunities. We cannot guarantee that every learner in our group will achieve, but every learner should have the same opportunity to do so. Although it can be challenging and bewildering dealing with such diverse groups, we should view the differences in individuals in a positive light. Learners will need to experience working with people who have different backgrounds, experiences, skills and beliefs in their working and social lives and the learning environment is an excellent way of breaking down barriers and eliminating prejudices. As teachers, we must be prepared to challenge discriminatory behaviour in the classroom and promote an atmosphere of mutual respect and appreciation.

☑ TASK 1.6

Think about your own practice. How can you promote the concepts of equality and diversity in the learning environment?

You might find the following questions useful, designed to help you think about how best to promote equality of opportunity and diversity.

Identifying learners' needs

Are individual needs diagnosed before the start of the course?
Do all learners have ILPs (Individual Learning Plans) or PLPs (Personal Learning Plans)?
Have all learners been made aware of the policies on equality and diversity in the induction process?

Delivery

> Are your methods of communication appropriate for all learners? (For example, do you use appropriate vocabulary which is understandable for all?)
> Do you use non-discriminatory language in your delivery?
> Do you use a variety of teaching strategies?

Learning environment

> Is the learning environment conducive to learning in terms of layout and accessibility?
> Do all learners feel safe and secure and able to express themselves without fear of reproach from their peers and teacher?
> Are you flexible in your approach, being prepared to renegotiate times of breaks, layout, location and so on?

Choice of materials and resources

> Are the resources culturally acceptable for all the learners?
> Do they challenge stereotypes? (For example, showing women working in typically male environments.)
> Have you made suitable adaptations to the materials to accommodate learners' needs?

Assessment

> Is the assessment fair for all learners?
> Have appropriate adjustments been put in place for learners who require additional support?
> Do you use the learners' names appropriately to check individual understanding, ensuring that you have pronounced them correctly?

These are only a few questions to get you thinking about the topic. The final point to make here is that promoting equality and diversity does not only refer to learners. It should be woven into all aspects of our professional life, for example in how we are treated at work, how we speak to each other, how employees are hired, and in our training and learning programmes.

TALKING POINT

We have looked mainly at how practitioners can promote equality and diversity. However, it is in the employer's best interest to ensure that these concepts are also being adhered to in the workplace. If students feel supported, achievement and retention rates might well be boosted, showing the educational provider in a positive light. If you are currently working in the further education and skills sector, have a look at your provider's policy on equal opportunities and consider the following questions. If you are not working in the sector, try to access one online.

you personally and your working practice. Of course, you don't need to finish all the laws, any
legislative reform of the past 30 years, and some acts will be more relevant to your role than
others, but being aware of what is required of you by law will help you to make learners aware
of their rights and responsibilities.

In this section, we will only touch upon some key legislation and you are encouraged to carry
out further research via the internet; some useful web links are provided at the end of the chapter.
Let's start by looking at the Equality Act of 2010 as the concepts of equality and diversity are
underpinned by this important legislation. This Act replaced existing legislation relating to
different aspects of equality such as the 1975 Sexual Discrimination Act, the 1976 Race Relations
Act and the 1995 Disability Act. The purpose of the new legislation was to provide one source
of anti-discrimination law and to ensure that particular groups were not victims of discrimination.
Within the Equality Act, there are nine protected characteristics:

> Age
> Disability
> Gender reassignment
> Marriage and civil partnership
> Pregnancy and maternity
> Race
> Religion and belief
> Sex
> Sexual orientation

We must be mindful that we do not treat learners less favourably or discriminate against them
because they have, or we perceive them to have, any one of these characteristics. Earlier, we
looked at ways of promoting equality and diversity in the learning environment. A key phrase to
take from this Act is 'reasonable adjustments'. This means that we have to make suitable
adjustments to our practice to ensure that an individual is not disadvantaged in any way and
has the same opportunities to access education as anyone else. An example of making a
reasonable adjustment in the workplace would be to put in ramps around the building for
wheelchair users.

☑ **TASK 1.7**

Choose three legislative policies from the list below which you think are most relevant to your own practice. Research the main points of the legislation and make a note of how it applies to your professional practice.

Health and safety legislation

- ❭ Health and Safety Act 1974
- ❭ The Manual Handling Operations Regulations 1992
- ❭ The Health and Safety (Display Screen Equipment) Regulations 1992
- ❭ The Reporting of Injuries, Diseases and Dangerous Occurrences Regulations (RIDDOR) (1995)
- ❭ Management of Health and Safety at Work Regulations 1999
- ❭ Control of Substances Hazardous to Health (COSHH) 2002

Safeguarding legislation

- ❭ Children Act 2004
- ❭ Safeguarding Vulnerable Adults 2006

Data protection legislation

- ❭ The Copyright, Designs and Patent Act 1988
- ❭ Data Protection Act 1998

Some key points are highlighted below.

Health and safety legislation

As far as possible, we need to ensure that learners are studying in a safe and secure environment. You will need to consult your employer's health and safety policy but you can adhere to the legislation by, for example:

- ❭ making learners aware of their personal responsibility to create a safe environment and of emergency procedures;
- ❭ ensuring the learning environment is safe and comfortable with, for example, appropriate ventilation, heating and lighting, no loose wires on the floor and an appropriate and accessible layout for all learners; and
- ❭ having suitable breaks between classes.

employment setting.

Data protection

This legislation refers to the processing and storing of data of both learners and employees. There are five key principles of data protection with regard to education:

》 Only collect necessary information.
》 Ensure information is in a secure place.
》 Ensure information is relevant and up to date.
》 Only keep as much information as is needed and for as long as is necessary.
》 Allow subject of information to access data if requested.

Examples of how you should take account of the different principles outlined in the act are the following:

》 Make individuals aware of how their personal data are processed and give them opportunities to access the information.
》 Ensure that individuals are not misusing the provider's internet or email systems, for example to send abusive messages. Although we have a right to privacy, policies need to be put in place for the welfare of all learners.
》 Secure permission from learners or parents when using personal images for assessment and promotional purposes.

✔ TASK 1.8

Consider the scenarios below. For each case, decide on the best course of action, considering the legal position.

1. Paula is an ESOL teacher. One of her groups will be delivering a presentation on a famous place in the UK. She would like to take the learners to visit a museum in preparation for their talks.

2. Adam is 17 and is studying hairdressing at a local college. He is planning on having gender reassignment surgery next year and wishes to be known as Diana. However, he is concerned about the reactions of the teacher and other learners in the class.
3. Aneela is a dyslexic learner who is concerned about an exam that is due to take place at the end of the college term.
4. One of your learners, aged 17, has told you he is self-harming.
5. Stephen teaches Geography A Level in a sixth-form college. His students are due to go on a field trip and Stephen wants to take photos of his learners carrying out research to put on the college website and to provide evidence for external verifiers.

1. This scenario relates to the Management of Health and Safety at Work Regulations 1999 which states that employers need to complete risk assessments to identify and assess potential hazards, and take precautionary measures to minimise risks. The teacher would need to do a risk assessment, and weigh up the options before submitting the report for approval. The teacher would need to consider:

❭ the learners themselves, for example their age (is parental permission required?), their general behaviour, any special medical needs or mobility issues, and so on;
❭ the number of learners;
❭ the modes of transport involved;
❭ weather conditions, for example are there any adverse conditions predicted for that day which affect travelling by public transport?;
❭ insurance arrangements for loss of goods or travel cancellations; and
❭ the location of the proposed trip, identifying any risks involved. Ideally, this would involve assessing the site prior to the visit or talking to somebody who works at the museum.

Although it is impossible to predict all potential hazards, contingency plans need to be put in place and learners need to be made aware of emergency procedures and how to keep themselves safe. The teacher would have to obtain emergency contact information for each learner and all details of the trip would be given to the appropriate members of staff dealing with risk management at the place of work.

2. This scenario relates to the 2010 Equality Act. The revised legislation now includes the protection against discrimination of those undergoing or considering undergoing gender reassignment. It is difficult to change people's perceptions and beliefs, but it is important that we handle such situations in a sensitive way. We need to ensure the learner feels safe in the learning environment, challenge derogatory language and set clear boundaries, reminding learners that discrimination will not be tolerated. Of course, the responsibility for taking proactive measures does not lie solely with the teacher. Your employer also needs to tackle prejudice. This could be done by:

❭ ensuring all incidents of discrimination are reported;
❭ training teachers to deal with instances of bullying and discrimination;
❭ ensuring all learners are aware of the institution's code of conduct and its zero tolerance approach to discrimination; and

4. This is a very serious safeguarding issue. We do not have the authority or expertise to counsel the learner ourselves but we do have a duty of care to our learners and we need to deal with such situations in a sensitive and appropriate manner. In this case, the best course of action would be to carry out the procedures outlined by your safeguarding team such as completing a disclosure or safeguarding referral form, outlining details in the person's own words as far as possible. The learner would then be referred to a suitable internal or external agency such as a counselling service.

5. Adhering to the principles of the Data Protection Act, the teacher needs to obtain permission from the learners or their parents before publishing any personal details, images or otherwise, on the website.

Code of practice

No matter what your job title in the further education and skills sector is, you will need to adhere to a code of professional behaviours as outlined by your educational provider. The code will provide a consistency of approach, outlining the responsibilities required of you and making it clear what is considered acceptable and unacceptable conduct. In all situations, you need to be responsible for your own conduct, ensure that you are acting in an ethical and responsible way and be aware of the consequences if you do not conform to the standards. This document is known as a code of practice. There may be separate codes of practice for particular groups, for example those working with learners with special educational needs. It may also be known as a 'corporate code of conduct'.

It is worth noting that in the new Ofsted inspection handbook for initial teacher education (ITE) provision, reference is made to the importance of all trainees adhering 'to an appropriate standard of professional conduct' (Ofsted, 2014), including checking that dress is appropriate for their work context.

☑ **TASK 1.9**

What kinds of standards outlining appropriate behaviour would you expect to see in a code of practice? If you have access to your institution's code of practice/conduct, it would be useful to refer to this.

You may have thought of examples of appropriate behaviour similar to the following:

- Dressing in a suitable manner
- Using appropriate and non-derogatory language
- Working collaboratively with colleagues
- Upholding the reputation of the place of work
- Not using force as a form of punishment
- Maintaining appropriate relationships with learners
- Using the institution's resources in an appropriate way (for example using computers for business use only)
- Ensuring learners are in a safe learning environment

Ethical values underpin the standards of behaviour expected of all employees. As an example, a key value to which all employees would be required to show commitment is respect. You need to be courteous towards learners and other employees, respecting and acknowledging the differences in individuals, and not imposing your own belief systems on others. You need to have integrity, for example disclosing any criminal offence when applying for employment. You have a duty of care to your learners, taking reasonable steps to ensure their safety and welfare, and reporting any incidents of bullying or discrimination. Finally, you are expected to be trustworthy, not doing anything that would bring the profession and educational provider into disrepute.

TALKING POINT

In 2008, the Institute for Learning (IfL) introduced a code of professional practice for all those teaching and training in post-compulsory education. It was brought out to highlight the behaviours expected of professionals in accordance with the Institute's professional values, outlined below:

- Integrity
- Respect
- Care
- Practice
- Disclosure
- Responsibility

Those who did not abide to any aspect of the code would undergo disciplinary procedures with the possibility of being struck off from the profession. However, it was found that taking action against members of the profession due to misconduct was difficult to implement and not a single member of the IfL was found to have been permanently excluded. The Lingfield Review panel concluded that 'establishing special national arrangements to disbar FE lecturers would be disproportionate' (LSIS, 2012). Those entering the profession were subject to rigorous screening checks and cases were dealt with independently between employers and employees, with possible intervention from trade unions.

What do you think? Should there be a professional body (membership to the IfL is now on a voluntary basis) in order to support the professional standards? Should all those working in the sector be obliged to subscribe to a professional code of practice or should the enforcement of appropriate conduct be employer-led?

REFERENCES AND FURTHER READING

Brookfield, S. (2006) *The Skillful Teacher on Technique, Trust, and Responsiveness in the Classroom*. San Francisco: Jossey-Bass.

Department for Business, Innovation and Skills (BIS) (2012) *Professionalism in Further Education: Final Report of the Independent Review Panel*.

Duckworth, V. and Tummons, J. (2010) *Contemporary Issues in Lifelong Learning*. Oxford: Oxford University Press.

Francis, M. and Gould, J. (2012) *Achieving your PTLLS Award: A Practical Guide to Teaching in the Lifelong Learning Sector*. London: Sage.

Gravells, A. and Simpson, S. (2012) *Planning and Enabling Learning in the Lifelong Learning Sector*. London: Learning Matters.

Hall, L. and Marsh, K. (2000) *Professionalism, Policies and Values* (Greenwich Readers). Greenwich: Greenwich University Press.

Keeley-Browne, L. (2007) *Training to Teach in the Learning and Skills Sector*. Harlow: Pearson.

Lingfield, R. (2012) *Professionalism in Further Education: Final Report of the Independent Review Panel. Established by the Minister of State for Further Education, Skills and Lifelong Learning*. October 2012, pp. 27–8.

Ofsted (2012) *Handbook for the Inspection of Further Education and Skills*.

Ofsted (2014) *Initial Teacher Education Inspection Handbook*, for use from June 2014.

Reece, I. and Walker, S. (2007) *Teaching, Training and Learning: A Practical Guide*. Sunderland: Business Education Publishers Limited.

Tummons, J. (2007) *Becoming a Professional Tutor in the Lifelong Learning Sector*. Exeter: Learning Matters.

Wallace, S. (2011) *Teaching, Tutoring and Training in the Lifelong Learning Sector*. Exeter: Learning Matters.

Websites

www.bis.gov.uk (Department for Business, Innovation and Skills)

www.ecu.ac.uk (Advancing equality and diversity in universities and colleges)

www.equalityhumanrights.com

www.et-foundation.co.uk (Education and Training Foundation)

www.hse.gov.uk/legislation/hswa.htm (Health and Safety Act)

www.ico.org.uk/for_organisations/data_protection/the_guide (Data protection)

www.ifl.ac.uk/membership/professional-standards (The Institute for Learning's code of practice)

www.legislation.gov.uk (All legislation)

www.niace.org.uk (National Institute of Adult Continuing Education)

www.ofsted.gov.uk/resources/initial-teacher-education-inspection-handbook (Guidance on what to expect from an Ofsted inspection)

www.safenetwork.org.uk (Advice on safeguarding)

By the end of this chapter, the reader will have a better understanding of:

> barriers to learning

> how to motivate learners

> relationships between teachers and learners

> learning styles

> using ground rules to promote learning

> teaching approaches to engage learners

> communication skills

> coping strategies

> giving instructions

> using learners' names

BARRIERS TO LEARNING

As you embark on your career in teaching, you may be feeling a number of things – anticipation, excitement, anxiety or fear. All of these are natural and it is realistic to expect that you are likely to experience any of these at some point; even the most experienced of teachers can feel trepidation before the start of a new term or when taking over a new class. Recognising these emotions will help you to manage them more effectively. More often than not, behaviour is at the top of the list of what new teachers worry about. *What do I do if they don't listen? How can I control the class? How do I stop them talking?* These questions are likely to resonate with you as you walk into a classroom for the first time, ready to put the principles underpinning teaching pedagogy into practice.

Ask any experienced teacher about how to engage students in learning and they will most likely say that motivation is the main ingredient – you have to get the students motivated to learn. Sounds simple enough, yet the reality is that engaging learners can sometimes be a complex process. As we saw in Chapter 1, the range of learners is wide and diverse and that brings real challenges. It is important to remember, though, that levels of motivation will vary considerably from individual to individual. Any classroom or workspace in a post 16 learning context comprises learners who are conscientious in their approach to study as well as those at the other end of the spectrum who aren't (not to mention all the others in between). It is our responsibility to create an environment conducive to learning and to do this effectively we have to find out what the potential barriers might be.

✔ TASK 2.1

Not all learners are naturally motivated to learn. Think about why. Make a list of the factors which can create a barrier to learning.

In thinking through the issues above, your list might include:

> inability to access the curriculum due to weak basic skills
> previous negative experience of education
> peer pressure to conform and fit in with the group (messing about 'is cool')
> weak study skills – not knowing how to take notes or write assignments
> economic reasons ('What's the point? There aren't any jobs anyway.')
> lack of knowledge and/or skills to cope with the level of study
> negative labelling ('I can't be bothered, I've already failed at school.')
> home environment – academic attainment isn't valued
> lack of access to appropriate resources for studying, such as a computer
> weak planning and teaching by the teacher
> lack of interest in the subject
> additional learning needs such as dyslexia
> low attention span

For any teacher, experienced or not, this is quite a range of factors to have to deal with. Yet if we are to fulfil the primary purpose of teaching, which is to help learners to learn, then we need to accept this as part and parcel of our day-to-day jobs. Sometimes there are things we cannot be responsible for, such as the current economic climate or learners' lack of interest in a subject. More often than not, though, careful planning, which is underpinned by an understanding of our students, can result in learning that is rich and inspiring. Let's bear two things in mind. Firstly, there are no 'bad' learners. Behaviour which is deemed to be 'challenging' is often the result of one or more of the above factors. If we can separate the behaviour from the individual and not personalise it, then we are in a better and more informed position to manage it. Secondly, the teaching is only as good as the learning which occurs as a result. If there is no good learning, then the teaching needs to be rethought and reconfigured.

2 things

NO bad learners.

behaviour

good teaching — good learning!
bad teaching — Bad learning!

MOTIVATING LEARNERS

If we can engage our students in learning, then we stand a good chance of minimising the potential for challenging behaviours to occur. Understanding what motivation is, and the role it plays in this process, will help you do this more effectively.

One of the best known models of motivation is the humanist psychologist Abraham Maslow's (1908–1970) 'Hierarchy of Needs', shown below. The basis for Maslow's theory was that human beings act because they are motivated to achieve certain needs. The first four levels in the triangle are low-level deficiency needs (*D-needs*) and are so-called because they are the basic needs that drive human behaviour. According to Maslow, individuals cannot reach their full potential as human beings (self-actualisation) until the lower order needs have been met;

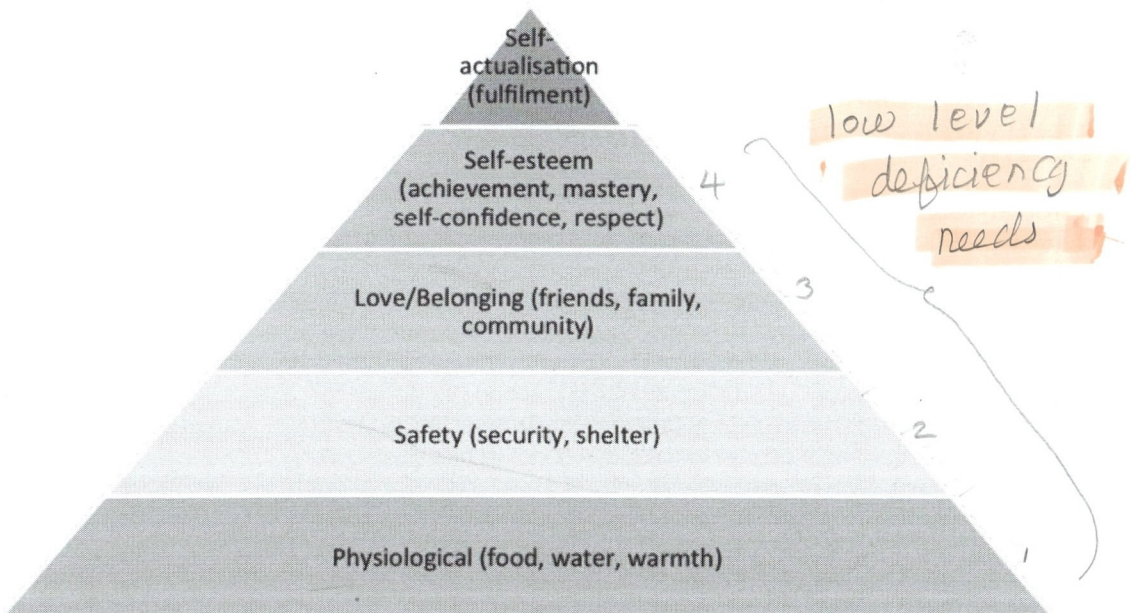

Self-actualisation
(fulfilment)

Self-esteem
(achievement, mastery,
self-confidence, respect)   4

Love/Belonging (friends, family,
community)   3

Safety (security, shelter)   2

Physiological (food, water, warmth)   1

low level
deficiency
needs

Level of need in Maslow's Hierarchy	Teaching and learning considerations
Physiological	• Is the room too hot? Too cold? • Do the learners have access to water? • Are there regular break times? • Is the room noisy? • Does everyone have a seat and desk space?
Safety	• Is the room/workplace tidy? • Are there any loose wires? • Is the furniture neatly arranged? • Is there space for the learners to store their coats and bags? • Is there any hazardous equipment that needs to be safely stored? • Do the learners know how to use the equipment? • Do they need to wear hard hats or goggles?
Belonging	• Do the learners feel comfortable with their peers? • Am I organising group work effectively? • Do I know all the learners' names? • Do the learners know each other's names? • Do they know how to ask for advice and guidance? • Can the learners make mistakes knowing that their efforts will be recognised?
Self-esteem	• Am I praising appropriately? • Do my learners feel valued? • Do my learners feel included? • Am I providing activities that meet individual needs? • Do my materials reflect equality and diversity issues?

progress at any point can be disrupted if the *D-needs* are unfulfilled. Failure to meet these lower level deficiency needs can prevent an individual from achieving self-actualisation. In other words, if barriers to learning exist, an individual will not achieve everything they are capable of. The barriers impede their progress.

Applied to an educational context, the model can offer us a useful insight into what causes our learners to act in the ways they do. How do we explain Ibrahim's continual reluctance to do any writing task you set? Or Sophie's refusal to work with any of her peers? Or Ana's repeated absences? All of these behaviours could be viewed as challenging. As teachers, we have a responsibility to do what we can to find out the possible underlying reasons. The most obvious

❯ *Extrinsic motivation* is external to the individual; he or she acts as a result of factors 'outside' themselves. For example, an individual might be motivated to study for an exam because of a promised reward such as a promotion at work. Alternatively, being motivated to act may be the result of wanting to avoid some kind of punishment such as not moving up a level to a new class.

❯ *Intrinsic motivation* is internal to the individual; he or she acts as a result of factors 'inside' themselves. An example is the desire to learn Spanish. A learner undertakes a programme of study because he/she loves languages and derives a natural sense of pleasure, rather than reward, from doing so.

In reality, individuals act for a variety of intrinsically and extrinsically motivated reasons and this is human nature. Students are not always naturally motivated to engage with a particular task or activity. Recognising this will help us to structure their learning experiences in a way that increases the chances of this happening.

☑ TASK 2.2

Maslow's Hierarchy of Needs provides us with one way of understanding what motivates human beings. It has, however, been criticised by some theorists. Why do you think this might be? What do you think may be the shortcomings?

You might have thought about the possibility that people may not always be aware of their needs and, even if they are, may not be able to verbalise them. Further, by virtue of the fact that self-actualisation is a rather abstract concept, it is very difficult to measure scientifically and is therefore open to the criticism that there is no 'truth' to it. Additionally, what self-actualisation means to one person may mean something entirely different to someone else. Individuals may have the same need but behave in very different ways; for example, the desire to be accepted as part of a group can mean individuals respond to this need in varying ways.

All things considered, it is true to say that if you know what really motivates your learners, you hold the key to unlocking what can be potentially very powerful learning opportunities. We will look at this in the next section.

TALKING POINT

Think about a time in your life when you were motivated to achieve something. What was it? Were you successful? Was it a positive experience? What were the factors that made it successful? If it was an unsuccessful experience, reflect on the reasons why. Relate your thoughts to the explanations of motivation you have read about.

MANAGING THE LEARNING ENVIRONMENT

TASK 2.3

Make a list of the factors that can contribute to the development of positive relationships between teachers and learners.

In the opening scene of a 1947 film published by McGraw-Hill Book Company entitled *Maintaining Classroom Discipline* (see References and further reading for a link), the main protagonist Mr Grimes, a maths teacher at a high school in the USA, is shown admonishing his students because of poor results in a recent test. The dialogue begins with him telling them,

> *"This is the poorest class I've had in a long, long time... most of you have no foundation at all. Now the trouble is with your attitude, you don't pay enough attention in class, you don't do enough work outside of it. You don't know what the word study means, you haven't the slightest idea. Don't you realise that mathematics is an important subject? I tell you right now that unless you get over your lazy habits and come up to the standards I've set for this class, many of you will have the pleasure of repeating this course next semester."*

As the scene continues, we witness him losing control of the class as the discipline deteriorates and he issues punishments for bad behaviour such as books being dropped on the floor and students throwing things. Although the film is more than 60 years old, the issues still resonate in today's classrooms and workplaces.

Undoubtedly, there is a lot to be learned about the way in which teachers manage their relationships with their learners and the impact their language has on them. If we unpack the above, we can see that Mr Grimes is sending out messages which are dismissive, humiliating and threatening; they speak to the students of failure, blame and lack of respect. For students who return to education in a post-16 context, such a negative approach is potentially very

The film is old-fashioned but nonetheless it is highly effective in demonstrating two things which maximise the potential for learning. These are

1. the powerful effect that establishing positive relationships with students has; and
2. the importance of students feeling valued and worthy in respect of their academic pursuits.

Another human psychologist, Carl Rogers, held the basic belief that human beings can only achieve their full potential if they have a positive self-image and unconditional positive regard from others. In other words, that they think of themselves positively and feel unconditionally respected by others around them. In practice, this means we need to recognise and reward the efforts that our learners make over and above the grades they achieve.

Broadly speaking, developing an understanding of how learners like to learn, showing enthusiasm for them and your subject area and using language which is free from blame is crucial to establishing and maintaining positive relationships.

GROUND RULES

In addition to enthusiasm, understanding your learners, using appropriate language and establishing clear ground rules are vital. Ground rules are the basic rules that underpin classroom behaviour. Being respectful and listening are just two examples of these. Other ground rules can include:

> no mobile phones
> arriving punctually for lessons
> completing homework on time
> no talking while you're talking
> valuing others' opinions

The setting of ground rules is hugely important and will help you to create the kind of learning environment that you want in your classroom. Learners need to understand what is and isn't acceptable with respect to their behaviour. As teachers, we can't assume that they will know, so a process which outlines this, ideally formulated at the start of a new term or at the point at which a new teacher takes over a class, is advisable. A set of ground rules which establish structure and routine is the bedrock of good behaviour because expectations are clear and learners know what their responsibilities are.

Here are some tips for implementing ground rules.

- Don't impose them – involve the learners to provide a sense of ownership and responsibility.
- Use positive language rather than language which is blameworthy and negative.
- Select a manageable number – don't overload the students as this increases the chances of the rules being broken.
- Change the rules as and when necessary.
- Consider cultural differences – what is acceptable in one culture may not be in another.
- Apply rules which relate to both learners' academic and social behaviour.
- Base them on what is acceptable rather than what isn't.
- Be consistent in your application – if a rule is broken and a sanction applies, then ensure it is followed through.

Following these suggestions will increase the chances of creating an environment conducive to learning. Remember, the list is not exhaustive and you will be able to amend the rules according to the profile of your group. Display them on the walls of your classroom or workplace and remind learners of them when you need to.

TALKING POINT

Mr Grimes wants to develop better relationships with his learners. What advice would you give him?

APPROACHES TO MOTIVATING LEARNERS

In *The Practice of English Language Teaching*, Jeremy Harmer (2001, p. 54) says 'Our attempts to initiate our students' motivation are absolutely critical for their learning success'. If we base our approach to teaching and learning on this very idea, we are in a strong position to produce an environment which promotes and increases the chances of learning. Remember that our learners' levels of motivation will differ so we must continually explore and experiment with a variety of strategies to engage our learners. A 'one size fits all' approach will not suffice. How, then, do we motivate our learners? What approaches should we use?

TASK 2.4

How can you engage learners in the process of learning? Think of some approaches and make a list. Compare your ideas with those listed on the next few pages.

previous experience of education, strengths and weaknesses, _____
results, additional support needs, and languages spoken. This information provides a really useful starting point from which to begin the process of planning. Profiles can also include information related to the way in which they like to learn. Among the most well known of the learning styles models are those produced by:

Fleming

This categorises learners as either predominantly visual, auditory or kinaesthetic in the way they best receive instructional stimuli.

- ❭ *Visually* stimulated learners tend to learn best through seeing things represented visually. The use of maps, graphs, pictures and drawings work well in the classroom.
- ❭ *Auditory* learners tend to learn to best when they hear things. The use of teacher-led explanations, lectures, presentations, or listening to peers work well in the classroom.
- ❭ *Kinaesthetic* learners tend to learn best by doing things and respond well to being given active tasks and making use of the physical space in the classroom or workplace.

Honey and Mumford

Basing their work on Kolb's experiential learning cycle, Honey and Mumford identified four distinct learning preferences:

- ❭ *Activists* like to learn by doing and being actively involved in a task.
- ❭ *Theorists* like to understand the theory, concept, principle or idea behind a task before engaging with it.
- ❭ *Pragmatists* like to experiment and understand how they can put the idea into practice in their real lives.
- ❭ *Reflectors* like to take a back seat and think about what they observe from different perspectives before reaching conclusions or forming opinions.

Howard Gardner

Gardner developed his Theory of Multiple Intelligences in opposition to the conventional ways to consider intelligence – as either mathematical or linguistic. He put forward the idea that grouping intelligences into seven different categories (later developed into nine categories) more accurately captured the ways in which individuals acquire knowledge. The categories are mathematical, linguistic, spatial, bodily-kinaesthetic, musical, intrapersonal and interpersonal. An interesting point to note is that the intelligences overlap rather than operating independently.

The models above provide us with a useful approach to tailoring our teaching approaches to meet our learners' needs. However, a note of caution is perhaps needed. Useful as they are, some educational researchers have criticised the overreliance on learning styles inventories for pedagogical use. In their examination of 13 of the most influential learning styles models, Coffield *et al.* (2004, p. 148) say 'Learning style researchers do not speak with one voice; there is widespread disagreement about the advice that should be offered to teachers, tutors or managers'.

In this respect, we should bear in mind that learning style taxonomies can provide us with a useful starting point from which to base our strategies. It is more important, however, to note that all good teaching requires teachers to vary the way in which information is presented as a way of sustaining motivation.

TALKING POINT

Think about the learning styles you have read about. Do you think the models suggested are useful? Think about the ways in which you like to learn. What is your learning style? Do you learn in more than one way?

2. Enabling learning

a) Interactions

The idea that learning is essentially a social phenomenon was first put forward by Bandura (1977). Lave and Wenger later developed the idea that 'communities of practice' are those social groupings which are bound together by a common purpose or aim. Although not an automatically direct consequence of collaboration, learning can, and often does, take place as a result of the process of interaction in the group and the discussing and sharing of ideas. Applying this to an educational setting means that having learners working together in pairs and groups to problem-solve, negotiate, determine solutions and seek out new strategies is rich in learning potential.

b) Resources

Varying the resources you use will stimulate and maintain the interest of your learners. Try not to over-rely on text-based materials, as learners with weak literacy and/or language skills will struggle. Don't put too much information on a PowerPoint presentation as this becomes tedious and you risk switching learners off. Prensky (2001, p. 1) says, 'Our students have changed radically. Today's students are no longer the people our educational system was designed to teach'. They have grown up around computer games, tablet devices, smartphones, the internet and a vast range of other mobile technologies. In practice, this means that the way in which they think and intellectualise has changed and as teachers we need to respond to this. In Chapter 10, you will find some ideas for teaching with technology.

connect with them.

d) Classroom layout

The physical appearance of a classroom can have a powerful effect on motivation levels. Drab classrooms can be brightened considerably with displays of your learners' work and sends clear messages about the extent to which you value it. Disorganised working spaces can lead to a decrease in motivation as the appearance can suggest that you do not value the learning environment. Think carefully about the kind of emotional atmosphere you want to create and how you want to encourage collaborative learning.

3. Assessing learning

Regular assessment that is designed to move students forward in their learning is motivating. The Assessment Reform Group (2002, p. 2) states that, 'assessment that encourages learning fosters motivation by emphasising progress and achievement rather than failure'. Feedback should be constructive and provide information about the quality of the work, rather than the learner, and what needs to be done to improve it. Links need to be made between each learning episode and progress should inform the individual learning plan. Another consideration is that it should focus on what can be done well in the future more than what was done wrong in the past. We will look at assessment in more detail in Chapter 6.

TALKING POINT

Think about your teaching specialism. How will you organise your classroom workspace? How useful will group work be to you? What information will you want to know about your learners? How will you adapt your strategies to get the best out of them?

COPING STRATEGIES

Busy teachers always need strategies to help them cope with the challenging behaviours they can face in the classroom.

> ☑ **TASK 2.5**
>
> How do you feel about managing learners' behaviour? What approaches will you take to handling behaviour that is challenging? Do you think you will be a 'strict' teacher or a more 'lenient' one?

What were your responses? What can you remember about how teachers managed behaviour when you went to school? What advice would you give a colleague? Generally speaking, when the going gets tough it is absolutely crucial to remain calm and composed. Hopefully a direct reminder about the ground rules that have been set will be enough to stem any further unwanted behaviours. Speaking quietly on a one-to-one basis with an 'offending' learner can stop a situation escalating. Try to remember that behaviour is always orientated toward a purpose in the sense that it attempts to gain something, whether attention or kudos, or to risk not losing respect or 'face' in front of peers. As we said at the beginning of this chapter, always separate the person from the behaviour – they are not the same thing: 'Livia, your talking is annoying because it's disrupting Abdul' is better than 'Livia, you're annoying', as the latter can lead to feelings of low self-esteem and lack of self-confidence. Susan Wallace (2007a) outlines a range of useful tips, which are summarised below:

> ❯ Always try to establish what the problem is so that you are better able to find a solution.
> ❯ When things seem stressful, it's really important to stay calm and maintain your composure. Never shout, raise your voice or be provocative or confrontational as this is likely to make matters worse and the situation is likely to escalate.
> ❯ Avoid making threats as the language is often emotionally charged and can lead to hostile relationships and worsening behaviour.
> ❯ Modelling good behaviour yourself will increase the chances of your learners replicating it.
> ❯ Whatever you do and no matter how hard it is, don't take things personally. Sometimes, learners may see 'the teacher' as a label –they don't see you as a person.
> ❯ Try to maintain a balanced outlook. Accept that not everything will go well all the time and when things have gone particularly badly, try to balance this with the things that have worked well for you.
> ❯ When we looked at ground rules, we said that consistency is really important. This means that if you apply a sanction for a particular behaviour, then you must see it through – learners need to know where they stand and anything else sends out mixed and confusing signals.
> ❯ Pick and choose your battles; punishing learners for every misdemeanour is unnecessary and exhausting. Some learners thrive on the attention they get by 'playing to the crowd'.

In the table below, there are some typical scenarios that teachers face in their classrooms and some suggested ways of managing them. Do you agree with them? What would you do differently?

Behaviour	Strategy
Two of the learners are having an argument and you hear one of them swearing.	Remind the learners about the ground rules. Give a warning that if it happens again, a sanction will be applied. If it does, make sure you follow it through.
One of your learners is texting on his mobile phone when he should be doing an activity.	Remind him of the ground rule stating that phones are not allowed during class time. Warn the learner that if you see him using his phone again, you will take if off him until the end of the lesson.
A group of learners has finished the activity and is now messing around at the back of the classroom.	Check that they have the correct answers to the task. Set another activity; make it more challenging.
You are trying to explain what to do and your learners are talking to each other and not listening to you.	Stop talking and wait for silence. Explain calmly that they need to listen in order to know what to do. Check they understand the task before they start. Monitor and support as necessary.
A learner turns up late then disrupts the class by asking what to do.	Ensure the class is doing the activity you set. Take the learner to one side and find out the reason for the lateness. Explain quickly what to do or ask a student to. If your institution has a penalty for lateness, make sure it is applied.

THE IMPORTANCE OF EFFECTIVE COMMUNICATION IN THE CLASSROOM

Good oral communication skills form the basis of effective working relationships between teachers and learners so it is essential that you consider the impact of what you say. The *Oxford English Dictionary* defines communication as 'the imparting or exchanging of information by speaking, writing or using some other medium', which seems relatively straightforward. However, in practice communication requires skilful handling by teachers if it is to have the desired impact on the classroom environment.

☑ TASK 2.6

Think about someone you know who you believe to be an effective communicator. Make a list of the reasons why.

Hopefully you will have come up with some or all of the reasons below.

1. Language

The power of language and its ability to connect individuals cannot be understated. Language choice is an active process and reflects the values that inform our identities both in and outside the classroom. For this reason, it is crucial that we understand the effect our language has on our learners' behaviour and motivation. The key principles are:

Do	Don't
be prepared to restructure language if the learners do not understand it. Simplify it and use vocabulary items and grammar structures with which they are familiar.	alienate learners by using language which is too complex or sophisticated. Language which is simple enough for the learners to understand is generally well received because it is meaningful and they can 'do something with it'.
provide learners with a glossary of terms and/or write key words/phrases on the board so that they are able to build up a bank of terms relating to the subject they are studying.	forget to ask learners for an example or definition of the language you are using as a way of checking they understand
use class time to teach useful phrases/words.	correct everything learners say. Think about when it is appropriate to do so and do it sensitively.

without conviction, then you risk disengaging the learners. Geoff Petty (2009) says, 'hypnotists can put people to sleep with monotone' so do be aware of the importance of a lively, enthusiastic delivery. Additional factors include the ability to articulate clearly and project the voice audibly without shouting. 'Chunking' relates to the pauses that we take between stretches of speech to allow learners time to digest and process what we mean, so avoid overloading them with too much language in one stretch. This is particularly important when you are teaching those for whom English is an additional language. These learners need longer to translate speech into their first language and process its meaning(s) before responding.

3. Non-verbal features

Non-verbal behaviours are really important in day-to-day communication. Given this fact, we need to capitalise on what can be conveyed using body language whilst being aware of the fact that non-verbal features are culture-bound; what one feature, such as folding arms, means in one culture can mean something entirely different in another. Selecting appropriate non-verbal signals as part and parcel of the process of communication greatly enhances our intrapersonal skills and enables us to become better senders and receivers of information. Needless to say, it is crucial to always consider the context within which language occurs and the way in which this can alter the way in which the intended message is interpreted.

4. Instructions

What do teachers spend a lot of time doing in the classroom? There are obviously a number of responses to this question, one of which is giving instructions. Given that our voice is one of our most valuable assets, the need to preserve it is really important. The worst-case scenario means repeating your instructions over and over again, either because learners don't understand them or they weren't listening. Implementing a few basic rules will help you to establish an orderly environment in which students are responsive and the learning time is maximised. Look at the instructions in the task on p.38. What are the issues? Think about how you would phrase the instructions if you were talking to your learners.

☑ TASK 2.7

1. 'OK, right, erm, what I'm asking you to do, erm, is to, er, get, get into pairs… no, erm, I meant threes… just a sec, erm, there's thirteen of you, so better make it threes and one four. Miriam, do you want to work in a three or four?'
2. 'Everybody stand up… now you're going to…'
3. 'Ask him over there.'
4. 'Work with your partner and then you'll be in a group with someone else from another group over there and you'll tell them what your partner thought. After that we'll hear everything with all of us listening and then you'll listen to the recording and take some notes that you can use for your homework.'
5. 'I'm handing out a piece of paper… I'm writing on the board.'
6. 'This is going to be really easy, what you need to do is listen and take notes.'

You might have thought that the teacher in (1) sounded hesitant whilst the one in (3) sounded rude. Perhaps you thought that the instructions in (4) sounded rather long-winded, while (5) is just unnecessary (isn't it obvious what you are doing?). (6) could be demotivating if the learners find it difficult. Finally, it would be better for the teacher who gave instruction (2) to tell the learners what to do before asking them to stand up. Giving good instructions is a really important aspect of classroom management and to do it well takes time and practice. Here are some tips for effective instruction-giving:

❯ Wait until you have the attention of the whole class before you give an instruction or you will find yourself talking over the learners and they will be talking over you and each other. Teachers do this differently: for example, some clap two or three times or knock on the whiteboard or a desk; some simply say 'listen to me' or 'can I have your attention please?' and wait until there is silence before moving on. Make sure all heads are turned towards you and that the focus is on them listening. You will need to experiment with different techniques and develop a style that you feel comfortable with.

❯ Stage the instructions if the activity is complex or has more than one part. Learners find it difficult to absorb a lot of information in one go so breaking down what they have to do is beneficial. This means telling them what's expected in part one before they need to know what's expected in parts two, three or four, and so on. Deliver information on a 'need-to-know' basis. An approach like this can help maintain good pace as you are able to effectively 'orchestrate' how the activity unfolds.

❯ Use simple concise language that learners understand. This is beneficial especially if English is not the learners' first language; for example, 'Farooq, work with Juan please' is better than 'Farooq, would you mind moving over there and sitting next to Juan?' as there is less language for him to understand. Accompanying your verbal instruction(s) with a non-verbal gesture is also helpful, as is writing the instruction on the whiteboard to maintain clarity.

this applies to all the others. Try the simple techniques listed here:

- Ask a learner to repeat back to you what they have to do – try not to use the strongest one.
- Demonstrate how an activity works – or ask the learners to.
- Ask questions such as, 'Are you working on exercise 1 or 2?', 'Mohamed, is your partner Mia or David?', and 'How long do you have for the reading exercise?'.

❯ Set a time limit for the activity as this helps establish and maintain good pace; however, this is really an approximation. For example, if you have given ten minutes for an activity and after five minutes everyone has finished, then it is clearly time to stop. On the other hand, if you have given ten minutes and after that time only one or two learners have finished, then obviously you need to extend the time. Use your professional judgement.

❯ Give a summary of the instructions before the learners start the activity.

It is a good idea to stand centrally at the front of the class and stand still when giving an instruction so that your voice projects clearly and everyone can hear you. Make eye contact to involve and engage the learners, and use any signs of non-comprehension (silence, quizzical expressions) to backtrack and repeat. A tip: give the instruction before distributing any materials or resources. If you don't, you'll lose the learners' attention as they'll think that it is more important to read what is on the paper than listen to you.

Until you become more experienced and confident, you may find that scripting your instructions (writing out what you'll say to the learners before the lesson) is helpful. This is fine – do whatever you need to do to boost your confidence levels. Following the guidelines above should result in clarity, direction and good pace.

5. Using names

When was the last time someone forgot your name? How did you feel? What about if you had met the person a few times before and they still couldn't remember your name? Chances are that the first time you wouldn't worry too much. You would, however, be much more likely to feel irritated the second, third or even fourth time around. Why is it important to use someone's name? Because it makes them feel valued and included (remember Maslow's triangle?), and shows that we are interested in them. The same is true for us as teachers. Failing to learn and use our learners' names is a recipe for disaster.

TASK 2.0

Make a list of ways in which you could remember a group of ten new names.

You may have come up with some of following ideas (adapted from Wallace [2007b]):

❯ Until you can do it automatically, ask learners to wear badges or stickers with their names. Alternatively, ask them to make name cards that they can display in front of the desk.
❯ Every time you ask a question, preface it with the learner's name. For example, 'Maria, what's the answer to number 8?'
❯ Use the learners' names at every opportunity until it becomes second nature.
❯ Use a name you and the learner feel comfortable with. Learners sometimes use a different name to the one on the register.
❯ Consider how you will address the learners as a group.

It is really important for us to learn and use our students' names. If we do, we increase the chances of establishing and maintaining respect and positive relationships with them.

TALKING POINT

In this section, you have read a lot about maintaining an orderly classroom/workplace and engaging students in learning. What have you discovered that is new? Have you changed your opinions about anything? What will you find easy and difficult about teaching your subject area?

SUMMARY

In this chapter, you have read about the importance of motivating learners and the strategies you can use to do this. You also looked at some models of motivation and considered their value in the classroom. You considered the nature of the learners who study in the further education and skills sector, and their potential barriers to learning. You explored the value of establishing positive teacher–student relationships and how these are underpinned by respect. You examined the ways in which you can help form these relationships in class. You discovered what ground rules are and how these can contribute to an environment conducive to learning. You read about the ways in which students learn and explored some different learning style models. You learned about the importance of tailoring teaching to suit different learners and the ways in which this can be done at different stages of the course. Finally, you read about how to manage the learning environment, including how to use language effectively, and the importance of giving good instructions and using learners' names.

Harmer, J. (2001) *The Practice of English Language Teaching*. Essex: Pearson Education Ltd.

Honey, P. and Mumford, A. (2000) *The Learning Styles: Helper's Guide*. Berks: Peter Honey Publications.

Kidd, W. and Czerniawski, G. (2010) *Successful Teaching 14–19: Theory, Practice and Reflection*. London: Sage.

Lemov, D. (2010) *Teach Like a Champion*. San Francisco: Jossey-Bass.

Petty, G. (2009) *Teaching Today: A Practical Guide* (4th edn). Cheltenham: Stanley Thornes.

Riddell, D. (2003) *Teaching English as a Foreign Language*. London: Hodder and Stoughton Ltd.

Rogers, B. (2012) *Cracking the Hard Class*. London: Sage.

Wallace, S. (2007a) *Getting the Buggers Motivated in FE*. London: Continuum Books.

Wallace, S. (2007b) *Managing Behaviour in the Lifelong Learning Sector* (2nd edn). Exeter: Learning Matters.

Websites

http://headguruteacher.com/2013/01/06/behaviour-management-a-bill-rogers-top-10/ (tips for behaviour management)

http://topnotchteaching.com/experts/behaviour-management-strategies/ (strategies for behaviour management)

https://www.teachit.co.uk/user_content/satellites/6/schoolplacements/Behaviour%20management%20advice%20leaflet%20Feb%202010.pdf

https://archive.org/details/Maintain1947 http://assessmentreformgroup.files.wordpress.com/2012/01/10principles_english.pdf (poster outlining ten assesment for learning principles)

www.marcprensky.com/writing/Prensky%20-%20Digital%20Natives,%20Digital%20Immigrants%20-%20Part1.pdf (reading about digital natives vs digital immigrants)

www.mcgraw-hill.co.uk/openup/chapters/9780335241125.pdf

www.simplypsychology.org/bandura.html (reading about social learning theory)

www.tes.co.uk/article.aspx?storycode=6008302 (TES article about the 'Mr Grimes' clip – see also p.28)

Video clip

Maintaining Classroom Discipline (1947), McGraw-Hill Book Company.
www.youtube.com/watch?v=oMYmaZm74k4

Identifying and accommodating individual needs

◎ LEARNING AIMS

By the end of this chapter, the reader will have a better understanding of:

❱ the concept of inclusive teaching and learning

❱ designing and carrying out appropriate initial assessments

❱ the importance of setting learning targets with learners

❱ selecting appropriate differentiation strategies to accommodate individual needs

THE CONCEPT OF INCLUSION

If you are new to the further education and skills sector, you may sometimes feel bombarded with the number of buzz words that you will encounter on a regular basis: achievement and retention, targets, learner voice and personalised learning, for example. One term you will come across again and again is 'inclusion'. You only need to look at the assessment for the Award in Education and Training to note how frequently the word 'inclusive' appears. As with equality and diversity (Chapter 1), promoting inclusion will be integrated into all aspects of your working practice. It is not always easy to implement but we should do everything we can to ensure that all learners feel included and valued.

✔ TASK 3.1

What do you understand by the term 'inclusion'? Write your own definition.

The concept of inclusion arose from an influential report by a national committee chaired by Tomlinson in 1996 to investigate post-compulsory provision for individuals with learning difficulties and disabilities. Instead of labelling these learners as 'disabled' and providing them with additional learning aids, the report proposed that it was the responsibility of the educational

make learning accessible for everyone. For example, ...
made to the learning environment, such as ensuring there are induction loops in each classroom to assist hard-of-hearing or deaf learners. Learning providers need to reach out to all learners, particularly those who feel reluctant to participate in education, to help them get back on track and gain a rich and rewarding learning experience.

AN INCLUSIVE LEARNING ENVIRONMENT

When you think about the word 'inclusion', what image of a classroom do you have? How are the learners seated? What is the role of the teacher and the learners in the learning process? As we will see in Chapter 5, we cannot say that there is only one way of delivering a lesson. We need to constantly reflect on our own practice to devise strategies to meet the diverse needs of our learners.

✔ TASK 3.2

What makes an inclusive learning environment? Read the extract below and identify some characteristics of inclusive teaching and learning.

Farah is an English teacher. In today's lesson, she wants her learners to be able to identify linguistic devices from different texts. Before the start of the lesson, she organises the classroom so that there are four desks adjacent to each other. She estimates 20 students will be attending and wants there to be five groups. One of the learners is visually impaired and requires assistive technology, a portable CCTV machine, to read information. This magnifies the material and allows the learner to view it as white writing on black paper. Farah has enlarged the typeface used to make it easier for this learner to read.

As the learners enter the classroom, Farah greets them by name and assigns them a seat, ensuring the number of learners in each group is approximately the same. In groups, the learners work on finding linguistic devices within different texts – one text per group. The teacher monitors and prompts the learners to steer them in the right direction if they are struggling. She asks questions such as, 'How has the writer aroused interest in this paragraph?' and 'Which words carry the most emotion?' One group finishes earlier than the others and Farah gives these learners an additional task to complete: to analyse the effectiveness of these linguistic devices.

Each group then presents its findings to the whole class. Some groups choose to represent the information using visuals or drama; others show the information using a mindmap. Each group is encouraged to evaluate its efforts.

We can only speculate as to the teacher's intentions but here are some general features that constitute an inclusive learning environment.

1. The layout of the learning environment

In Farah's lesson, the desks have been organised so that the learners have to collaborate with each other; no learner is excluded and the teacher is able to walk freely among the groups to help provide support. The teacher will need to match the seating plan to the activity but it is important that there is no barrier between the teacher and the learners. Having desks in rows can make it difficult for cooperative learning to occur, a fundamental element of inclusion.

2. Teaching materials, activities and resources

Within any lesson, there should be a variety of activities, materials and resources to engage and accommodate the needs of all learners. By using different approaches, we can engage learners, find out what interests them and encourage them to contribute. As we shall see in the next section, it is important to find out as much as you can about your learners in the initial stages of a course so that you are more likely to 'connect' with them and plan appropriate activities. Hopefully, they will also be more successful in their learning.

3. Teacher relationship with learners

It is important that we establish a positive relationship with our learners. In Farah's lesson, all learners were made to feel welcome as soon as they came into the classroom. She used their names and assigned them a seat. It was clear that no time was to be wasted; the lesson was to begin promptly to enable maximum opportunities for learning. In an inclusive setting, teachers will ask questions to promote discussion and encourage participation, valuing all learners' contributions.

4. Support

Farah was aware of the support needs of one of her learners and had made appropriate adjustments to the material. The individual was assigned the same task as the other learners but was provided with appropriate assistive technology to support him. As Wright *et al.* (2006, p.3) point out, no learners should be made to feel excluded from the educational process just because they have different needs:

> "…they are part of the mainstream learning community and are free to make choices and to find their place within the curriculum and to access the support they may need."

5. Differentiating instruction

We shall look at this in more detail later but it is important to recognise that learners work at different speeds and require different levels of challenge. Farah noticed that one group had finished an activity earlier than others so gave the learners an extension task to examine the information they had discovered in more depth.

been asked to do this or they may have chosen it themselves. It is important also evaluate their own progress if they are to develop their learning, so we need to provide opportunities for peer- and self-assessment.

TALKING POINT

It is difficult to argue against promoting inclusion in education. However, in practice it is not always easy to be as fully inclusive in our approach to teaching and learning as we would like. There may be constraints which have an impact on the planning and delivery of sessions. For example, if you are teaching several groups, with a large number of students in each class, it is not always easy to identify and respond to each individual's needs. What other constraints might there be?

In addition, if learners are being offered additional support outside the course hours, is there an argument that they are receiving discrete provision, being treated differently from others? What impact does offering more learning support have on educational providers?

INITIAL ASSESSMENT

When you come face to face with a new learning cohort, you are likely to encounter a heterogeneous group of individuals, all with diverse needs, abilities and interests. It is important to recognise but embrace these differences:

> *"There are no students who are 'different' or 'normal' or 'traditional' or 'stereotyped': there are just students who are all individuals, and who need to be spoken to and responded to on their own terms." (Powell, S. and Tummons, J., 2011, p.52)*

TASK 3.3

What kinds of individual differences connected to learning and studying can you think of?

You will probably have come up with a long list of how learners differ. Hartley (2000) categorises the differences in learning under four headings: fundamental differences, cognitive styles, learning strategies and preferences. Fundamental differences are concerned with aspects which are difficult to change, such as age, gender, culture, religious beliefs and level of motivation. Cognitive styles relate to the preferred way individuals process information. Some learners do not respond well to ambiguity; others relish problem-solving tasks and desire a more flexible approach from the teacher. Learning strategies are the methods that learners choose to help them progress in their learning. Some learners may only want to recall information to pass an assessment, for example, whereas others will actively search for deeper meaning. Finally, individuals have different preferences with regard to learning. Some learners are more alert in the morning, while others need time to warm up. Individuals often like to sit in the same place in the learning environment and work with the same people. This is not necessarily a bad thing but it is a good idea to mix up the groupings from time to time.

So, how can we find out useful information about our learners which will enable us to plan for inclusive teaching and learning? An important starting point is initial assessment. You may not be responsible for carrying this out yourself but you will still need to be involved in the process as the results of the assessment will help inform your planning and determine appropriate support for your learners. Initial assessment often takes place before the start of the learning programme and has a number of aims.

1. It allows the teacher to establish the learner's prior knowledge which will assist in future planning. It may be that learners can be exempt from course modules through APEL (Accreditation of Prior Experiential Learning). It may also be the case that the learner does not currently possess the skills necessary to pursue a vocational or academic learning programme, and will then be provided with alternative pathways. If learners are placed on the wrong course, they will struggle to meet the demands of the programme and drop out. This is not a positive outcome for the learner, tutor or educational provider.

2. Initial assessment enables the teacher to find out about the learner's goals, level of motivation (see Chapter 2) and particular support needs. Individuals can, although they are not required to, declare any learning disabilities or difficulties on the application form. It is important to discuss the level of support they need so that they feel included in the planning process and feel valued, and appropriate adjustments can be made in good time. It may be that some learners require materials to be sent in advance of the sessions or produced on different coloured paper, or the materials may need to be presented in a different format altogether. For example, learners could have access to recordings of the course content via podcasts.

3. It gives the learners the opportunity to find out about the learning programme. They may be feeling anxious about studying again and having an opportunity to discuss their fears with a member of staff may put their minds at rest.

4. An initial assessment can be used to determine learners' level of functional skills (see Chapter 10). Knowing how individuals will cope with written assignments, for example, is essential. They may need additional external support or, as a tutor, you may realise that you will need to help the learners with specific skills such as making notes, delivering presentations and

basic numeracy. Some learners may lack confidence in ICT and will benefit from a refresher course to keep them up to speed and boost their confidence.

☑ TASK 3.4

Can you recall your own experience of initial assessment, perhaps to gain entry on to the Level 3 Award in Education and Training course? What did you have to do? A written test? An interview? How did you feel about having to do an initial assessment?

Hopefully, your experience of initial assessment was a positive one. The initial assessment process should be an holistic one. In other words, a variety of assessment methods should be used to gain an overall impression of the learner's abilities, personality, goals and preferences. The type of initial assessment used will depend on the nature of the learning programme and it may be organised by other teams in your institution. Nevertheless, as was mentioned earlier, you will need to be made aware of the results of the initial assessment so that you can plan your lessons accordingly. Initial assessment methods can include:

> application forms (these provide a summary of the learner's qualifications and abilities);
> interviews (these enable you to gain a rounded profile of the learner and identify aspirations);
> tasks (for example, summarising an article, writing a short essay to determine the learner's level of literacy, a numeracy initial assessment tool);
> psychometric tests (used to measure aspects of your mind such as verbal or numerical reasoning);
> problem-solving tasks related to the academic or vocational area;
> a presentation/microteaching session (relevant for candidates wishing to be selected for teacher training courses); and
> a needs analysis questionnaire (see p.48 for an example of a needs analysis questionnaire for an ESOL group).

NEEDS ANALYSIS   Put a tick (✓) as required (learners to complete with support)

I would like to improve my English in order to:	Important	Not important
Communicate with my GP/school teachers/neighbours		
Help children with homework		
Read and follow instructions		
Deal with clients/customers		
Deal with phone calls		
Write emails to colleagues		
Deal with travel needs		
Give presentations		
Take part in interviews		
Prepare for higher education		
Find a better job		
Other:		

It is important that whatever assessment method is used, the staff administrating it have been trained so that they are able to negotiate a learning programme with the individual or provide appropriate guidance on alternative routes.

TALKING POINT

Given the importance of inclusion in education, how we can we ensure that the process of initial assessment is inclusive? Is there a danger that setting a written task will disadvantage dyslexic learners? Powell and Tummons (2011) maintain that learners with mental health difficulties may find interviews stressful and not portray themselves in the best way. Some learners will also require specialist support to complete an initial assessment, which may not have come to light prior to the assessment. What can be done to ensure the initial assessment process runs as smoothly as possible?

INDIVIDUAL LEARNING PLANS

The information gleaned from the initial assessment will inform the content of an individual learning plan (ILP), also known as a personal learning plan (PLP) or personal development plan (PDP). This can be completed manually or online. It helps formalise the process of analysing learners' skills and abilities, and indicates gaps in their knowledge. Because the learners are responsible for setting their own goals under the guidance of the tutor, they should feel more motivated to learn as they can see how they are developing. Progress needs to be monitored at regular intervals to see whether the learners have achieved their targets and are developing strategies to become more self-reliant. As a tutor, you can design learning activities which play to the learners' strengths and accommodate their needs.

☑ TASK 3.5

What information would you expect to find in an individual learning plan?

Here is some information that might appear in an ILP:

- **Results of initial and diagnostic tests**. Diagnostic assessment is carried out in the initial stages of the learning programme to check the learners are studying at the right level and for the tutor to see how they are progressing.
- **Learner's attendance and punctuality**.
- **Long-term and short-term goals**. It is useful to find out what learners can already do (their starting points) and what they want to be able to do. For example, a learner's long-term goal might be to go to university. A short-term goal could be being able to cite and reference academic sources appropriately.
- **Development needs**. For example, a strength might be cooperating with peers and a weakness could be proofreading work for grammar, punctuation and spelling errors. Learners should be encouraged to record their own targets so that they take ownership of their learning. These can be then discussed and negotiated with the tutor or support worker.
- **Support needs**. Other individuals may be interested in viewing ILPs: other tutors, support workers, managers and external verifiers, for example. There needs to be a record of how the learner has been supported. For example, a learner may require support from the dyslexia team to assist with written assignments.

THE INDUCTION PROCESS

The learners' first impressions of the learning environment, course, teachers and other students are likely to stay with them for a long time so it is important to try to make their initial experience a positive one. Can you recall your first day at school, college of work and how you felt? What influenced your feelings? If learners have a negative experience of their place of study, they might not choose to stay. We want to stop them from walking away!

The settling-in period which occurs in the first few days or weeks of a learning programme is known as induction. During the induction process, the learners should receive information about the following:

❭ **The learning programme**. This should include the content of the course, assessment methods, support systems such as tutorials, and types of activities in which they will be expected to participate. Some learners have a very traditional view of teaching and learning and the role of the teacher. It is a good idea from the outset to outline your expectations of your learners. For example, you can explain that the learners will need to take some responsibility for their learning and be expected to collaborate with their peers. You will be guiding the learners through their assessments but not spoonfeeding them!

❭ **The learning environment**. It is a good idea, particularly if you work in a large institution, to take the learners on a short tour of the place where they are going to study. They need to know where basic amenities are found such as the toilets, vending machines, telephones and refreshments in addition to knowing the location of the library and student support and being aware of first aid and emergency evacuation procedures. They should also be introduced to the VLE (Virtual Learning Environment) if there is one so that they have the opportunity to access materials remotely.

Learners also need to know what behaviour is appropriate in the place of study and classroom. For example, if they need an ID card to get into the institution, they should be informed that if they leave this at home, they may not be allowed in. In Chapter 2, we looked at the importance of negotiating ground rules as a class early on in the course in order to promote an atmosphere of mutual respect.

❭ **Information about their peers.** It is worth remembering that even if learners appear confident on the outside, they are likely to have some qualms about studying, particularly if they have been away from education for a while. Therefore, to make this transition a little smoother, an 'icebreaker' is a good way of getting the learners to find out some information about each other. For instance, learners could interview each other in pairs and then feed back to the whole class. One of our favourite icebreakers is the 'star of life'. The teacher draws or writes some personal information around a five-point star and encourages the learners to predict how this information is relevant.

For example, the picture of a piano depicts one of the teacher's hobbies and the place names are cities where the teacher has taught. The learners could then do the same in pairs. Not all learners like to reveal information about themselves and it is important to monitor this kind of activity to prevent it from going on for too long; the learners want to come away with something concrete from the first session of a course. Nevertheless, icebreakers are good way of encouraging collaboration, relaxing learners and creating a positive learning atmosphere.

> **Answers to any queries they might have**. Finally, and most importantly, the learners need to be given an opportunity to express themselves. If they are confused about any matter relating to the course, this should be cleared up straightaway. By the end of the induction process, the learners should be ready to participate wholeheartedly in their learning programme.

☑ TASK 3.6

It is a good idea to evaluate the learners' experience of induction so that you can use the results to improve the process next time. This is especially important if learners are doing an online course as they may be feeling a little lost. In this case, you will need to find out whether the learners received materials promptly and are aware of how they can make contact should there be any issues. One way of evaluating the induction process is to ask learners to complete a short questionnaire such as the one below. You might want to rate your own experience if you have recently enrolled on a course.

Statement	Rating 1 = strongly agree 5 = strongly disagree	Additional comments (optional)
1. Information about the programme was clear, accessible and comprehensive.	1 2 3 4 5	
2. The initial assessment process was a positive experience.	1 2 3 4 5	
3. The registration process was clear and straightforward.	1 2 3 4 5	
4. The induction activities were useful.	1 2 3 4 5	
5. I know how I will be assessed.	1 2 3 4 5	
6. I know how to access the facilities I need.	1 2 3 4 5	
7. I know what to do if I have a personal or study support need.	1 2 3 4 5	
8. Initial contact with my tutor was positive.	1 2 3 4 5	
9. Overall, I am looking forward to studying on my course.	1 2 3 4 5	

DIFFERENTIATION STRATEGIES

If you are currently working in the further education and skills sector, you will probably already be employing differentiation strategies, consciously or without even realising it. For example, if you ask questions and nominate individual learners according to their ability, you are differentiating your checks on learning. You are targeting your questions so that all learners are given an opportunity to extend their knowledge. If you ask a student to support another learner, you are differentiating because you are encouraging individuals to learn from each other. Although you are trying to ensure that each individual has a positive learning experience, differentiation should not mean you are spending hours creating discrete tasks for each individual. There are many ways in which you can differentiate and the more you do it, the easier it will become.

So, what do we mean by differentiation? One way to describe it is 'an approach to teaching that attempts to ensure that <u>all</u> students learn well, despite their many differences' (Perry, 2003, p.22). We need to ensure that we match activities to abilities and needs, offer appropriate support and provide a suitable level of challenge so that all learners are working to their full potential.

☑ TASK 3.7

There are a variety of differentiation strategies. How many can you think of?

Below are some of the more common ways of differentiating. We shall briefly look at each strategy in turn, thinking about how we can make the process a meaningful one.

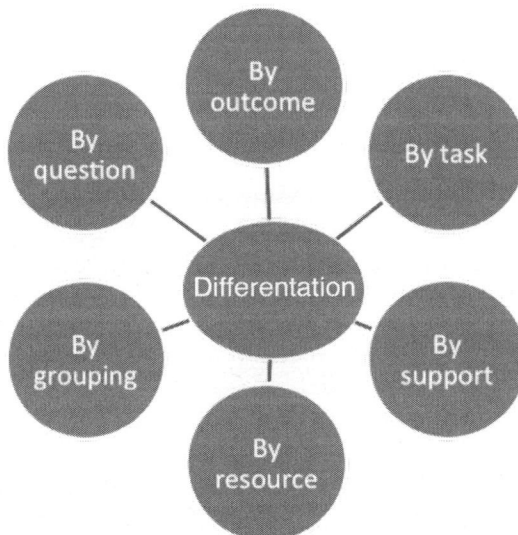

Differentiation by outcome

This is one of the most common ways of differentiating. Learners are given the same task to do but will produce very different results. For example, if the task is to look at the different components of the hospitality industry, some learners may produce a list while others may mention their own experiences and adopt a more evaluative approach. Learning outcomes (see Chapter 4) can also be differentiated to facilitate progress for individuals in the class (see the picture below). You can devise 'core' objectives (represented by the trunk of the tree), outcomes which *all* learners will be able to achieve by the end of the session and 'extension' outcomes which stretch the stronger individuals in the group (the branches and twigs of the tree). For example, you might envisage that *most* learners will be able to explain why the hospitality industry is important to an area and *some* learners will be able to assess the impact of the world economy on the industry.

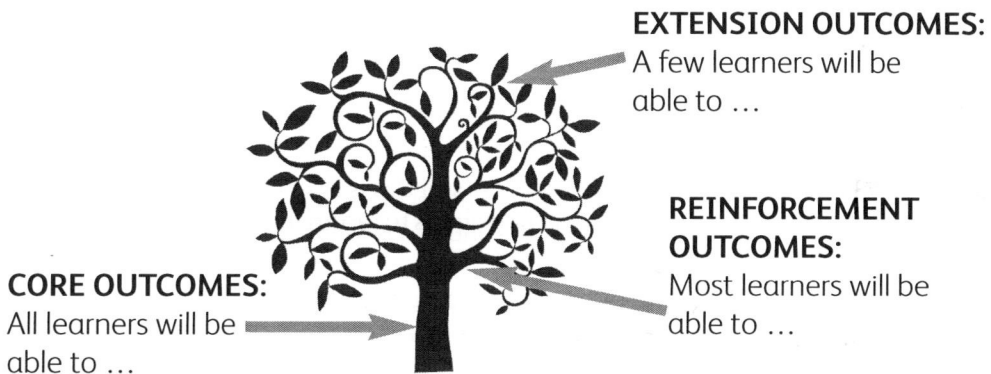

EXTENSION OUTCOMES:
A few learners will be able to …

REINFORCEMENT OUTCOMES:
Most learners will be able to …

CORE OUTCOMES:
All learners will be able to …

(Adapted from an example in Convery and Coyle, 1993)

The difficulty with implementing differentiation by outcome is ensuring that all learners are really working to the best of their ability and not taking the simplest route. It is easy to label learners as strong or weak but we need to be careful of pigeonholing our learners and not having high enough expectations of them. All learners need to be challenged, not only the 'stronger' individuals. Differentiation by outcome is a useful way of diagnosing ability and using the information to set individual targets. However, be wary of only using this approach to differentiate instruction.

Differentiation by task

One way of making differentiation more meaningful is to differentiate by task. For example, you can use graduated worksheets; the tasks become more challenging as the learners progress. Not every individual will be expected to complete all the tasks (again, you could have a set of core tasks which you expect all learners to be able to complete successfully) but individuals can work at their own pace, and, in theory, learning should be more effective. Producing varied worksheets can be time consuming for the teacher but you don't necessarily have to plan different tasks for different learners. Cowley (2013) suggests using the 'top and tail technique' to cater for all abilities. Tasks should be pitched at just the right level for the learners in the middle; the lower

"To accommodate the different learners' needs, I often differentiate by task. I give the learners graduated worksheets to support them. One of Learner A's short-term goals is to be able to read a short text and answer a series of comprehension questions on it, thus improving her extensive and intensive skills. She needs sufficient time to complete more straightforward questions. Learner B, who needs to be stretched, is provided with more open-ended probing questions once he has completed the easier tasks. I also give the learners individual work in accordance with their learning targets. For example, Learner B has been given additional grammar exercises to be done as homework.

Differentiation through variety of strategy and resource helps to motivate learners. I use a wide range of learning resources such as flashcards, the interactive whiteboard, sticky notes, realia and music to stimulate learners and create a classroom atmosphere conducive to learning. One of Learner B's targets is to improve his spelling. By discussing different strategies to help him improve this, he has found a method which is effective for him. I use pair and group work to facilitate differentiation. Learners can pool their resources and learn from others. Group work helps to provide a non-threatening atmosphere because it provides more opportunities for bonding. Learner A has more time to sound out her ideas and hopefully she is beginning to gain in confidence. She is gradually beginning to join in more and feel less insecure.

Finally, where possible, I also find it useful to provide learners with an element of choice on how to express the required learning, for example in the form of a presentation or written report. Giving the students an opportunity to reflect on their work also gives me an idea of how well they can assess their own learning. Learner B is beginning to develop his reflective skills so that learning is more effective for him."

Catering for individual needs is one of the most challenging aspects of being a teacher or support worker. It is our responsibility to create a positive learning atmosphere in the classroom where it is accepted that learners are working at different levels and on different tasks, where each learner has his or her personal targets, and where each learner's contribution is accepted and valued by everyone. It is important to plan how best to differentiate instruction with your learners, rather than hoping for the best. As you gain more experience, you will become more skilful at considering the needs of your learners but we would suggest, at least initially, that you formalise the process of differentiation by recording the strategies you will employ in your lesson or support plan. Think also about how you might differentiate homework to encourage learners to work on their areas for development and improve their study skills.

TALKING POINT

'Time is the reason why so many teachers feel they cannot differentiate whether it is by task or outcome. This is because teachers see differentiation as extra and not part of the delivery of the curriculum' (McNamara and Moreton, 1997). We can all appreciate the importance of differentiation but each strategy has its positive points and limitations. You also have to consider which strategy is appropriate within your teaching context and for your learners. Which strategies of differentiation do you currently, or plan to, use with your learners? Are they effective? Do they have any limitations?

SUMMARY

In this chapter you have read about the concept of inclusion which will influence everything we do in the learning environment from identifying learners' needs, planning and facilitating learning to assessing and evaluating the learning process. The need to carry out appropriate initial assessments to gauge individuals' starting points and diagnose any support needs they might have was also discussed. You looked at the importance of individual learning plans, with individual targets set for each learner. Finally, we summarised and evaluated some common differentiation strategies which you might use in your professional practice to cater for the needs of your learners.

REFERENCES AND FURTHER READING

Convery, A. and Coyle, D. (1993) *Differentation: Taking the Initiative (Pathfinder)*. London: CILT.

Cowley, S. (2013) *The Seven T's of Practical Differentiation*. Bristol: Sue Cowley Books Ltd.

Francis, M. and Gould, J. (2012) *Achieving your PTLLS Award: A Practical Guide to Teaching in the Lifelong Learning Sector*. London: Sage.

Hartley, J. (2000) 'Individual differences and learning.' *Perspectives on Learning*. M. Bloor and A. Lahiff (eds). London: Greenwich University Press.

Kerry, T. (2002) *Learning Objectives, Task Setting and Differentiation*. Cheltenham: Nelson Thornes.

McNamara, S. and Moreton, G. (1997) *Understanding Differentiation: A Teacher's Guide*. London: David Fulton.

Perry, D. (2003) 'Differentiation – policy and practice.' *Language Issues: The Journal of NATECLA*, 15(1), pp. 22–23.

Petty, G. (2009) *Teaching Today* (4th edn). Cheltenham: Nelson Thornes.

Powell, S. and Tummons, J. (2011) *Inclusive Practice in the Lifelong Learning Sector.* Exeter: Learning Matters.

Tomlinson, J. (1996) *Inclusive Learning: Report of the Learning Difficulties and Disabilities Subcommittee.* Further Education Funding Council.

Wright, A., Abdi-Jama, S., Colquhoun, S., Speare, J. and Partridge, J. (2006) *FE Lecturer's Guide to Diversity and Inclusion.* London: Continuum.

Websites

http://archive.excellencegateway.org.uk/pdf/Good_Practice_Guide.pdf (Guidance on effective initial assessment)

www.newteachers.tes.co.uk/content/using-differentiation-mixed-ability-classes (Guidance on differentiation)

Planning learning

LEARNING AIMS

By the end of this chapter, the reader will have a better understanding of:

❭ the reasons for lesson planning

❭ how to devise and create inclusive lesson plans and schemes of work

❭ the difference between aims and objectives

❭ the relevance of SMART objectives

LESSON PLANNING

A lesson plan, sometimes known as a teaching and learning or session plan, is a document, usually formal, which outlines the content you want your students to learn and the process of how this should be achieved. Lesson planning is a very useful exercise and something from which all teachers, even experienced ones, benefit. Initially, you may find that it takes a while to formulate your ideas and record the stages of your plan. However, the process becomes easier the more you do it. You are usually required to produce formal lesson plans on teacher training courses (see Appendix C for an example pro forma for the Level 3 Award) and may have to keep a record of lesson planning in your place of work for quality assurance purposes.

Bear in mind that what is recorded in the lesson plan will not necessarily be the same as what happens in the lesson; it should be a guide rather than an instruction manual. What goes in your lesson plan may be largely dictated by the requirements of an internal or external syllabus, but you should never lose sight of the fact that the learners' needs will always be at the heart of the planning process. Experienced teachers will continue to produce lesson plans because even though the material may be familiar, the learners are different. There is no guarantee that what 'works' with one group will be successful with another. We always have to consider how best to plan for individual learning and make any appropriate adjustments to material and our delivery (see Chapter 3).

The amount of detail that goes into the lesson plan will depend on your approach towards planning, how well you know your learners, your experience, the type of lesson you are teaching and your familiarity with the content.

☑ TASK 4.1

What are the reasons for writing a lesson plan? Write down what you consider to be the key aims of lesson planning.

SOME REASONS FOR LESSON PLANNING

Your list may include something similar to the following:

❭ A lesson plan provides a framework for the lesson, giving it a sense of direction and purpose. It can help learners to move towards specific learning outcomes and, provided you have considered the aim of each activity from the learners' point of view and the transitions between each stage, the lesson should feel more cohesive and less like a list of activities. Simply writing a lesson plan and recording your thoughts will help you to think through the different processes of the lesson.

❭ A plan provides a useful means of support or aide-memoire. This is especially useful if you are new to teaching as you may not have the confidence to deviate greatly from your lesson plan and think on your feet. If you are worried about your own use of language, for example when giving instructions for a complex activity, it can be a useful exercise to write down exactly what you want to say to help you grade your language appropriately. Bear in mind that your lesson plan should be a clear working document. In other words, you, above all, should be able to follow it. You may find it helpful to highlight key stages or phrases to focus you when you are teaching. There is no shame in having to refer to your plan during the lesson although you will, of course, not want to read from it verbatim.

❭ It helps with the timing of activities. We have found that teacher trainees can find it difficult to allocate appropriate timings to each activity, perhaps because they or their learners get distracted, or they feel all the activities need to have been completed for the learning objectives to be met. There will need to be a certain amount of flexibility here depending on how the learners are coping with the activities set, but it is useful to estimate the duration of each activity to maintain momentum and pace.

❭ It can help you to think about how to make your lesson inclusive, incorporating differentiated activities depending on your learners' needs, abilities and interests. Some learners will need more support, while others will need to be challenged (see Chapter 3). As you gain more experience, you will think about what shapes your attitudes towards teaching and learning, namely the pedagogical approaches you have adopted and your role in the process. For example, is there group work included? Are learners encouraged to work together to solve a problem or do you provide them with the solution?

❭ A lesson plan is a useful record. You can use it as an evaluation tool to reflect on what you consider went well in the lesson and what you would change were you to teach the same topic again. In theory, if you are unable to deliver the lesson for any reason, the plan would also be a useful guide for another teacher to follow. This is not always the case in reality as what makes sense to us may be unclear to someone else.

❱ A final point is that lesson planning may also have a positive impact on learners. If the learners can see a teacher is working from a lesson plan, they may consider the teacher to be professional and appreciate a clear structure to a lesson. Again, this depends on the learners themselves and what they expect from a teacher and the learning process. Some learners may become frustrated if they feel activities are cut short purely to move the lesson on.

WHAT SHOULD BE INCLUDED IN A LESSON PLAN?

You may have to produce your own lesson plan but your place of work is likely to have a template which you should use for the planning process. There is usually at least one cover sheet which outlines the topic of the lesson, the learning outcomes, the duration and the venue. There should also be a procedural document which will outline each stage of the lesson, showing what the learners will be doing and how learning will be assessed.

☑ **TASK 4.2**

Look at the following elements which may be seen in a lesson plan. Which do you believe should be included? If they are not evidenced here, where else might they appear?

❱ Aims and objectives
❱ Personal (teacher's aims)
❱ Stage aims
❱ Group (or individual, if teaching a one-to-one lesson) profile
❱ Presumed knowledge
❱ Differentiation strategies
❱ Assessment methods
❱ Anticipated problems and solutions
❱ Timetable fit: links to past and future lessons
❱ Resources
❱ Starter and closing activity
❱ Evidence that the learning environment is safe
❱ Timings
❱ Interaction pattern
❱ Functional skills
❱ Evaluation

On the next page is an example of a lesson plan written by a trainee teacher of chemistry. You may not be familiar with the topic but, as you can see, the front page outlines the topic area and lesson objectives. These are differentiated (see Chapter 3); it is clear what the core and extension lesson objectives are. The lesson procedure is quite detailed, with differentiation strategies included. Although the aim of each stage is not identified explicitly, there are some key words to help signpost the teacher and each activity is mapped to the lesson outcomes. There are interesting starter and closing activities mentioned and a range of techniques and multimedia are integrated in the lesson. Functional skills are also embedded and a space is left at the end of the lesson place for the teacher to evaluate the lesson.

Learner activity plan

Date: 17/4/13	**Teacher:** PB	**Learning Area:** GCSE
Module/Unit: 1	**Course:** GCSE Science	**Length of Course:** 1 year
Week Number: 11	**Length of session**: 2 hours	

Start of lesson activities

Split the class in two; teams have to describe a word on the board to someone who can't see what the word is. They also have to use certain words in their descriptions: all words refer to last week's session.

Learning objectives

All students will be able to :
1. State why we do cracking and what kind of reaction it is
2. Distinguish between an alkene and an alkane
3. Define monomer and polymer
4. Draw the structure of an alkene

Most students will be able to:
5. Compare and contrast the structures of alkanes and alkenes
6. Determine the polymer name if the monomer is given
7. Explain the test for an alkene

Some students will be able to:
8. Draw alkenes with double bond in different places
9. Draw the displayed formula of a polymer

Teaching and learning activities related to the learning objectives

Duration	Teaching and learning activities	Differentiation
Activity 1 (20 mins)	What is cracking? (LO1) Supply and demand graphic: show students the graft with questions for them to figure out the relationship between what's in crude oil and what bits we actually need. Students think independently, then with peer. Use molymod	Peer support Provide prompts to support students if necessary

	kit to show cracking of molecule – a picture of apparatus for cracking in the lab. Elicit from students what kind of reaction is going on. On post-it notes, students write a definition: snowball – share in groups to make one definition. Compare with own definition: 'Thermally decomposing large hydrocarbons so that they are split into smaller, more useful fractions.'	Pictorial representation as a visual stimulus followed by class discussion (aural stimulus). Differentiation by response: students coming up with own response but scaffolding (own definition) to help learners who are struggling.
Activity 2 **(15 mins)**	**Alkanes vs alkenes (LOs 2, 4, 5)** Worksheet: students name an alkane or alkene, draw the formula and write the molecular formula for a set of examples.	Will be revision for some learners – can be encouraged to support students who were absent (TM, AB, WW). Extension work for more advanced learners.
Activity 3 **(10 mins)**	**Test for alkene (LO7)** Pre-video work: students look for colour changes and to think about what is happening in the reaction. Watch video to compare answers. After video: draw the molecules on the board and ask students to see if they can figure out what happened. Elicit addition reaction.	Problem-solving activity: group support.
Activity 4 **(15 mins)**	Recap on cracking: find someone who can answer each question (LOs 1, 2, 4, 5, 6, 7) Revision task: learners given a sheet with nine questions; students ask around and find someone who can answer each question. They can't have the same person more than twice.	Students asked privately if they can answer a question before being put on the spot in front of the class.
Activity 5 **(10 mins)**	**Define monomer and polymer (LO3, 6)** Get one student up with arms folded to represent an alkene monomer and them to open their arms and link arms (or put a hand on the shoulder of the person next to them if they aren't comfortable linking arms) with someone else, get the whole class together as a chain, or polymer. Define monomer and polymer.	Kinaesthetic learner activity to help visualise new concept before oral and visual descriptions. Differentiation by response.

| Activity 6 (20 mins) | **Drawing polymers (LO9)** Questions about how ethane becomes polyethene. Ask students to draw propene becoming polypropene. Extension task: students try polytetrafluoroethene. | Model provided as support. More able learners pushed with harder questions to figure out structure. |
| **Flexi activity** | If time, students tackle exam questions 1, 2, 3 – finish for homework. | Questions structured to test different skills, not just writing ability. |

Assessment of learning linked to lesson objectives

Objective 1: targeted question and answer with oral and written feedback
Objective 2: successful completion of exercise, self-assessment and peer assessment
Objective 3: feedback; question and answer
Objective 4: successful feedback, peer assessment
Objective 5: observation, response to questions
Objective 6: observation, feedback
Objective 7: observation and feedback
Objective 8: self- and peer assessment, comparison with own model
Objective 9: self- and peer assessment, comparison with own model

End of lesson activities

Sentence matching of key themes – mingle activity

Learning resources	**Homework**	**Functional skills**
IWB PowerPoint Worksheets Whiteboard Molymod kids Post-it notes	Exam questions 1, 2 and 3	Spoken language use: defining key terms Identifying key terms and synonyms Writing short summaries/definitions Problem-solving/discussion with colleagues Listening skills from audio-visual stimulus (video) Note-taking and note-making Forming and responding to questions

Evaluation

REASONS FOR DEVIATING FROM YOUR LESSON PLAN

There may be instances during your lessons when you feel you need to deviate from your lesson plan. For example, you may decide it is in the learners' best interests to go with the flow. If they are particularly engaged in a discussion or activity, it is worthwhile continuing with this rather than starting a new task only because it is included in your lesson plan. Learners may also need more time to understand something than you had originally thought. We cannot predict everything learners might find difficult with a task or concept and we will constantly have to review material so that it is more digestible for learners. You may also find that learners are not engaged with a topic or you feel for whatever reason that it would be insensitive to continue with the subject matter. All these are valid reasons for moving in a different direction from what is recorded in your lesson plan. It is always useful to have contingency plans so that you can omit exercises or have additional tasks prepared should the need arise.

ALTERNATIVE WAYS OF RECORDING THE LESSON PLANNING PROCESS

There may be instances when you cannot produce a formal lesson plan. Perhaps you have to cover a class at short notice, for example. However, this does not mean that you should skirt the lesson planning process; you still need to think through the stages of the lesson, how you are going to check learning and respond to individual needs. You might want to use one of the following approaches to planning outlined below.

1. Using sticky notes

This is a very quick way of recording the key stages of the lesson so that you still have something concrete to which you can refer when delivering the session (see below).

1. STARTER – Ask each other Qs about last week's lesson
2. LEAD-IN – Show visuals re healthy eating. Elicit ideas.
3. T/F exercise – Mark true/false on handout (facts about healthy eating).
4. FEEDBACk via IWB. Peer correction.
5. GROUP EX. – Work out their BMI and report back.
6. WRITING – Students produce tips (leaflet) – how to eat healthily (*may need to help with key language)
7. CLOSING EX – Think –pair –share

2. Using mindmaps

You might also want to jot down some ideas and connect them, in the form of a mindmap or bubble diagram (see below).

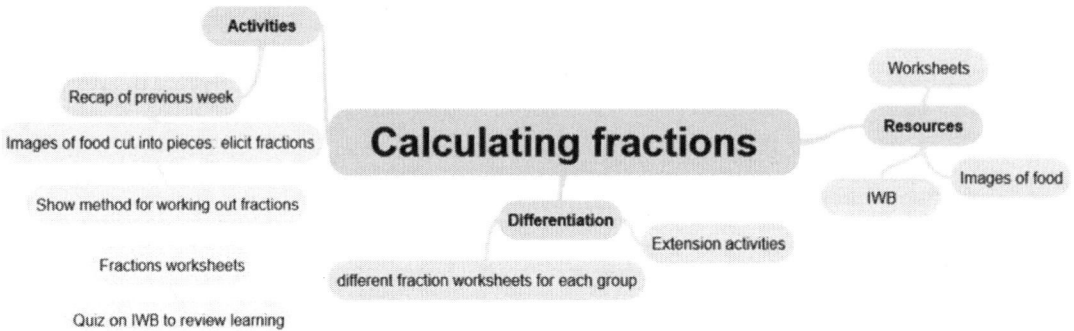

Activities

Recap of previous week

Images of food cut into pieces: elicit fractions

Show method for working out fractions

Fractions worksheets

Quiz on IWB to review learning

Calculating fractions

Differentiation

different fraction worksheets for each group

Extension activities

Worksheets

Resources

Images of food

IWB

(Created using www.examtime.com)

3. Planning backwards

It might feel a bit strange to plan from the end back to the start but this can be useful if you know you want your learners to produce or create something by the end of the lesson (such as a dance routine, a C.V., a fish dish). Thinking back through the stages, considering how each one builds on the next can help provide focus to the lesson.

TALKING POINT

How do you feel about lesson planning? What aspects do you think might be the most challenging?

SETTING LEARNING AIMS AND OUTCOMES

Whenever we deliver a lesson, we need to think about in what direction we want the lesson to go: what we are trying to achieve. This can be described as the aim of a session. Aims are broad statements of intent and should give you and the learners an overall idea of what the lesson is going to be about. For example, an aim for learners studying on a hairdressing course might be to improve their understanding of different colouring techniques.

Connected to aims are objectives or learning outcomes which are specific statements that can be observed or measured. They specify what a learner should be able to do by the end of the lesson in order for the teacher to assess whether or not there is evidence of learning having taken place. We can think of lesson objectives as the different building blocks or steps we need to achieve on our way to reaching our goals or aims. Setting learning outcomes at the beginning of the lesson will provide a sense of a purpose and direction to your lesson and may help to ease anxiety as the learners have an idea of what is expected of them. They should be understood by the learners and written from their point of view rather than for the benefit of another teacher or trainer. You might also like to consider some problems with setting objectives, something we shall visit at the end of this section.

A useful way of recording lesson objectives is to use the acronym SMART. There are different variations of this but our way of remembering it is the following:

» **S**pecific: the lesson objectives describes exactly what is going to happen, in concrete terms, where and for whom. There should be no ambiguity here.
» **M**easurable: the markers we have to observe and assess progress to demonstrate that the objective has been achieved. For example, learners are able to *explain* what is meant by capital budgeting.
» **A**chievable: how feasible a learning outcome is in terms of the learners' ability, the resources and support you have available.
» **R**elevant: whether the goal will be useful for the learners and relevant to the subject area.
» **T**ime-bound: when the outcome of the learning objective should be met. This may be by the end of the lesson or over a longer period of time depending on the nature of the lesson.

SMART objectives are written using verbs which express actions such as analyse, assess, recognise, explain, identify and construct. They usually begin with the phrase 'by the end of the lesson the learner will be able to…', or with a 'can' statement, for example 'the learner can…'. Learners studying on vocational courses such as NVQs will need to demonstrate their ability to perform different skills in the workplace. They need to show what they can do already and receive appropriate support to develop their knowledge and skills.

☑ TASK 4.3

Look at the statements below and decide whether the objectives are SMART. All of them are related to a specific timescale so you do not need to worry about the time-bound aspect.

Statement	SMART?
1. Raise awareness of different organisational structures used in business.	
2. Use capital letters for people's names.	
3. Know how to speak Arabic fluently.	
4. Learn how lifestyle factors can affect major body systems.	
5. Read a chapter on Macbeth.	
6. Convert fractions into decimals.	
7. Evaluate the values and underpinning care principles used in social care.	

Points to consider

You will probably have noticed a difference in the language used to express the outcomes. Some of the objectives expressed on p.67 are non-behavioural. This means it is difficult to say whether there is evidence of successful learning. In general, when writing objectives, we avoid using verbs such as 'know', 'understand', 'appreciate' and 'learn' because it is difficult to observe and measure learning, knowledge, appreciation and understanding. Can we be certain, for example, that our learners know something? They may be able to recite something back to us but knowledge is far too abstract a concept to measure. Behavioural objectives describe a change in behaviour that has resulted from learning taking place. Statements 2, 6 and 7 all use 'action' verbs and can be described as behavioural objectives. Statement 2 is very specific and might appear as a personal target for an individual learner. Statement 1 uses the phrase, 'raise awareness of'; this would be fine as a lesson aim but, again, is not specific enough to be classed as a lesson objective. Finally, be careful of confusing activities with objectives. Statement 5 uses the verb 'read'. This is a general skill but needs to mention what they will extract from the reading process: for example, learners will be able to identify three key points about child development from the text.

BLOOM'S TAXONOMY OF LEARNING DOMAINS

Most of the objectives we have just examined fall into the cognitive (thinking) area of learning. However, there is evidently more to learning than that. Bloom's taxonomy (1956) identified three domains of learning:

- ❯ Cognitive (thinking)
- ❯ Affective (feeling)
- ❯ Psychomotor (doing)

Certain subjects or skills may be more disposed to one domain than another but all areas of learning will be covered to a certain extent in a curriculum. For example, in a music lesson individuals will learn about theory (cognitive domain), they may express their feelings about a particular piece of music (affective domain) before producing a piece of music through their voice or via an instrument (psychomotor domain). Bloom's hierarchy of learning focuses on the different steps that learners need to take in order to progress, starting from the simplest and moving to the most complex. The ladder opposite shows the different levels of learning in the cognitive domain alongside examples of appropriate action verbs which could be used to express behavioural objectives.

6. Evaluation (making judgements)	appraise, argue, assess, choose, compare, conclude, estimate, evaluate, judge, measure, perceive, rank, rate, support, value
5. Synthesis (putting elements together)	arrange, assemble, combine, compose, construct, create, design, formulate, manage, organise, plan, predict, propose, unite
4. Analysis (breaking material down and seeing how elements relate to each other)	analyse, categorise, classify, contrast, debate, differentiate, divide, experiment, inspect, investigate, simplify, solve
3. Application (putting something into practice)	administer, apply, build, calculate, construct, demonstrate, develop, dramatise, organise, produce, select, sketch, solve, use
2. Comprehension (constructing, making sense of information)	describe, discuss, explain, express, illustrate, locate, recognise, rephrase, report, review, show, summarise, translate
1. Knowledge (retrieving and recalling information)	arrange, cite, list, name, define, identify, label, match, memorise, recall, recite, record, relate, reproduce, spell, state, underline

There should be both 'lower' and 'higher' order objectives in a lesson and all learners should be stretched and challenged to a degree. We want to move away from only surface learning which focuses more on recall and memorisation to a deeper understanding of a topic. With deeper learning, we want to encourage learners to think more critically and apply their knowledge to different situations. Hopefully, this knowledge will then be retained in their long-term memory.

Although more emphasis is generally given to the cognitive domain, a hierarchy of learning outcomes can also be seen in the affective and psychomotor domains. For example, within the psychomotor domain (Simpson, 1972), objectives could range from reproducing mathematical equations to creating a dance routine. Similarly, in the affective domain (Krathwohl *et al.*, 1964), learners would need to display different behaviours with a view to becoming more self-reliant and developing their own values and belief systems. When setting objectives, it is important to consider all three domains and ensure there is variety in your planning.

☑ TASK 4.4

Write three learning outcomes for a lesson you are about to teach or for your microteaching session using Bloom's cognitive domain as a guide. Have you used both lower (knowledge and comprehension) and higher order (application, analysis, synthesis, evaluation) objectives?

Bloom's model has proven to be very influential, particularly in the planning and evaluation of lesson outcomes. However, it has been criticised for being too neat and linear in its design (Furst, 1994) with the assumption that learners go through different stages of cognitive development in ascending order of difficulty. Who's to say, for example, that you can't create something before you are able to explain it? The taxonomy was revised in 2001 by Anderson *et al.* to account for developments in cognitive psychology. One of the aims of the new model was to make the language used to describe the different stages of development more up to date. The nouns were replaced with verbs and the subcategories renamed, with creating being considered a higher order skill than evaluating.

Creating
Evaluating
Analysing
Applying
Understanding
Remembering

TALKING POINT

SMART objectives are based on a behaviourist view of learning (see Chapter 5): the idea that learning can be observed and measured. However, they have their limitations. For example, by setting SMART objectives, are we implying that learning is rather like a checklist of competences that we can tick off once we believe the learners are doing what we want them to do? Petty (2009, p.420) argues that learners should be in charge of their learning, not the teacher, and questions whether objectives offer a limited view of learning: 'What of developing motivation, appreciation, interest and curiosity? What about ethics, joy, beauty and the human spirit?'

What is your view on setting SMART objectives?

SCHEMES OF WORK

As we have seen, a lesson plan focuses on the content of a particular lesson. If you are teaching learners over a series of lessons, a course plan or scheme of work should be developed before thinking about the more detailed plan to enable us to sequence our lessons in a coherent way: to consider the overall shape of the course and the skills and knowledge the learners are expected to develop. Reece and Walker (2007, p. 240) define a scheme of work as 'a series of planned learning experiences, sequenced to achieve the course aims in the most effective way'. A scheme of work can be for a long- or short-term course and the content will depend on a number of factors:

- The course aims and objectives: these may be dictated by modules or units mapped to an awarding body's syllabus or national curriculum.
- The learners, including their age, ability, interests and needs.
- The time and resources available.
- Whether you need to embed functional skills (maths, English and ICT) and help learners develop their study skills, for example how to take notes.
- The teaching and learning strategies you are going to employ: there is no one right method but adopting an inclusive approach is essential.
- Equality and diversity considerations (see Chapters 1 and 3).
- Assessment methods: there will need to be scope for revision, particularly if the learners are preparing for an exam or coursework. There should also be opportunities for peer- and self-assessment and study outside the course hours.
- How the course will be evaluated.

The next few pages contain an example of a scheme of work created for a 24-week course: the first five weeks are provided. A brief profile of the learners has been provided from the results of the initial assessment. As the learners are working towards a qualification, links have been made to the syllabus of an awarding body. Nevertheless, there should still be opportunities for negotiation with learners. A scheme of work is a working document: it should guide the programme of learning rather than dictate it. As we saw with lesson planning, there may be times when you need to deviate from your scheme of work to accommodate the needs of your learners.

Course title:
NOCN STEP UP DIPLOMA IN HUMANITIES AND SCIENCE

Aim of the course:
- For learners who are interested in taking further qualifications in Science and/or Humanities. This course provides a taster of the different modules.

Module/Unit reference
HEALTHY LIVING

Class profile:
- 24 learners (mostly aged between 16 and 19)
- 16 female, 8 male
- Most learners have completed entry courses but are lacking necessary study skills to progress to GSCE courses.
- One dyslexic learner (DB): resources prepared in advance on yellow paper

Week	Topic/ Module/ Unit	Lesson outcomes	Learning activities (including E & D considerations and differentiation strategies)	Functional skills	Assessment	Resources	Homework
1	Intro: lifestyle factors 1.	1.1 LO1: Define what a lifestyle factor is LO2: List some lifestyle factors and explain whether they are good or bad for an individual's health	Odd one out – lifestyle factors Venn diagram of environmental/genetic factors Fitness questionnaire (extension task – evaluate the questionnaire and answer questions)	Development of speaking, reading and writing skills via various class activities related to lifestyle factors. Correct spelling of key terminology (DB needs monitoring)	Successful completion of exercises F/back	PowerPoint – lifestyle factors and healthy living Fitness/Health questionnaire Images – prompts of lifestyle factors	Research- To find about some major diseases and illnesses that can be caused by an unhealthy lifestyle

Week	Topic/ Module/ Unit	Lesson outcomes	Learning activities (including E & D considerations and differentiation strategies)	Functional skills	Assessment	Resources	Homework
			Discussion: consider why each of the questions is important to the fitness facility and needs to be completed before the client uses the facilities	Language used in formal fitness questionnaires Contribute to discussion by giving opinions and presenting ideas		Video clip	
2	1.1 Identify different lifestyle factors that can affect the health of an individual	LO1: Identify factors that can affect health LO2: Explain in detail how each lifestyle factor (alcohol, exercise, sleep, smoke, diet, stress) can affect health LO3: Outline factors in your own life that are healthy / unhealthy and explain how they affect your general health and wellbeing.	Recap activity: cartoon: compare the lifestyles of two different people Diary of my daily activities: brief diary entry Table: good vs bad lifestyle factors Quiz	Comparison and evaluation of key ideas Listening and responding appropriately	Response to Qs and As Successful completion of exercises Self-assessment (from criteria)	Cartoon Diary entry Table Quiz	Design a poster
3	MAJOR BODY SYSTEMS	1.2 LO1: List the main body	Warm up activity: Show posters (from homework)	Monitoring of spelling and grammar on	Response to questions	Card match system to function	Respond to question on the blog in

Week	Topic/Module/Unit	Lesson outcomes	Learning activities (including E & D considerations and differentiation strategies)	Functional skills	Assessment	Resources	Homework
	1.2 Outline how lifestyle factors can affect major body systems	systems LO2: Describe the main functions of the major body systems LO3: Explain how each system works and common implications when it does not function efficiently LO4: Produce a factsheet	Presentation: introduction of different systems Matching systems to functions (pairwork) Designing factsheets – presentation to class	factsheets (provide PB with factsheets Vocabulary connected to major body systems Participating in discussions Delivery and clarify of information via presentations	Successful completion of exercises matching activity Peer assessment of mini-presentations	Images of different body systems and keywords PowerPoint presentation – on all 4 different body systems Group quiz questions	preparation for next week's session
4	Unhealthy lifestyle Diseases/ illness	1.2 LO1: Describe the diseases linked to an unhealthy lifestyle LO2: Outline some common health problems that arise from smoking, drinking alcohol, poor diet, lack of exercise and sleep LO3: Compare and other	Warm up activity: recap on last lesson – Q&A session using lollipop sticks Video clip: on lifestyle and health – linked to homework Role play: characters' different lifestyles (*give learners thinking time – have prompts ready for learners who	Communication skills during group work and role play session Using correct spelling of key terminology related to the body systems Encouraging development of note-taking skills	Role plays Monitoring and observation Successful completion of activities	MCQ quiz Video Flipchart paper Handouts	Worksheet to consolidate their understanding of human body systems and the main functions

Week	Topic/Module/Unit	Lesson outcomes	Learning activities (including E & D considerations and differentiation strategies)	Functional skills	Assessment	Resources	Homework
		indirect factors that may affect an individual's lifestyle	are struggling) Discussion: explain links between different systems Worksheet Mindmaps: group work and then presentations	(mind maps) Delivering information succinctly and clearly (presentations)			
5	1.3 Describe the key elements of a healthy lifestyle	LO1: Define what a healthy lifestyle is LO2: Explain the components of a healthy lifestyle and explain each one LO3: Evaluate the importance of leading a healthy lifestyle	Key words ex on sticky notes Discussion: compare pictures of healthy and unhealthy lifestyles ICT research: ideas about smoking, junk food and obesity to prepare for debate session (*explain how to navigate the web using an appropriate search engine)	Listening and responding to information (*introduce language for polite disagreement) ICT – how to search the web Note-taking skills – recording key words	Response to questions Successful completion of handout Monitoring and observation Peer and self-assessment of debate	Sticky notes Flipchart paper Images – different lifestyles Newspaper articles Computers Video clip – link to website on BBC learning zone	Produce a leaflet to show the key elements of a healthy lifestyle and promote healthy living

Week	Topic/ Module/ Unit	Lesson outcomes	Learning activities (including E & D considerations and differentiation strategies)	Functional skills	Assessment	Resources	Homework
			Debate: students choose idea (*provide list of ideas if necessary)				

✔ TASK 4.5

Who do you think would be interested in a scheme of work? Make a list of individuals or groups of people who might need to see one and their reasons for doing so.

You may have noted that a scheme of work should be most beneficial for those teaching or learning on the course. It will be a useful starting point on which you can build, tailoring the content to suit your learners' needs and your own style of delivery. It will also provide you with a benchmark to monitor progress. You may not have been involved in devising the document but it should influence your lesson planning or support plan. A scheme of work should also be shared with your learners. They may like to look ahead to future topics so they can prepare in advance and be clear on assessment schedules. If they have missed a session, they can see where it fits into the overall learning programme and catch up by accessing the appropriate material and resources. Other interested parties could include the following:

- Parents, if you are teaching younger learners
- Colleagues and members of other faculties as a cross-communication tool to ensure that there is a consistency of approach
- Line managers
- Work supervisors: they will be keen to see whether the training meets the needs of their employees
- Quality assurance teams
- Human Resources departments
- External verifiers
- Ofsted inspectors

One of the hardest aspects of planning a scheme of work is deciding on the sequencing of topics or activities. As we saw earlier, the course content will need to be mapped to the units or modules of a curriculum or external syllabus, but this does not necessarily mean we want to cover the units in chronological order.

✔ TASK 4.6

How will you decide how to sequence content in a scheme of work? List some factors which will influence the prioritising of topics or acquisition of skills.

Your list may include the following points.

1. The different starting points of your learners

It seems logical to sequence the activities in a scheme of work from easiest topic or skill to most challenging. Of course, this is a subjective assessment as what is easier for some may prove more challenging for others. However, using the data from initial and diagnostic assessments (see Chapter 3) there will be some indication of what is likely to be known and unknown for the learners. When devising a scheme of work, it is essential that you have considered the different needs and attainment levels of your learners and considered how to support and challenge them.

It is also worth remembering that some topics or skills will need to be allocated more time. It is not always easy to assess this before knowing the capabilities of your learners and this is one of the reasons why there should be flexibility in a scheme of work.

2. The different personalities of your learners

It often takes time for learners to get used to their teacher's delivery and to the other members of the group. Some learners may be forthcoming in discussions and willing to take risks, while others will lack confidence and be reluctant to experiment with different approaches to learning. You will have to consider the diverse personalities of your group when devising a scheme of work, encouraging learners to become more self-reliant and move out of their comfort zones during the course. For example, without really knowing your learners, it could be risky to set a discussion on a controversial topic for the first session of a learning programme.

3. Access to resources and the learning environment

If you are delivering a vocational course, there will be both practical and theoretical components to consider; these may be delivered in different venues. You will need to ensure that these aspects are linked to each other to maximise opportunities for learning. For example, on a hairdressing course, learners could study different colour combinations used in colouring hair (theory) before trying out the processes in a salon (practical).

4. Themes

You may find that you can extract particular themes from a syllabus and organise topics or skills to be acquired around these. You may have to play around with the sequence to suit your learners. If you have taught the course before, it is worth obtaining feedback on the order of particular topics; for example, which topics they found easiest and most challenging, and use this for future planning.

The danger with a topic-based scheme of work, particularly for a long programme of study, is that learners will forget what was covered earlier on in the course. The aim of a spiral curriculum, proposed by Bruner (1960) is to revisit themes to allow learners to consolidate and deepen their knowledge. Within a scheme of work, there should be plenty of opportunities for review.

QUESTIONS TO CONSIDER WHEN PLANNING COURSES AND INDIVIDUAL SESSIONS

You might find the following checklist helpful.

		✔
Needs	• What do your learners already know about the topic? • Is there room for manoeuvre, for example to support learners and stretch those who are more able? Have you considered the needs of the learners, their abilities, age and personalities? • What do you want the learners to be able to do by the end of each lesson? • Are there links to prior and future learning? • Have differentiated activities been included to accommodate the diverse nature of your group?	
Structure	• Is the content mapped to an external syllabus or curriculum? • Is the content organised in a logical way? • Are there opportunities for review? • Is there a sufficient amount of variety (activities and resources) in the lesson? • Is there a focus on the learners actively participating? • Are all learners potentially included in the learning process? • Have functional and study skills been embedded if appropriate?	
Assessment and evaluation	• Are formative methods of assessment varied and appropriate? • Are learners aware of the schedule of summative assessments? • Are there opportunities for self- and peer assessment? • Are there opportunities for learners to evaluate the course? • Have sufficient opportunities been provided for feedback? • Are there opportunities for further development on the topic, such as setting homework?	
Support	• Are support systems in place, for example through supported independent study sessions, tutorials? • Is preparation for assignments, exams and coursework included?	

TALKING POINT

In an ideal world, you would be able to include everything you wanted in a scheme of work with access to all the materials and resources you need. However, in reality there will be constraints placed on the planning of a scheme of work such as time restrictions, availability of resources, or lack of access to a suitable learning environment. What factors can you think of which might have an impact on the construction of a scheme of work for your subject area?

SUMMARY

In this chapter you have read about the importance of devising and creating lesson plans, placing the learners' needs and interests at the centre of the planning process. We discussed when it is better to be more flexible and deviate from the lesson plan. If you are working directly with learners, it is a good idea to set clear aims and SMART objectives for each lesson and ensure that you can observe and measure progress. Lesson objectives should be differentiated so that all learners are encouraged to use higher-order skills at some stage of the learning process. Finally, as part of your job role, you may be expected to create or follow schemes of work, which are designed to show the content to be covered in each lesson, and how learners should build on their learning and develop their knowledge and skills.

REFERENCES AND FURTHER READING

Bloom, B. S. (1956) *Taxonomy of Educational Objectives Book 1: Cognitive Domain*. New York: David McKay.

Bruner, J. (1960) *The Process of Education*. Cambridge, MA: The President and Fellows of Harvard College.

Fawbert, F. (2004) *Teaching in Post-Compulsory Education Learning, Skills and Standards*. New York: Continuum.

Furst, E. J. (1994) 'Bloom's Taxonomy: Philosophical and Educational Issues'. In L. Anderson and L. Sosniak (eds), *Bloom's Taxonomy. A Forty-Year Retrospective*, pp. 28–40. Chicago: The National Society of the Study of Education.

Keeley-Browne, L. (2007) *Training to Teach in the Learning and Skills Sector*. Harlow: Pearson.

Krathwohl, D. R., Bloom, B. S. and Masia, B. B. (1964) *Taxonomy of Educational Objectives: The Classification of Educational Goals*. New York: David McKay.

Petty, G. (2009) *Teaching Today: A practical guide* (4th edn). Cheltenham: Nelson Thornes.

Reece, I. and Walker, S. (2007) *Teaching, Training and Learning: A Practical Guide*. Sunderland: Business Education Publishers Limited.

Richards, J. C. and Farrell, S. C. (2011) *Practical Teaching: A Reflective Approach*. Cambridge: Cambridge University Press.

Simpson, E. J. (1972) *The Classification of Educational Objectives in the Psychomotor Domain*. Washington, DC: Gryphon House.

Website

www.tes.co.uk (Useful templates and ideas for lesson plans)

Enabling learning

LEARNING AIMS

By the end of this chapter, the reader will have a better understanding of:

❱ the difference between learning- and teaching-centred approaches

❱ how to manage group work

❱ how to use different types of group work

❱ approaches to understanding learning

❱ teaching and learning methods

LEARNING-CENTRED VS TEACHING-CENTRED TEACHING

Read the two scenarios below. Which approach do you prefer?

Joanne
'Ok… look at these three different types of hair. Anila's hair is Asian, Janet's is Caucasian and Samantha's is Black Caribbean. Work in your groups to compare and contrast the hair types… then we'll discuss the differences.'

Farzana
'In today's lesson, we're looking at hair types. I'm going to describe the differences and I want you to listen and take some notes. At the end, there'll be some time to ask questions. Ok, let's go.'

What are your thoughts? Whose style would you most like to emulate? Clearly, both teachers approach their classes in different ways. Joanne prefers to allow the learners some time to work things out for themselves. She poses a scenario, provides some information in the form of props then lets the learners get on with it. Discussion and questioning form the basis of the approach. She knows the answers but wants the learners to work things out for themselves. Of course, there is always the possibility that they will get things wrong but this doesn't matter because she can correct their misconceptions. At the heart of the approach is the value that can be gained from students learning to reason and problem-solve, which leads to the creation of meaning. This approach is known as *guided discovery* and it is a *student-centred* method.

Farzana prefers a controlled environment. She likes to know that she has given her learners the information they need to know. She has prepared the PowerPoint in advance, so she knows what is coming up. She can predict the kinds of questions learners might ask because she has used the same material with other classes. She knows she is preparing them well for their assessment as she has read through the syllabus and selected the information she knows they need. She has structured the information on the PowerPoint so that it makes sense to the learners; she doesn't want to overload them. She has allowed time at the end for the learners to ask questions. This approach is a *didactic* or *teaching-centred* method.

Let's explore the two approaches in a little more detail. Have you ever heard this well-known proverb by the Chinese philosopher Confucius? How do you think it relates to education and learning?

> *"Tell me and I'll forget. Show me and I'll remember. Involve me and I'll understand."*

This captures the continuum between teaching and learning-centred learning effectively. Learning-centred learning places the focus of instruction on students' needs, interests and abilities. It involves them in the process of learning and they take an active part in constructing meaning. In this approach the teacher questions the students to elicit existing knowledge from them and uses their responses to build on and extend it. It relies heavily on the 'student voice' as central to the learning experience. It requires learners to bring any and all of their knowledge to the learning situation and to be active participants in the construction of new knowledge. In contrast, a teaching-centred approach places the focus of instruction squarely at the feet of the teacher. In this situation, teachers teach by telling rather than by eliciting and questioning. They control the information to be learned and the way in which it is delivered. Learners are passive recipients rather than active constructors of meaning. Learning-centred methods require learners to be responsible for and take ownership of their learning. The role of the teacher is different. In learning-centred methods, teachers are facilitators of learning and in teaching-centred methods, teachers are transmitters of knowledge. Learners are 'jugs to be filled up'. There are many benefits to gain from using learning-centred methods in addition to some classroom management decisions to make. Below are some of them.

Benefits

Learning-centred methods:

- encourage engagement and collaborative working;
- are motivating because they draw on learners' prior knowledge and experience;
- are a dynamic, interactive way of learning;
- allow teachers to adjust their input based on learners' responses;
- encourage learner independence, freedom and choice; and
- encourage group cohesion.

Classroom management considerations

Think about:

- encouraging everyone to contribute to the task;
- ensuring one learner doesn't dominate discussion tasks;
- explaining the purpose and expected outcome of the task;
- checking that everyone knows who they are working with in the pair or group;
- feeding back on any errors the learners make in their language use;
- explaining the rationale for the activity so that learners know how it links to their course; and
- balancing your approach against other methods of delivery.

When deciding which approach to take, think about your learners' characteristics and be guided by their levels of motivation, ability, needs and interests. What works for one group of learners may not work for another group. Learn from your experience and try to reflect on why something didn't work when you expected it to. Try to vary the approaches you use and don't always use the one that works for you. It's what works for your learners that matters.

TALKING POINT

In your opinion, which is a better: a learning-centred or teaching-centred approach? Why? Which approaches will work for your teaching specialism?

THE MANAGEMENT OF GROUP WORK

Research shows that pair and group work are good practice teaching methods that facilitate learner articulation and deep learning. Group work has many advantages but to work truly effectively, it needs to be thought about in advance of the lesson. Consider the scenarios below. What are the problems?

✔ TASK 5.1

Marta is teaching a Level 1 Business class. There are 18 learners aged between 18 and 27. She wants the learners to work in groups and write their ideas down on the flipchart paper she has provided. She is having problems managing the behaviour of some of the learners.

In group 1, Ahmad isn't listening to what Luisa is saying. Jess and Carla are talking to each other about their plans for the weekend.

In group 2, Miriam and Yasmin are complaining that they're bored while Abdul tries to write down Malgorzata's ideas on the flipchart paper they have been given but is getting frustrated because the pen doesn't work.

In group 3, Richard and Kamal have filled the flipchart with ideas and are now texting on their phones. Keisha is shouting out to Marta that her group has finished.

In group 4, Jakub is asking Pieter what they have to do in their first language. Rachel has wandered over to group 3 to see what they have written on their flipchart and is telling Jakub in a loud voice that their group's ideas are better.

In group 5, Patrice is grumbling loudly to Nancy that they always do the same activity. Josh is twiddling his thumbs. Amir is drawing pictures on the flipchart paper which have nothing to do with the task.

Marta is feeling downtrodden and isn't sure what to do. Can you help?

What did you think of? What advice would you give to Marta? You might say to her that in group 1, Ahmad needs to listen to Luisa's opinion even if he doesn't agree with it as this is the right and respectful thing to do. Jess and Carla need to contribute to the group discussion. In group 2, it would be better for Marta to give each group member something to do so that each feels valued and is kept engaged. She needs to check her resources before the lesson starts. In group 3, Marta needs to be more aware of the fact that some of her learners need something to do while the rest of the class finish the task. Keisha needs to understand that shouting out in class is unacceptable and disruptive. Jakub and Pieter clearly do not understand what they have to do so this needed to be made clear at the outset of the class. Like Keisha, Rachel needs to understand the impact that her behaviour can have on the rest of the class. Patrice is bored because there is no variety. Josh and Amir need to be given some level of responsibility within the group so that the activity is meaningful and they are kept engaged. As mentioned earlier, effective group work needs to be carefully planned for and managed. Marta would have benefited from thinking about roles within the groups, levels of ability, task outcomes and resources more thoughtfully.

Highly effective groups are well organised, with each individual having a role to play. It is really important to ensure that group work you set up is tightly structured. Without this, it can easily be derailed. Bruce Tuckman's theory of group formation is a useful way to think about dynamics within groups.

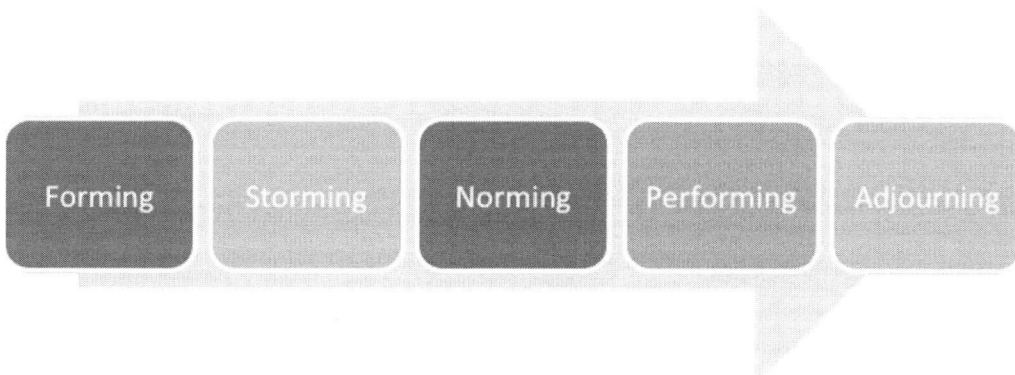

Forming Storming Norming Performing Adjourning

Put simply, his model has five stages which are:

1 **Forming.** At this stage, there is little structure. Individuals are uncertain about their roles and responsibilities. As yet, there are no ground rules. It is effectively a 'finding out what to do' stage. Members of the team need to be clearly directed by someone in charge.

2 **Storming.** This is a conflict stage. Disagreements can occur about purpose and there may be personality clashes between team members. There may be rebellion against the leader. Power struggles may persist.

3 **Norming.** Commitment and group cohesion are established. Aims and purposes are clear as are individual roles and responsibilities. Harmony reigns, allowing the group to stabilise.

4 **Performing.** The group works toward the task in unison. Mutual support is offered and individuals have shared ownership of and responsibility for the task.

5 **Adjourning.** The group has successfully fulfilled its purposes. The task is complete and the group breaks up.

Tuckman's model provides a useful framework that we can use to understand the ways in which dynamics can affect how individuals within groups operate. We need to take individual personalities into consideration when organising group work so that they function successfully. Some of your learners will be natural leaders, whereas others will naturally want to take more of a back seat. This shouldn't mean that they get a 'free ride' (Petty, 2009) but that you recognise this and allocate a role which will allow them have a voice in a way that feels comfortable. Your lesson plan gives you the time to think about this in advance so that group work tasks can be optimised and time is not wasted.

To maximise levels of student engagement and increase the sense of purpose, and minimise the potential for learners to go 'off-task', follow these guidelines:

 ❱ Make sure each learner is allocated a role – this can be note-taker, organiser, contributor or the person who does feedback.
 ❱ Explain how the group work contributes toward the lesson outcomes.
 ❱ Explain the activity clearly – check instructions.
 ❱ Ensure you check that the materials and resources you want to use are in good working order before the lesson starts.
 ❱ Try to either have a mix of levels in each group (and genders) or learners of similar ability working together.
 ❱ Plan the seating arrangement in advance.
 ❱ Set a time limit for the task – remind them when the time is nearly up.
 ❱ Have extension tasks ready for groups who finish and need something to do.
 ❱ Set clear ground rules – listen to each other, don't walk around the classroom, respect each other's opinions and communicate in English.
 ❱ If the activity requires learners to record ideas from their discussions, try to vary the way in which this happens – for example, don't always use flipchart paper.
 ❱ Ensure the level of challenge is appropriate – stretch the learners but not so much so that they become demotivated if they can't do it.
 ❱ Encourage collaboration in the groups.

❱ Ask learners to elect someone in their group to feedback, so that not everybody is shouting out at the same time.

❱ Actively monitor – don't stand in the same place. Move around so that you see how each group is progressing with the task. Support and troubleshoot as necessary.

❱ When monitoring, keep a mental (or written) note of the common problems.

❱ Give praise in feedback for good work – indicate areas for improvement.

❱ Don't let the activity go on for too long – change it if you feel the pace is beginning to flag.

TALKING POINT

How useful will group work be for teaching your learners? Can you foresee any problems with organisation? What factors will you bear in mind? How can you ensure it works effectively?

DIFFERENT TYPES OF GROUP WORK

TASK 5.2

Look at these different ways of organising group work. What does each layout tell you about the teaching and learning environment?

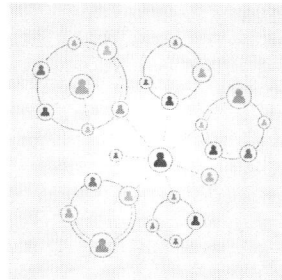

Images © Shutterstock.com

1   2   3

The first layout suggests the teacher may want to create a collaborative environment that encourages debate and discussion; he or she is able to monitor the activities set. The exam-style layout (2) suggests the teacher would like the learners to focus on him/her and/or a board/projector; he or she can easily check the work the learners are doing. Similar to the first layout, the table groups (3) suggest the teacher wants the learners to be able to talk to each other within small groups; he or she can easily monitor and help each group as needed.

Kidd and Czerniaswski (2010) say that moving learners around the classroom/workspace is an effective and dynamic way of increasing learner motivation and maintaining good pace. Using a variety of group work configurations is one way of doing this. According to the authors, the advantages of moving learners around are that:

> ❱ collaboration with others maximises learning opportunities;
> ❱ differentiation can be effectively accounted for through groupings based on learner ability;
> ❱ interaction with others is enjoyable;
> ❱ it's fun and adds variety;
> ❱ group bonds strengthen when learners work with each other;
> ❱ student talk time, as opposed to teacher talk time, is maximised; and
> ❱ students can take ownership of the learning.

However, group work only works successfully if it is carefully planned and managed. Following the guidelines outlined in the previous section will enable you to do this.

As mentioned earlier, there is a variety of teaching methods. In the same way, there are different ways of organising group work and you should alter the ways in which you manage it to minimise the chances of the learners becoming bored (remember Patrice's comment about 'always doing the same activity'). Below, you will find some interesting ways of managing group work that through action research projects have been found to lead to effective learning.

a) Jigsawing

This is based on the principle that learners only have access to some of the information some of the time; regrouping enables them to share it, so that by the end of the activity everyone has all the information they need. It is a good way to convey a lot of information quickly, which is particularly good if time is short. It has the added advantage of encouraging learners to work together toward a common aim. For learners who have English as an additional language, it is particularly beneficial as it forces them to communicate in English.

How does it work?

Split the learners into two groups (A and B).

1 Give group A some information and give a different set of information to group B. Ideally prepare this on different sets of coloured paper or card to avoid confusion.
2 Set a time limit for the groups to read their information. Give them some questions to focus the reading activity.
3 Regroup the learners so that one learner from group A is working with one learner from group B. Do this by allocating numbers within each group (1, 2, 3, 4…).
4 Tell the number 1s from both groups to work together, the 2s, the 3s, and so on.

5 Set a time limit for them to share information.
6 Conduct plenary feedback.

b) Pyramiding

This is based on the principle of enlarging the size of the groups to move toward an agreed outcome. Through a process of explaining and justifying responses and problem-solving, learners develop deeper levels of understanding.

How does it work?

1 Set a question or series of questions to be answered or a problem to be solved.
2 Set a time limit for individuals to think about their responses.
3 When the time is up, ask learners to work in pairs to share their ideas. Set a time limit. Ask learners to try to agree on a common outcome.
4 When the time is up, ask pairs to join another pair to share their ideas. Set a time limit. Ask learners to try to agree on a common outcome.
5 You can repeat step four so that groups of four make groups of eight depending on the size of the group.
6 Conduct whole-group feedback.

c) Market place

Based on an idea put forward by Geoff Petty, market place is based on the same principle as jigsaw and appeals to visual and kinaesthetic learners. It is a particularly effective way of familiarising learners with assessments they have to do.

How does it work?

1 Divide the class into three groups.*
2 Give each group the assessment brief for a module they will be assessed on. Make sure each group gets a different module. Different coloured paper helps avoid confusion.
3 The task is to summarise the brief and explain it to other groups.
4 Give each group some flipchart paper (or poster) and pens. They must summarise the information in pictures and use no more than a specified number of words (ten is a good number).
5 Set a time limit.
6 Tell each group to elect a market stall holder. They must stay at the tables. Their task is to answer questions put to them by other class members but they cannot offer any information. The other members of the group are shoppers whose job it is to 'shop' for information from other market stall holders. Tell them they can take notes. They must get as much information as they can as their task is to take it back to their original group and explain it to the holder.
7 Set a time limit for the information gathering. When this is up, instruct everyone to return to their original groups and share the information with their holder.
8 Finish the activity off with a short quiz to see who remembers most.

* This can be adapted depending on numbers and modules

d) Speed-dating

This is based on the principle of rapid exchange of information. It is an effective way of developing summarising skills. It works well at the beginning of a lesson to review learning from a previous lesson or at the end to recap learning that has taken place. It appeals to auditory and kinaesthetic learners.

How does it work?

1 Organise two rows of chairs each with equal numbers of learners (for example two rows each with four learners).
2 Ask each learner to face each other.
3 In row 1, allocate each learner a number. In row 2, allocate each learner a letter.
4 Stand at the head of the rows and ask a question based on learning the students have already done or will do.
5 Give them a minute to discuss their answers with the person sitting opposite.
6 When the time is up, tell the learners in row 2 to move to the chair next to them. They must move in a clockwise direction.
7 Now, there is a different set of pairings. Tell them to summarise the information from their previous discussion then add any *new* information that hasn't been discussed.
8 Repeat the clockwise-moving process and set a new question.
9 Finish the activity when the original pairs are back together.

e) Circulating

This is based on the principle of deconstructing information to deepen learning. It is an effective way for students to see things from a perspective other than their own.

How does it work?

1 Decide which topic you want to review.
2 Organise groups of three or four.
3 Give each group a related question written on an A3 poster or flipchart. The questions/themes must be different.
4 Tell each group to write down as many ideas as they can. Set a time limit.
5 When the time limit is up, clap your hands once loudly. Tell the groups to circulate the posters clockwise to the next group.
6 The task is for the new group to add ideas to the poster that haven't already been thought of. They can also amend or delete them. Set a time limit.
7 Repeat step 5 as many times as you need to until the posters are back with the original group.
8 Tell each group to summarise their learning based on the information on the posters.
9 Conduct feedback.

These are just a few strategies for encouraging your learners to collaborate. Experiment with them to see which ones work for you and your learners. At the planning stage, always think through the organisation aspect carefully. If you can anticipate potential problems at an early stage (such as odd numbers of learners), you will be better able to manage them when you are in the classroom. If you follow this advice, your learners will see you as a teacher who is creative, structured and imaginative in their approaches to teaching.

Remember that group work is a valuable and engaging teaching method, which is widely used in teaching classrooms and workspaces. There are, however, other ways to configure the learners. For many teachers, pair work is the basic way of organising learners when it comes to seating arrangements. This can be an effective way for learners to work as they are able to share ideas and support each other. Setting it up is straightforward and you can plan who you want to (and don't want to) work together. Don't forget that there are times when learners will benefit from working alone and many learners respond positively to this way of operating. As we have said before, try to vary your approach.

UNDERSTANDING LEARNING

TALKING POINT

Think back to your school days. What can you remember? Did you enjoy going there? What can you remember about studying? Did you have strict teachers? How did it make you feel? What can you remember about the classroom environment? Was it welcoming? Did you feel secure?

Thinking about the questions above may have invoked a range of different memories of your early school years. It is true to say that individuals experience education in different ways in addition to the fact that we are likely to have some idea about the ways in which we prefer to learn. For these reasons, it is important for teachers to be aware of some of the fundamental principles underlying different approaches to understanding how people learn. There are many such approaches and many ways of grouping and categorising them. There can be considerable overlap between categories too. For the purpose of this introductory book, we have chosen a few approaches for you to consider.

Learning and behaviour

Behaviourism

Behaviourist theories, generally speaking, focus on what is external to the human being and define learning as a change in an individual's behaviour. They offer us a scientific view of what learning is. The theories are broadly based on a stimulus–response approach to moulding behaviour. For example, desirable behaviour can be positively reinforced by the giving of rewards such as praise ('Well done, Jack'), a smile or some other recognition of good work. Conversely, undesirable behaviour can be eliminated by ignoring these. Additionally, negative reinforcement can take the form of punishments such as detention or extra work.

Behaviourist approaches to learning emphasise the fact that the content to be learned in a lesson or the skills to be developed should be very clearly outlined at the outset of the class. This is often phrased as, 'By the end of the lesson, you will be able to…'. Careful planning and teaching should result in observable changes in behaviour, which is the learning that has occurred as a result of the instruction. Behaviourist theories place value on the centrality of the teacher as the giver of knowledge. Among the most well-known behaviourist theorists are Watson, Pavlov and Skinner.

Social learning theory

Bandura's (1977) social learning theory emphasises the role of imitation, or modelling, in learning; individuals observe and copy the behaviour and attitudes of others. According to Jarvis (2006, p. 151) the emphasis in this theory is 'more on the learner and less on the one who provides the stimulus' as it involves the individual thinking about the consequences of their behaviour. Although there are similarities with behaviourism, the process of imitation does not necessarily result in a change of behaviour. Modelling involves four processes: attention (paying attention to the thing you want to copy), retention (remembering the thing that you paid attention to), reproduction (reproducing the behaviour or attitude you remember) and motivation (having a reason to imitate, such as a reward). Applying this to an educational context suggests that teachers can model the behaviours that we would like our students to replicate; these can include paying attention, listening actively, concentrating and modelling study skills such as note-taking.

Learning and thinking

Cognitivism

Cognitivism offers a set of theories about how people learn as well as how they think (Jarvis, 2006). It contrasts with behaviourism as the emphasis is on the thought processes behind the behaviour rather than the behaviour itself. Cognitive theories emphasise what happens inside our heads when learning is taking place. The focus is on the thought processes an individual has when they are in a learning situation. In contrast to behaviourism, learning is not measurable or observable. Cognitive theories start from the premise that knowledge is created, not given. An individual thinks and rethinks what they see or hear until they have made sense of it. They connect the new information with what they already know and process it until it has become personal and meaningful for them. This is what learning is. This theory places the student at the centre of the learning process. It requires them to be active 'meaning-makers'. Teaching and learning methods require learners to engage with ideas proactively until they have made their own sense of them and 'made room for' them in their existing knowledge bank. Students should think about what they are learning and engage with it. Making mistakes is a rich source of new learning potential. Some of the theorists associated with cognitivism are Piaget, Ausubel, Bruner and Vygotsky.

Learning and emotions

Jarvis (2006, p. 175) says 'emotions play a major role in behaviour and in human learning since they are at the heart of our personhood'. This is resonant with the principles underpinning humanist theories which place the individual at the heart of learning and value self-esteem, personal growth and self-fulfilment highly. Given this, it is important for us to recognise that a person's emotional state can influence the extent to which they choose to engage with educational activities or not. An individual who feels valued, safe and secure in the learning environment is more likely to achieve than one who feels stressed or anxious.

Emotional intelligence

Broadly speaking, emotional intelligence refers to the ability to understand one's own feelings and those of others. Individuals with high emotional intelligence can succeed at work, achieve personal goals and ambitions, and fulfil their potential. Daniel Goleman (1998) provided a framework of five elements that constitute emotional intelligence. These are:

- self-awareness (knowing your own emotions, strengths and weaknesses, values and goals)
- self-regulation (managing your emotions and redirecting them if necessary)
- empathy (recognising and understanding other people's emotions)
- social skill (managing relationships)
- motivation (motivating oneself to achieve goals and ambitions).

In a classroom environment, individuals need to be able to communicate with others, work in teams, collaborate to solve problems, avoid reacting on impulse, establish friendships, make thoughtful decisions and park personal or home issues that get in the way of learning. It is therefore important to help our students understand their emotions and the role they play in learning.

Learning and intelligence

As we saw in Chapter 2, Howard Gardner's theory of multiple intelligences challenges traditionally-held beliefs that IQ is a single fixed entity that is inherited. He originally listed seven distinct intelligences, which individuals possess in varying degrees of strength. These are: visual/spatial, bodily/kinaesthetic, musical, linguistic, logical/mathematical, interpersonal (understanding and interacting with others) and intrapersonal (understanding oneself). Applying this theory to an educational context challenges the high value that is often placed on logical and mathematical intelligences. It also means that we need to seek out different ways of presenting instructional material in order to appeal to the separate and distinctive ways in which students learn.

Learning and context

Situated learning

As we touched on in Chapter 2, Lave and Wenger (1990) developed the theory that learning is 'situated', i.e. learning occurs within the context of an activity that students are engaged with; this is often unintentionally. In this model, learners work collaboratively in a 'community of practice' to problem-solve and negotiate, and in doing so construct their own meanings which leads to learning. In a classroom setting, it is important to present the materials, ideas, knowledge and principles to be learned in a realistic context.

In this section, we have given you an overview of the main theories of learning. If you are interested in developing your learning further, you can do your own research.

☑ TASK 5.3

Look at the snapshots of these lessons. Which theory underpins each teacher's approach?

Scenario 1
Paula has been given a new Level 1 ESOL class to teach. It's a 24-week course. She is keen to involve the students in the learning, so on the first day does a needs analysis questionnaire with them. This requires them to say what activities best help them to learn. She also gives them the opportunity to say what activities they don't like. The learners respond well to this because they feel that she is interested in them and their opinions.

Scenario 2
Sajeda sets her class an assignment task. With the exception of two learners, everyone completes it and hands it in on time. She recognises their efforts by rewarding them with positive feedback which clearly signals she is pleased with their progress. The learners who did not submit feel left behind. She explains to them the importance of completing tasks. The next time she sets homework, they not only do it but submit it on time as well.

Scenario 3
Anna is teaching a GCSE Maths lesson. She starts the session by asking the learners what they can remember about the quadratic equations they studied in the last lesson. The learners discuss what they remember and Anna writes their ideas on the board. She then sets them an exercise on quadratic equations, which is more complex than previously. She asks them to work in pairs to solve the problems. She tells them to use what they already know in their calculations. During the feedback stage, she encourages the learners to explain their answers and directs them to correct their own work and that of their peers.

What were your thoughts? You might have thought that Paula in scenario 1 is drawing on humanist principles in her lesson. She is interested in what the learners think and gives them choices about what and how they learn. In scenario 2, Sajeda sends out clear signals about the kind of behaviour she wants to encourage – learners completing homework and handing it in – by praising the two learners. Her approach is effective because when she next sets the class homework, they all do it. She is drawing on principles of behaviourism. In scenario 3, Anna draws on her learners' existing knowledge and encourages them to use it to make new forms of knowledge. She doesn't directly 'teach' them; she creates a situation in which they can use what they already know to solve what they don't. Anna is drawing on constructivist principles.

TEACHING AND LEARNING METHODS

In Chapter 4 we looked at lesson planning. A key element of this process is thinking about which methods you will use to enable learning. There are many different options available to you and you need to think carefully about which ones to use. Before reading on, though, think about what we mean when we talk about a 'learning method'. What do you understand by it? Think back to a time when you were a learner yourself either at school or in a post-16 context. What did your teacher do to convey the information? How did you learn? Did you learn by yourself or by working with others? Did you like listening to explanations by the teacher? Did you like taking notes or listening to audio? A method is an approach a teacher uses to organise the classroom/workspace and manage the resources which helps achieve the learning outcomes in a lesson. We can select from a range of methods and the approach we use depends on the information to be learned and the characteristics of the students.

☑ TASK 5.4

Think about your teaching specialism. Which teaching methods will you use? What will determine your choices? What factors will you take into consideration?

Selecting a method for your learners

Choosing the appropriate teaching methods to use with our learners is important and there is a wide variety to choose from. Broadly speaking, teaching methods can be formal, such as a lecture, or informal, such as a quiz. You should try to use a variety of methods to keep your learners engaged and interested. If you are using several methods all the time, the chances are you are varying things. A clear understanding of what you are aiming to achieve in the lesson as well as knowing your learners will guide you toward selecting the right approach. Remember that the content of the lesson is a key driver in selecting the right teaching method and resources for your learners. The questions below will help you decide.

a) What is the profile of the group?

You need to consider the make-up of the class. What is the age range? Do you have any students with additional learning needs? If so, you may need to adapt your approach so that the information to be presented is inclusive and accessible to everybody. What is the age range? A group of adult learners may respond in a different way to a particular method than a group of 14–16 year olds. It is important to know your group and how they like to learn.

b) What is the timetable?

What time is the class? If it is first thing on Monday morning, you might find that the learners are sluggish so you should do something lively to wake them up! The same principle applies if the lesson is straight after lunch. Using a kinaesthetic task which requires some kind of activity will energise them. If you are teaching in the evening, it is likely that your learners work during the day and are tired when they arrive for your lesson. An activity with an element of fun will energise them and establish good pace.

c) What did I do last lesson?

The opening to your lesson can begin with a review of what you covered in the previous lesson as this helps to consolidate learning. You can use a puzzle or quiz to revisit the key points. If there is a good dynamic in the group, a game or competition can be an effective way of doing this. Alternatively, the starter activity can be used to launch the lesson you are about to teach. The activity you choose to do this needs to have a clear purpose and learners need to understand how it links to the learning outcomes for the lesson.

d) What's the environment like?

You need to be familiar with your classroom or workspace in which you are teaching so that you know what you can realistically do in the lesson. For example, if you want to use a PowerPoint, you need to ensure there is a projector in the room. If you want the learners to stand up and move around, you need to ensure that the furniture in the room allows for this – too many tables and chairs can be a real hindrance! If you want your learners to make posters to display, you need to make sure there is enough space for them on the walls. Take into consideration any health and safety issues. Where possible, try to check the environment beforehand.

Variety is the key to a good lesson so try to ensure that you use a range of different methods. Don't always stick to the same ones. Experimenting with new ways of delivering learning will keep you and your learners interested.

✔ TASK 5.5

Read through the scenarios below and the profile of each group. Think about which teaching method(s) the teacher in each could use to maximise the potential for learning.

Scenario 1
Trevor teaches motor vehicle maintenance to a group of mainly male 16 to 19 year olds. He sees them twice a week from 1–3 pm. The course requires a mix of theory and practical work.

Scenario 2
Georgia teaches an NVQ Level 2 Hairdressing class. She has 15 female learners in her class. She teaches them twice a week and the lessons are two hours long. One of the learners is dyslexic.

Scenario 3
Vanessa teaches a BTEC Business class. There is a mix of male and female learners in the group, and the ages range from 18 to 50. She sees them on Tuesday mornings for a two-hour lesson and Friday afternoons for a 90-minute lesson. Four of the learners have English as an additional language.

Scenario 4
Lynne teaches a GCSE English class. The learners are 16 to 18 and there is a mix of males and females. The learners are resitting their GCSE. She sees them once a week for a two-hour lesson. Some of them struggle with reading and writing.

As you considered the scenarios, you may have found yourself wondering about the learning outcomes the students are working toward and which method(s) most effectively helps them meet them. Compare your answers to the suggestions below. Are they the same or different?

Scenario 1. In this lesson, a demonstration of a motor vehicle maintenance technique by Trevor followed by practice by the learners, which he monitors, would work well. He might also decide to use handouts with step-by-step instructions to help the learners remember what to do. As the lesson takes place in a workshop environment, he would also need to carry out a risk assessment (see Chapter 1) to ensure his learners are safe. What issues would a risk assessment cover? For example, he might need to consider the layout of the room and number of learners, or the equipment they are using and whether it is has been checked for safety purposes.

Scenario 2. In this lesson, inviting a guest speaker from a local salon in to talk to the learners about working in the industry would be a good way of motivating them. Georgia could spend some time with them beforehand, helping them prepare questions to ask. As she has a dyslexic learner, she would need to ensure that any materials she distributes are adapted accordingly so that they are inclusive. For example, she may need to enlarge the size of the font on a worksheet or print it out on coloured paper.

Scenario 3. In this lesson, Vanessa could use a PowerPoint presentation followed by group discussion. Some of the learners do not have English as a first language so her teaching method needs to be able to accommodate this. What should she do? She might, for example, need to provide dictionaries (or allow them to use Google Translate on their phones) so that the learners can check language they don't know). She might also work with them on an individual basis and/or organise peer support.

Scenario 4. In this lesson, Lynne could organise the learners into pairs to do some online research about the characters in the book they are studying for their exam. She could then ask them to discuss their findings and record the results in a mind map. As some of them struggle with reading and writing, she might organise some after-class support in which she targets the areas they find difficult.

There are no right or wrong answers. The main thing to bear in mind is that you need to know how the method you are using works and then clearly communicate this to the learners. Learners work best when they know exactly what is expected of them and how what you are asking them to do contributes to the learning objectives. Clarity and structure are the key words.

Here is a list of teaching and learning methods along with a description of their advantages and things you need to consider in regard to classroom management. Compare them with the ideas you had above. Have you changed your mind?

Method	Description	Advantages	Classroom management considerations
Demonstration	A practical 'hands-on' way of showing how something works	The key learning points are immediate Learners can see exactly how something works Learning can be supported by handouts, visuals and other resources Learners can apply the new knowledge immediately	Keep it short so the learners don't get bored Follow it up with practical work Make sure everyone can see you properly
Discussion	A group activity which involves learners talking about a topic or theme related to the lesson	It is interactive It develops teamwork and collaboration skills Everyone can contribute It can generate a lot of ideas Learners can see things from a perspective other than their own	Group your learners so that dominant people don't take over Instruct them that they must feedback what someone else has said If you have a student whose spoken English is at entry level, pair them with a supportive colleague to help them follow the discussion Write key words on the board first and discuss meanings with the whole class
Game/quiz/puzzle	A way of learning which often involves problem solving and teamwork.	It is fun and engaging It is good for pace, energy and momentum It can be used at any	Explain the rules clearly Make sure everyone understands what to do by asking checking questions

Method	Description	Advantages	Classroom management considerations
		stage in the lesson It can make learning memorable A healthy sense of competition can be instilled	Give an example and/or demonstration of how the activity works
Independent study	A way of studying which takes place outside of the classroom or workspace Learners study independently of the teacher and classmates	It encourages independence It broadens the way in which learners can access information Learners take responsibility for and ownership of their learning Learners can study at a time that best suits them	Make sure everyone knows the purpose of the study Support those with weak study skills by showing them how to organise their files, take notes and access information online Balance independent study with face-to-face and tutorial time Organise a study-buddy system to encourage peer support
Journal/diary/log	A way of recording a learner's private thoughts and reflections It can be done online or in a book	Encourages independent thinking Encourages deep thinking skills, which enhances the potential for learning It adds variety to taught class or workplace delivery Learners have time after class to reflect on their learning	Ensure the learners know how to complete the log Show some examples of logs to give the learners an idea about possible content Mark the logs regularly so that you are able to keep in touch with how the learner is feeling Explain how the log will be assessed

Method	Description	Advantages	Classroom management considerations
Mind map	A way of recording learners' ideas centrally so that everyone can see them A mindmap is usually a circle which can have branches for sub-headings	Everyone can contribute It is an effective way of gathering ideas quickly Learners can 'bounce off' each other No preparation time needed It lends itself to other formats Links between ideas can be made	Encourage everyone to contribute Organise the ideas neatly so that the learners can write them down easily if you want them to Have a main title (food, for example) and use sub-categories (such as protein, carbohydrates) to help the organisation of the map Ensure everyone can see the board
Online learning	Learning which takes place on a computer or other mobile device There is a connection to the internet and/or virtual learning environment	Learning is current Younger learners often like learning in this way Information can be accessed from a variety of sources Different mobile devices can be used to access information	Ensure everyone has access to a device with an internet connection and knows how to access, store and retrieve information Ensure that learners have the technical skills to complete the tasks you set Do the tasks you set yourself before the lesson so that you can see how they work
Practical work	Practical hands-on tasks which are carried out by the learners usually observed by a teacher	It helps learners develop the skills they need for industry or the workplace It is relevant and adds variety	Make sure everyone can see while you demonstrate the skill/task If competency

Method	Description	Advantages	Classroom management considerations
		The teacher can assess progress easily Learners' work can be recorded for assessment and/or verification purposes	checklists are being used, make sure the learners know how they will be assessed Monitor the learners' progress frequently and provide one-to-one support where needed Encourage the learners to make links between the practical and theoretical aspects of their course Encourage peer-to-peer support where appropriate
Presentation	A formal talk-based way of presenting information It is a teacher-centred method	The teacher can organise and present information in a structured manner The teacher can present a lot of information Other aids can be used to support meaning	Don't overload the PowerPoint (or other presentation tool) with too much information – try to limit it to three key bullet points and use them to expand on, and explore and emphasise the key issues Use graphics to support your explanations when appropriate Ensure the projector is working prior to teaching

Method	Description	Advantages	Classroom management considerations
Reading	Students learn by reading different kinds of text, for example newspaper and magazine articles or journals	Learners can read at their own pace Different sub-skills of reading can be developed, such as reading for general or specific information Learners can access a lot of information Other skills can be integrated, such as speaking or writing	Make sure you allow adequate time for the reading and set tasks that develop the sub-skills of reading Pre-teach any difficult words needed for the tasks before the learners start to read Integrate a 'pre-reading' phase during which you build interest in the text and elicit learners' opinions of/thoughts on the content Differentiate the texts according to ability if appropriate
Research	An in-depth way of finding out information about a topic or theme related to the learners' course It can be carried out individually or in pairs or small groups	It encourages teamwork skills and a sense of cooperative learning Learning is deepened by extra study Topics can be explored in a more in-depth way than in class Learners can choose the information they want to access It encourages independence	Provide learners with a source list to begin with, to focus the research If the research is to take place over a period of time, integrate regular checks on progress and support as necessary Ensure everyone has the appropriate technical skills if the research is being done online
Trip/visit	A visit to a place external to where a lesson usually takes place	A change of environment is good for maintaining interest	Ensure the chosen venue is of interest to everyone

Method	Description	Advantages	Classroom management considerations
	The venue is of relevance to the learners and the course	Learners can see the point of their learning It adds variety Learners can link the learning outcomes of their course to a real-life context	Ensure everyone knows how the visit links to their programme of study Ensure a risk assessment is carried out prior to the visit Ensure everyone knows about the logistics of the visit (venue, cost, travel time)
Visiting speaker	A speaker who is an expert in the learners' subject area	Speaker can bring relevant and up-to-date knowledge It adds variety to the classroom Learners can ask questions and get immediate answers	Prepare the learners for the visit with some preparation time beforehand (to write questions, for example) Ensure the visitor knows the logistics of the visit (address, group profile)
Worksheet	Learning by completing tasks provided on a handout (or electronically)	Tasks can easily be varied – circling or ticking answers, underlining the correct information or filling in gaps, for example It is easy to check answers Extension tasks can be provided at the bottom of the handout It is easy to prepare	Ensure the worksheets are professionally presented Check the text on the worksheet for language accuracy before photocopying Add variety by using colour and graphics when appropriate Encourage learners to organise them in files for ease of access after the lesson

Method	Description	Advantages	Classroom management considerations
			Use titles and headings on the worksheets so that learners can access and file them easily

Make sure learners don't leave them lying around in the classroom or workspace |

✔ TASK 5.6

Look at the teaching methods in the table. Which ones would you say are more learning-centred? Which ones are more teaching-centred? Rank them on a scale of 1–5.

1   5
Teaching-centred <--> Learning-centred

What did you think? Where did you put the methods on the scale? How did you make your decisions? At the teaching-centred end of the scale, you may well have put 'presentation' because it entails teachers deciding on the content to be taught and assuming control for teaching it. At the opposite end of the scale, you might have thought that 'discussion' was the most learning-centred method because it involves learners talking to each other. There is no right or wrong answer. A presentation can become more learning-centred if the teacher integrates lots of question and answer to involve the learners. Further, teachers can put varying levels of control onto a discussion for example by limiting the topics to be talked about, setting time limits and providing particular language for students to use. Teaching methods can, and should, be adapted according to the needs of your learners and the learning outcomes to be achieved.

SUMMARY

In this chapter, you have looked at learning-centred and teaching-centred approaches; you also considered the benefits as well as possible classroom management decisions relating to learning-centred methods. You discussed how to manage group work and some different types of group work you can use in your lessons. You then reviewed a variety of different approaches to understanding how people learn. Finally, you looked at different teaching methods, and considered the advantages of each in addition to a range of classroom management decisions relating to each one.

REFERENCES AND FURTHER READING

Fawbert, F. (ed.) (2008) *Teaching in Post-Compulsory Education: Skills, Standards and Lifelong Learning.* London: Continuum Books.

Goleman, D. (1995) *Emotional Intelligence: Why it Can Matter More Than IQ.* Bloomsbury. London.

Gould, J. (2009) *Learning Theory and Classroom Practice in the Lifelong Learning Sector,* Exeter: Learning Matters.

Gravells, A. (2008) *Preparing to Teach in the Lifelong Learning Sector* (3rd edn). Exeter: Learning Matters.

Gravells, A. and Simpson, S. (2008) *Planning and Enabling Learning in the Lifelong Learning Sector.* Exeter: Learning Matters.

Gray, D., Griffin, C. and Nasta, T. (2005) Training to Teach in Further and Adult Education (2nd edn). Cheltenham: Nelson Thornes.

Hattie, J. (2012) *Visible Learning for Teachers Maximising Impact on Learning.* New York: Routledge.

Jarvis, P. (2006) *Towards a Comprehensive Theory of Human Learning.* Abingdon: Routledge.

Kidd, W. and Czerniawski, G. (2010) *Successful Teaching 14–19: Theory, Practice and Reflection.* London: Sage.

Lave, J. and Wenger, E. (1991) *Situated Learning: Legitimate Peripheral Participation.* Cambridge: Cambridge University Press.

Petty, G. (2009a) *Evidence-Based Teaching: A Practical Approach.* Cheltenham: Nelson Thornes.

Petty, G. (2009b) *Teaching Today: A practical guide* (4th edn). Cheltenham: Nelson Thornes.

Websites

www.infed.org

www.education.cu-portland.edu

www.learning-theories.com (summary of the theories about the ways in which people learn)

http://infed.org/mobi/bruce-w-tuckman-forming-storming-norming-and-performing-in-groups/ (reading on Bruce Tuckman and group formation)

Assessing learning

LEARNING AIMS

By the end of this chapter, the reader will have a better understanding of:

❭ what assessment is

❭ assessment practices

❭ self- and peer-assessment

❭ effective feedback

❭ fitness for purpose

❭ methods of assessment

❭ quality assurance processes

❭ record keeping

WHAT IS ASSESSMENT?

Assessment is an integral part of the process of teaching and learning; without assessing learners' progress, we have no way of knowing how effective our teaching has been. Assessment measures the depth and breadth of learning, and the results triggered by its associated practices are used to plan future learning. In *Inside the Black Box* (2001, p. 2), Black and Wiliam state,

> *"... the term 'assessment' refers to all those activities undertaken by teachers, and by their students in assessing themselves, which provide information to be used as feedback to modify the teaching and learning activities in which they are engaged."*

Assessment is a dynamic process. It captures the quality of a learner's knowledge or skill set at any given time. Used effectively, the results that assessments yield should be used to feed learning forward. It is the most important aspect of a teacher's job. If a teacher isn't assessing their learners, then they aren't doing their job.

✔ TASK 6.1

Think about why it is important for teachers to assess their learners. What is the purpose? Why do we do it?

Your first response to these questions might be 'because we have to' or 'because learners expect it' and you would be right. As stated above, assessment provides us with invaluable information about the effectiveness of our teaching and the extent to which it has moved learners on. The snapshot of learning which assessment provides allows us to create future learning opportunities; and learners expect it because this is often the educational tradition from which they come. From a quality assurance perspective, assessment provides evidence about the effectiveness of a learning programme and this is suggestive about the degree to which it is viable or fit for purpose. This is particularly pertinent given the context of the UK target-driven education system, where success equals funding.

✔ TASK 6.2

The descriptions of assessment below are from the perspective of different people working in a post-16 sector context. Which one(s) do you agree with?

Assessment is…..

'A way of establishing your learners' position in the learning process'

'A way of the teacher checking that the learners have learned what you planned for them'

'Checking learning, making sure all learners understand what they've been taught'

(Practising teachers and professional learning advisers)

A common theme of the definitions above is the idea of *checking* learning: finding out 'where our learners are'. Assessment is about whether learners are learning so we need to constantly look out for evidence of this in aspects of our students' classroom behaviour. There are different ways that we can do this. For example, we can do *formative* assessment, which basically answers the question 'What progress have you made?'. This type of assessment is often known as assessment *for* learning and is an ongoing feature of the instructional process. It identifies what the learners can and can't do, and the planning process is then geared toward 'plugging up the gaps'. The Assessment Reform Group (2002, p. 2) defines assessment for learning as,

"the process of seeking and interpreting evidence for use by learners and their teachers to decide where the learners are in their learning, where they need to go and how best to get there."

Formative assessment happens all the time in a real teaching situation; we are constantly looking for clues as to what our learners know and don't know. This process can be more or less formal. For example, a textiles teacher might decide to see how much his/her students have learned about stitching techniques by watching them do it. Alternatively, a science teacher might decide to use a quiz to see how much the learners had remembered about the periodic table. It is always important to interpret learners' non-verbal responses too. Silence or a quizzical face speaks volumes.

A key point to note is that the emphasis of formative assessment is on not on marks or grades but on the *feedback* given to students about their progress in relation to their learning goal(s). In this context, feedback is *information*. Professor John Hattie (2009) has clearly demonstrated the power of feedback and the value that it adds to students' learning. We will look at feedback later on.

In contrast, *summative assessment* takes place when the instructional process is finished. It captures the learning at the end of a programme of study through tests or exams, and results in a certificate or qualification. This hopefully leads to employment or further training. It is often known as assessment *of* learning.

There are other kinds of assessment that are part and parcel of teaching and training in the sector. As we saw in Chapter 3, *initial assessment* is a useful way to establish whether the learner has the skills set to join the course. It is a basic screening check and often, although not always, happens at the pre-entry stage (before the course has started). For example, if you teach hairdressing, you would want to know that your learners are interested in developing a career in the industry and that their literacy skills were good enough to cope with the reading and writing they would have to do on the course. You'd also need to check their numeracy skills as hairdressing involves working with numbers. If a learner is to mix colouring solutions properly, he/she needs to know about proportion. Working out bills for customers is another key area involving working with figures. Initial assessments can also identify additional learning needs, such as dyslexia. Broadly speaking, then, an initial assessment should include clear information, advice and guidance so that learners are directed to an appropriate course of study matched to their skills and aspirations.

Secondly, *diagnostic assessment* is a more detailed check on the learners' aptitudes and knowledge, and usually takes place once the learner has started the course; this is sometimes called the on-course stage. Diagnostic assessment is a useful way for you to find out what their strengths and weaknesses are so that you can plan learning activities matched to their needs. For example, if you are an ESOL teacher, you need to know how developed your learners' writing skills are. To do this you could ask them to complete a job application form; this would be an effective way to find out how good their punctuation and grammar skills are. Initial and diagnostic assessments can involve a range of different tasks such as completing an application form, doing a literacy and/or numeracy task, having an interview with a member of the teaching team, doing a test, writing a profile statement or checking on existing qualifications. Learning providers have their own processes and you need to be familiar with those that your department use. At some stage you, as the course tutor, will be involved.

Finally, *ipsative assessment* is one which encourages autonomy by asking the learner to self-assess. In ipsative assessment, learners compare their current performance to previous performance. A question such as 'How do you think that went?' will encourage them to self-evaluate. It can be very motivating as it requires the learner to diagnose their own strengths and weaknesses, and set their own targets in relation to the learning aims of the course independently of a teacher, trainer or assessor.

SELF- AND PEER-ASSESSMENT

Read through the dialogue between a performing arts teacher and his learner below, and consider how self-evaluation can move learning forward.

✔ TASK 6.3

Teacher 'Alex, let's look at your assignment. How do you think you did?'

Alex 'Hmm, I think I managed to get across the main points about drama techniques… I gave quite a few examples and remembered to say what I thought was good and not so good about them. I forgot to write about improvisation, though, so I've probably lost some marks there.'

Teacher 'OK, well done, we're in agreement there. What might you do differently next time?'

Alex 'Well I'd definitely remember to write about improvisation! I don't think the conclusion was very good so I'll work on bringing my ideas together.'

This is a small snapshot of the type of conversation that might occur between a teacher and learner. What stands out for you? Something you might have noticed is the fact that the teacher doesn't *tell* Alex what he/she thinks; in this case, he *elicits* the main points from him by using questions. This is beneficial because it encourages Alex to think through the main issues rather than have someone else do it for him. By using questions which encourage self-reflection, we can help our learners take ownership of their learning in a way which is meaningful for them. By guiding our learners toward thinking about their learning, we can help them see what they can *already* do and what they *still* need to work on to meet the outcomes. The goals should be captured in the Individual Learning Plan in the form of an action plan and/or targets (see Chapter 3). Black and Wiliam (2001, p. 7) say, 'self-assessment by pupils, far from being a luxury, is in fact an essential component of formative assessment'. For this reason, we should ensure that we make time to factor it in. Self-assessment can be carried out not just by reflective questions but also by:

❭ using a mark scheme or set of criteria against which the learners marks their own work;
❭ marking their work against a prescribed or exemplar answer;
❭ marking the learning outcome number next to each section or paragraph of a written response;
❭ using a traffic-light system (Green = I can do this, Amber = I need more help with this, Red = I don't understand this);
❭ setting themselves targets against the learning outcomes for the unit/module; and
❭ writing a response in a reflective log or journal so that their learning journey can be charted.

(Adapted from Petty, 2009b)

Make sure you add variety to keep the learners engaged and motivated toward improving themselves.

In the same way that self-assessment contributes to moving learning forward, peer assessment can have a similarly powerful effect so why not encourage learners to learn from each other? Peer assessment basically involves classmates assessing each other's work. It works most effectively when done in a supportive collaborative environment where learners feel comfortable with other. As with self-assessment, understanding the learning outcomes is an important part of the process. Geoff Petty (2009) outlines the various ways in which peer assessment can be done.

Students can:

❭ mark their classmate's work then tell them what they thought;
❭ write an overall comment on a piece of written work or activity worksheet;
❭ have a group discussion about a classmate's work;
❭ do an individual or group presentation. A class discussion can then take place about the good points and points to work on;
❭ mark work against a model answer; and
❭ edit their classmate's work using a marking scheme or correction code.

The advantages of peer assessment are that we can see the problems the class are having as a whole and take remedial steps to solve them. It is also helpful to see things from someone else's perspective. Learners may take more pride in their work if they know a friend is going to assess it. Finally, it may be that they take criticism more openly and willingly from a classmate than from you. When using peer assessment, check that the learners feel comfortable doing it and understand what to do. Additionally, set clear ground rules; these can include looking for two positives first before setting any development points. Learners need to feel secure that they won't be publically criticised so make sure they know they shouldn't make fun of each other's mistakes.

TALKING POINT

Go back to the scenario at the start of this section. How might Alex's teacher have integrated peer assessment?

HOW DOES ASSESSMENT SUPPORT LEARNING?

Feedback

 **TASK 6.4**

What does feedback mean? Have you ever been given feedback? How did you feel? Did you feel positive about yourself and your work? Did it help you improve? Have you ever given feedback to anyone else?

Hopefully, your experience of receiving feedback was a positive one and you will be able to use this experience to inform your own practice. Good feedback is a learning conversation between teacher and student, not a monologue by the former. The power of feedback in relation to teaching and learning cannot be understated. Research into this field has led academics such as Professor John Hattie (2009) to state that feedback is one of the most powerful influences on students' learning. Following on from Black and Wiliam's (2001) report into assessment for learning, feedback should be used to improve the quality of learning rather than as a measure of final outcomes.

Managed effectively, we can use feedback to motivate learners and move them forward in their learning. Feedback helps learners to see where they are in relation to the desired outcomes for the course, unit or module. From a teaching perspective, it helps us identify what we need to do to ensure they are on the right track. An important point to remember is that the most effective feedback is information in relation to the student's work rather than a grade or mark. Feedback can be verbal or non-verbal and it is up to you to decide which option to go with. Ideally you will be able to do both but this will depend on time. Giving effective feedback can take time to develop so here are some tips to get you going.

Do	Don't
ensure the feedback is constructive and developmental in nature - learners need to know what they can do to improve.	just focus on what is good. Learners need to know how they can improve their work so they can move on. The praise sandwich is a useful analogy: start and end with the positives – the middle bit is the 'filling', the points the learner needs to work on.
use language that the learner can understand and which is, as far as possible, free of teacher jargon.	use negative language (for example, 'Ibi that was terrible') – this is demotivating.
if you are giving group feedback, summarise areas for development for the class as a whole then set individual targets.	make sweeping statements – give a specific example to illustrate your point.

Do	Don't
take ownership of the feedback by using 'I' (for example, 'I saw you deal with X very well because…', 'I thought that was good because…').	overload the learner - prioritise the main areas for development.
encourage self-reflection – use questions such as 'How do you think you did in your assignment?', 'What worked well?', or 'What would you do differently next time?'.	compare a learner with their classmates – focus on the work they have produced and not the learner him/herself.
make a comment on language use as well as subject content – this helps the learner identify how they can improve their speaking and writing skills.	forget to be attentive to your body language – a frown can be off-putting.
make sure the learner understands the feedback; ask them to summarise what you have said or written to check.	forget to record the areas for development on the ILP.
give feedback as soon as possible after the assessment has taken place, so that it is fresh in the learner's mind – and yours.	give oral feedback in an open public place if you can avoid it.

Black and Wiliam's research (1998) into formative assessment led them to describe an approach to feedback, which can be summarised as the 'Medal and Mission' approach. In this model, *medal* relates to rewards for what the learner has done well and *mission* relates to targets that the learner still needs to achieve. It is a useful way to think about the way in which we approach feedback with our learners.

☑ TASK 6.5

Look at the feedback below. Rewrite it so that it is more developmental.

1. 'That was excellent.'
2. 'You're always making the same mistake.'
3. 'Work on punctuation.'
4. 'You need to work harder or else you'll never pass.'

There are clearly many possible different ways of rewriting the comments. Here are some suggestions:

1. 'Excellent, Marcia, you remembered to use the correct knife blade to bone the salmon.'
2. 'You need to keep developing your knowledge of quadratic equations. Look back at the examples we did in class and ask me if you need more help. You're doing well with fractions so keep up the good work.'
3. 'Work on using the apostrophe to show possession – for example, '*Tom's pen*'.'
4. 'Well done, Jamal, you have made progress in your assignment writing. Keep working hard."

TALKING POINT

Look at the tips above. Think about feedback you have been given or feedback that you have given someone else. On a scale of 1–5, how effective was the feedback? (1 = excellent, 5 = poor).

Fitness for purpose

One of the main responsibilities we have as teachers is to make sure the assessment we are asking our learners to do is a fair one. We do not want our learners to be disadvantaged because we have not thought through carefully enough what we have asked them to do or how we have asked them to do it. There are some terms that you need to be familiar with in order to ensure the assessment is fit for purpose.

Validity

Broadly speaking, a *valid* assessment is one which assesses what it is meant to assess. Here is an example: if you are a plumbing teacher and you want to check your learners' understanding of gas installation procedures, then you need to ensure that you have covered this area of the syllabus first. The assessment would be invalid if you hadn't because you would be assessing something the learners didn't know about. Validity also relates to the type of assessment method you choose. Here is another example: if you teach hairdressing and want to check your learners' ability to use different cutting techniques, then it is sensible to actually observe them using the techniques they have learned about. This is a *valid* assessment because it replicates an authentic workplace situation. Asking them to write an assignment is not valid because they would never be expected to do this in a salon environment.

Reliability

Reliability means consistency, and relates to both learners and teachers. A reliable assessment is one which produces broadly similar results at different times, and with different learners and assessors. For example, you may have two different groups of learners all of whom are studying maths but one group studies full time during the day and is made up of 16–18 year olds, and the other studies part time in the evening and is mainly 19+. Your assessment is reliable if the results of a test they take are broadly similar; that means, it doesn't matter who the learners are or when they take their test – the end result is the same. Your assessment is also reliable if you award the same results if you mark it on two different occasions, for example on a Monday morning or a Thursday evening. Finally if two different assessors award a similar mark to a singular piece of work, then it is likely that the assessment is a reliable one.

Authenticity

Authenticity can mean different things depending on the context. If we are assessing a piece of work, we need to be sure that it belongs to the learner in question and that it hasn't been plagiarised from another source such as the internet – we need to know that the learner hasn't cheated. It is common for learners who are being assessed through portfolios to submit a signed authenticity statement to say the work belongs to them.

Sufficiency

Teachers need enough information to make a decision about a learner's level of understanding, knowledge or skills. Without this, we are doing them a disservice. *Sufficiency* therefore relates to the amount of assessment evidence that is needed to demonstrate that a learner has met the learning outcomes for a module or unit. Ask yourself, 'How much evidence do I need to make a judgement?' Evidence may be demonstrated through assignments, witness testimonies, reports, presentations and so on. Often, a learner can show they have met not just one but a number of learning outcomes through the same piece of work. Our job is to map the evidence against the unit or module specifications to ensure the learner has successfully achieved them.

Fairness

A *fair* assessment is one which is free of bias of any kind. Bias can relate to factors such as language, gender, disability, culture or age. Let's take an example: we would have to question whether it would be fair to give an assessment which relied on knowledge about western European culture to a recently-arrived immigrant with a low level of English. As far as possible, assessment content should reflect a broad range of ethnic backgrounds, ages, genders and (dis)abilities.

Transparency

For learners to know what is expected of them, they need clear and unambiguous guidelines. In other words, they need to adhere to the assessment criteria. Transparency (or 'openness') is the term that we use for this. It basically answers the questions, 'Do you know what I am looking for?' and 'Do you understand the assessment criteria?' Learners need to know this in advance of taking the assessment so any queries they have can be addressed before they begin. Transparency adds to the reliability of an assessment.

The more you are involved in assessing your learners, the more you will become familiar with these terms. Whenever you have an assessment to prepare, ask yourself the following questions:

❭ Is the assessment valid?
❭ Is the assessment reliable?

❱ Do the learners know how they are going to be assessed?
❱ Are the criteria clear?
❱ Do they understand what they have to do?
❱ Is the language clear and understandable?
❱ Will the assessment method give me enough information about my learners?
❱ Is the assessment method resistant to cheating?

If you can answer 'yes' to all of the above, then your chosen method is highly likely to be fit for purpose.

TALKING POINT

What factors do you think might make an assessment invalid or unreliable? What will you do to ensure you have collected enough assessment evidence? How will you ensure that your learners understand how they will be assessed?

HOW DO WE ASSESS OUR LEARNERS?

There is a wide variety of methods available for assessment purposes and it is up to you to make a decision about which one best suits your learners. Assessment can be internally created by your team or department or externally prescribed by the awarding body which validates the course you are teaching. In each case you should ensure that you understand how the assessment works and how it contributes to the learning outcomes for the unit or module. You will also need to know about how to record the assessment results. We will look at record keeping later.

If you and/or your team are responsible for creating an assessment, you essentially have a menu of possible methods to choose from. How do you decide which one to use? In answering this question, you will need to think about issues such as the purpose of the assessment – is it formative or summative? How much time do you have? How easy is the assessment to mark? What is the profile of the learners? Have you used the method before? Will it provide you with the information you need? Thinking about these in advance will enable you to make an informed choice. Remember that you should try to vary the methods you use to engage the learners and appeal to the different ways in which they learn. Read the descriptions below and see which one(s) you could use with your learners.

Observation

An observation involves watching our learners at work and taking note of what we see and hear. It can be an effective way of assessing a subject such as catering and hospitality or beauty therapy where the learners are required to demonstrate their knowledge in a practical hands-on way. Observation has the advantage of seeing the learners using their skills in a real-time situation which replicates what happens in the workplace. NVQ assessors often use a checklist of performance criteria or competency statements to 'tick off' what they see, for example 'the learner can use communication skills effectively' or 'the learner can carry out a client consultation confidently' and this increases the reliability of the judgement made. One possible disadvantage of observation is that different assessors may interpret the evidence they see in different ways. For this reason, assessors often undergo a period of professional training so that they know how to use the checklists and interpret the evidence they observe.

Assignment

An assignment is basically a piece of written work produced by the learner, which allows us to establish the degree to which he or she has understood the principles or ideas that they have learned about. They are often linked to the learning outcomes for the unit, module or particular period of learning and provide the opportunity for the learners to demonstrate their creative thinking or problem-solving skills. For example, a learner on a sociology course might be asked to write an assignment on the causes of crime and deviance in society and justify their responses. Assignments can also provide an opportunity for us to capture our learners' attitudes or opinions on certain themes related to the area of the syllabus they are working on; for example an English literature student might be asked to compare and contrast two poems and give their opinion about which one they prefer. Assignments are an effective way to assess areas of learning holistically but, from our point of view, can be time-consuming to mark. They can also be open to criticisms of bias as what one assessor thinks is a good piece of writing may be different to what another assessor thinks. This can, however, be overcome with the use of mark schemes and training.

Presentation

A presentation involves verbally explaining the content of a topic to an audience, which often includes other learners as well as you in your assessing role. Learners may be allowed to use resources such as PowerPoint slides or other visual/audio aids to help them get their points across. Presentations are often an effective assessment method for those who learn in an auditory or visual way or those who have weak language and literacy skills, as they do not have to rely on the written word to demonstrate their learning. On the downside, presentations can make those who do not like public speaking nervous. The most effective presenters are those who can make eye contact, use their body language and gesture and voice to communicate their message. The skills needed to deliver good presentations can be practised and developed.

Professional discussion

A professional discussion is a conversation between the teacher and learner about aspects of a learning programme in relation to its outcomes. This is a useful way to capture information about the learner's knowledge or understanding, which may not be reflected in other areas of their course work. For the teacher, it is a way of checking that assessment criteria have been met. A professional discussion is an effective method for those learners who find expressing themselves in writing difficult. You will need to be careful about the wording of your questions. Remember this is an opportunity for the learner to tell you about what they know, so be careful not to answer the questions for them. Recording the discussion means you can capture the evidence and return to it at a later point if you need to. Don't forget to record the evidence of your discussion so that the learner, and others, can access it at a later point if they need to.

Learning journal

Learning journals or logbooks are a common assessment feature of many different types of learning programme, such as counselling, health and social care, and teacher training. They are a valuable way to assess learning when changes in attitudes or opinions are as important as assessing knowledge or competency. Learning journals usually require learners to reflect on their practice or the practice of others. They are a useful tool for those who have recently returned to education or who have not written formal assignments for a while. The best journals are often those which are organised with sub-headings or mapped to assessment criteria as these provide a sense of structure. When they are not, the reflection may be 'rambling' or off-point.

Case study

A case study is a detailed study of a person, group or situation based on a hypothetical or real-life scenario. Case studies often have human interest value because we can recognise the dilemmas they capture. They require learners to make decisions or problem-solve and are an effective way to assess those learners who are doing vocational courses, preparing them for working with others. Case studies allow learners to demonstrate their existing knowledge and experience in an authentic way. For example, a learner on a business course could compare and contrast the profiles of two new companies with a view to deciding which one has the most potential to be profitable. We should remember to ensure that the assessment outcomes are made clear so that learners know what they are working towards.

Quiz

A quiz can be a fun way to assess learning. You can use quizzes to create a healthy sense of competition and the advantage is that they can be quick and easy to create. We can tailor them to fit the areas we want to assess; alternatively, there is a wealth of online quizzes and puzzles ready to be downloaded. (See Chapter 13 for some fun and engaging activities to use with your learners.)

Role play

A role play is an enactment of a real-life scenario. It requires the participation of one or more learners demonstrating the practical application of skills, knowledge or understanding. It can be an engaging method of assessment for those students who learn kinaesthetically. Role plays require learners to speak to each other and the evidence for the assessment can be captured through the use of audio or visual recording equipment. This adds to the reliability of the assessment outcome because others can also listen to or see it, too. A role play could be used by an ESOL teacher who wanted to assess her learners' ability to ask and respond to questions in an interview situation. A possible disadvantage of role play is that learners who are shy or who lack the confidence to speak in public may not want to participate. Teachers can overcome this with adequate preparation during class time.

Previous experience

Recognising a learner's previous education and/or experience is a way of valuing what he or she did before starting your programme of study. The common terms are APL, APEL and APCL but there is a difference between them. APL (Accreditation of Prior Learning) is the general term for previous learning, whether this this is through experience or qualification. APEL (Accreditation of Prior Experiential Learning) is a way of recognising a candidate's previous experience and may include any paid or voluntary work they have done. APCL (Accreditation of Prior Certificated Learning) is a way of recognising a certificate that a candidate has gained from another provider or in another context.

Portfolio

A portfolio is basically a file (electronic or hard copy) containing evidence of the learner's engagement with the programme of study. It acts as an account of progress through the course and may contain documents such as witness statements, reports, letters, observation records and forms. It is our responsibility to check that the learning outcomes for the course have been met through this collection of materials and resources and to put plans in place if not. A portfolio can provide a sense of ownership and achievement as it is the learner's responsibility to collate it and present it for assessment. Learners often need guidance in putting together the information in a portfolio so that it is neatly ordered and easy to access. Portfolios which are poorly presented do not create a good impression.

Tests

Tests can be formal or informal. You can set up a test to run under exam-type conditions with time limits, no discussion or collaboration and invigilation. Alternatively, tests can be used formatively and in a more relaxed, less pressurised way than the former. The format of the test depends on your purposes. A test can be a multiple-choice worksheet, a short answer quiz, a set of true/false statements or gapped sentences for learners to complete. The good news is that there is a wide range of different ways of formatting, administering and marking tests. Tests can be quick and easy to mark which, for a busy teacher, is always a good thing!

Questions

Question and answer, or Q and A, is probably the most commonly used method of formative assessment. It is the staple ingredient of a teacher's diet and a powerful tool to assess learning. Teachers spend so much of their time questioning that it is worth reflecting on the kind of questions we ask. Questions can be verbal or written. They can also be *closed* which only require a simple 'yes/no' response ('Does the sun rise in the east?' 'Yes.') or *open*, which requires deeper-level thinking ('What were the causes of the Second World War?') and often begin with *who, why, what, where,* or *how*. Questions provide the opportunity for our learners to demonstrate their knowledge from a very basic level to a more complex one. In Chapter 4, we referred to Bloom's taxonomy and saw that questions range from a lower order, which only requires learners to explain, define or label, to a higher one, which requires much more sophisticated thinking skills such evaluation, analysis or appraisal. We must use our judgement to decide what kinds of questions to ask our learners. Needless to say, there should always be variety in what we do. Furthermore, questions should be scaffolded in such a way that they build learners' confidence and develop their knowledge. Below are some tips for effective questioning.

Do	Don't
nominate the person being asked the question ('Laura, what do you think?') as this helps create an inclusive environment and encourages less vocal learners to contribute.	answer your own questions – this is more common than you think.
differentiate the question – ask a lower order question to a weaker learner and a more difficult one to stretch and challenge a more able one.	multi-layer the question, embedding one or more questions within another.
allow enough time for the learner(s) to think about the response to the question you have asked.	use negative questions ('Did you not do your homework?").
ask questions to the whole class – this can create momentum and energy and can stimulate discussion.	ask rhetorical questions, those which make a statement rather than require an answer.
'snowball' the questions – when a learner asks you a question, throw it back to the rest of the class to see who can answer.	be led by the strongest and most vocal learners – spread your questions so that everyone is included.
use simple language that the learners understand.	overpraise a learner if they get a question right – it is easy for the word 'excellent' to become devalued if used too often.
encourage learners to ask each other questions.	give up if learners don't respond first time round – ask again.

You might find the *Pose, Pause, Pounce, Bounce* technique (http://teachertoolkit. me/2013/01/04/pppb-version2) to be a useful framework for questioning. In this analogy:

> ❱ *pose* means ask a question or series of questions making sure you have the attention of the whole class first;
> ❱ *pause* means wait some time, for as long as you can, before taking any answers – this builds tension and anticipation;
> ❱ *pounce* means ask student A for the answer; and
> ❱ *bounce* means throw student A's response back to Student B, who can throw it to Student C and so on. In this phase, it doesn't really matter if the answer is correct or not – the quality of the debate that can be created is more important.

Try it and see how effectively it works.

To summarise, skilful questioning is a basic technique for assessing what our learners know and making decisions about how to move them on. To become a skilful questioner, you need to practise the art until it becomes second nature.

PLANNING ASSESSMENT

Assessment is a key part of our learners' experience. It is an opportunity for them to demonstrate what they know so we must ensure that they are well prepared for it. This takes careful planning. You will need to consider a range of issues, including making sure the learners:

❱ have covered the content they will be assessed on;
❱ know the assessment dates and the equipment they need to bring (if any);
❱ know how long the assessment will take;
❱ know the criteria you will be using to mark their assessments;
❱ do not have any other assessments timetabled for the same day and time; and
❱ are registered with the exam or awarding body.

Finally, you will need to know the procedures for registering any disabilities learners have so that adjustments can be made. We will look at supporting learners with disabilities in Chapter 9.

☑ **TASK 6.6**

Read through the scenarios below and decide which assessment method is most appropriate.

1. An NVQ motor vehicle maintenance tutor needs to check whether the learners can replace the engine of a car.
2. A GCSE English teacher wants to know to what extent the learners have understood the relationship between George and Lenny in *Of Mice and Men*.
3. An NVQ beauty therapy tutor wants to know whether the learners can carry out a health and safety risk assessment check of the salon.
4. A BTEC Health and Social Care teacher needs to find out whether her learners understand the factors that contribute to health and well-being.
5. A Business teacher wants to assess the learners' understanding of marketing strategies.
6. An A2 Biology teacher wants to find out whether the learners understand the process of photosynthesis.
7. An A level Accountancy teacher wants to know how much the learners understand about the relationship between profit and loss.
8. An ICT teacher needs to find out whether the learners can produce a spreadsheet.

In scenario 1, the teacher might observe his learners in action, while in scenario 2 the teacher could ask the learners to write an assignment or do a presentation. In scenario 3, the teacher might ask the learners a series of questions and in scenario 4 the teacher could prepare a quiz. Scenario 5 lends itself to a discussion of a case study and in scenario 6 the teacher could ask differentiated questions to ensure everyone understood the process. In scenario 7, the learners could do a test and, finally, in scenario 8 the teacher could observe the learners at their computers.

TALKING POINT

As you can see, there are many methods with which to assess our learners. Which ones would be suitable for your subject area? What methods could you use? Why? Are there any you would not select? Why?

HOW DO WE QUALITY ASSURE ASSESSMENT?

In an educational context, quality assurance is an important feature of the assessment process. We need to be confident that our judgements reflect the quality of learners' work. For this reason, learning providers have certain systems in place to ensure that the decisions we make accurately capture this. The systems will differ from place to place but at some point, you will be involved.

Standardisation

Standardisation is a form of quality assurance. It relates to the reliability and fairness of assessment decisions. Broadly speaking, an assessment which has been standardised has been marked by different people to ensure consistency. Let's look at an example: an English teacher marks an assignment using an exam board's set of criteria and awards it 68%; a colleague teaching the same course independently marks the same assignment using the same criteria and gives it a similar mark; they then compare their marks and discuss their decision-making. This is good practice as it gives both teachers an opportunity to engage with the quality of the work in relation to the criteria. It is uncommon and not necessary for assessors to agree on everything all the time; the aim is to be in broad agreement.

Internal verification (IV)

Internal verification involves a judgement being made about the assessor's feedback rather than the learner's work. This role is carried out by an internal verifier, who is usually someone from the same team or department as the assessor. They need to be familiar with the course, assessment criteria and learning outcomes. It is good practice for internal verifiers to make an overall judgement about the assessor's feedback and provide some development points if they think it is necessary.

External verification (EV)

External verification is the process by which a person who works independently of the learning provider makes a judgement about the quality of a learning programme. It is a role which is provided by an awarding organisation where their assessments are being used. External verifiers are qualified and experienced in the curriculum area they are assessing. Verification can include inspection of elements relating to the course such as: the quality of the learners' work; the accuracy of the assessor's feedback; the learning materials; initial assessment procedures; and recruitment. Sometimes the external verifier will want to meet the students on the course to hear about their experiences first hand. External verifiers often provide a schedule for the visit, outlining what they will be assessing so that the requirements are transparent.

Course evaluations

At the end of a course, it is good practice for the learners to evaluate it. This is often done by questionnaire. The results should be used by the teaching team to assess the quality of the provision and provide a basis from which to make amendments to the course delivery. Teachers should also follow the same process. Thinking about what went well and what could be done differently are effective ways to maintain and enhance overall quality.

TALKING POINT

In this section, we have looked at different 'layers' of quality assurance. Think about your teaching specialism. What can you do to ensure that your assessment decisions are fair and equal? What will your organisation's involvement be? Can you foresee any problems? How will you overcome them?

RECORD-KEEPING

Complaints about the amount of paperwork in post-16 education are not uncommon. However, we must accept that working in the sector entails complying with rules and regulations relating to keeping records. This includes those which relate to assessment. Broadly speaking, assessment records are documents which capture information about 'who, why, what, when, where and how' (Gravells, 2008):

> Who was assessed?
> Why were they assessed?
> What was the assessment method?
> When were the learners assessed?
> Where did the assessment take place?
> How did the assessment take place?

Records such as assessment schedules and assessment trackers chart a learner's progress through a learning programme. These should be available for auditing purposes either by a provider's internal team or an external body such as Ofsted. Individual learning plans (see Chapter 3) are the personal records which outline SMART targets and/or action plans. These can either be stored electronically or in hard copy format. Check your provider's policies on record storage as you will need to be sure you are not contravening rules and regulations.

SUMMARY

In this chapter you have read about the purposes of assessment and why it is important. You also read about assessment practices including formative, summative, initial, diagnostic and ipsative. You then explored the value of self- and peer-assessment. You then moved onto reading about the value of feedback and the role it has to play in moving learning forward. This was followed by a focus on fitness for purposes and you read about the terms reliability, validity, sufficiency, transparency and fairness. You then examined a range of assessment methods and paid particular attention to the use of questions. You considered the importance of quality assurance and the roles of the internal and external verifier. Finally, you read about a range of assessment records that need to be kept and the reasons why.

REFERENCES AND FURTHER READING

Black, P. and Wiliam, D. (2001) *Inside the Black Box. Raising Standards Through Classroom Assessment*. BERA.

Ecclestone, K. (2010) *Transforming Formative Assessment in Lifelong Learning*. Maidenhead: McGraw-Hill Education.

Gravells, A. (2008) *Preparing to Teach in the Lifelong Learning Sector*. Exeter: Learning Matters.

Hattie, J. (2012) *Invisible Learning: Maximizing Impact on Learning*. Abingdon: Routledge.

Kidd, W. and Czerniawski, G. (2010) *Successful Teaching 14–19: Theory, Practice and Reflection*. London: Sage.

Petty, G. (2009a) *Evidence-Based Teaching* (2nd edn). Cheltenham. Nelson Thornes.

Petty, G. (2009b) *Teaching Today*. Cheltenham: Nelson Thornes.

Tummons, J. (2007) *Assessing Learning in the Lifelong Learning Sector*. Exeter: Learning Matters.

Wiliam, D. (2011) *Embedded Formative Assessment*. Bloomington, IN: Solution Tree Press.

Websites

www.gov.uk/definition-of-disability-under-equality-act-2010 (for guidance on disability)

www.excellencegateway.org.uk/node/25581

http://assessmentreformgroup.files.wordpress.com/2012/01/10principles_english.pdf (poster outlining ten assessment for learning principles)

http://teachertoolkit.me/2013/11/10/the-5minaflplan-by-teachertoolkit-and-pivotalpaul/ (information about the '5 minute assessment for learning plan')

http://geoffpetty.com/for-teachers/feedback-and-questions/ (Geoff Petty reading about the Medal and Mission approach)

http://teachertoolkit.me/2013/01/04/pppb-version27 (further information on the Pose, Pause, Pounce, Bounce questioning technique)

Evaluation and reflection

LEARNING AIMS

By the end of this chapter, the reader will have a better understanding of:

❭ the process of evaluation

❭ how to evaluate a course

❭ the nature of reflection

❭ models of reflection

COURSE EVALUATION

Let's take a moment to think about the cycle of teaching and learning. What are the elements? Your response to this question is likely to include planning learning – the point at which you decide what your aims are, how you will deliver the information and how you will meet the needs of the learners. You will also have thought about enabling learning and the processes that make this possible, for example preparing the materials and resources, checking the room beforehand, arranging the learners into groups and choosing the activities to engage the learners. You will also have considered assessing learning, where you select the best method to check how much your students have learned and how to move them forward. This, however, is not the end of the cycle. After the planning, enabling and assessing is complete, it is important for you to reflect on the whole process with a view to making decisions about what worked well and what didn't. We call this the *evaluation* stage.

☑ TASK 7.1

Think about the last time you went on a course. Were you asked to evaluate it? How did you do this? What did you comment on?

Evaluation is a process of gathering different kinds of information, which can be used to make judgements about how effective a learning event was. Whether you are teaching a one-day workshop, a short three-day programme, a long one-year course or a series of evening classes, evaluation should be part of the process. Without evaluating our teaching, we cannot think about improvement or how we might do things differently. We would not be able to identify problems or issues that needed addressing. We would continue in the same fashion regardless of our learners' experiences. Capturing the learner voice provides us with an opportunity to view our teaching objectively and make decisions about what to do differently next time. It is ultimately a form of quality assurance.

What can you evaluate? Generally speaking, any element of the learning programme that will help you to improve the learners' experience next time you teach it. This might include finding out whether the learners liked the resources you used or if the classroom environment was suitable. You will probably want to know if they enjoyed the learning activities or the way in which you presented the information. You might want to find out whether they got as much support with their learning as they wanted. Finally, you might want to know if the course administration was carried out smoothly. Their responses to these questions will form the basis of how you teach the course the next time round. They also give you an opportunity to give feedback to other departments in your organisation or workplace on the effectiveness of the services they provide; this might include the library, enrolment or student support team.

The question you need to keep in mind when you engage with evaluation is 'How do I gather the information I need?', so think carefully about the way in which you do this. One method is a questionnaire, which is easy to administer, and can include a mix of different question types. Here are some examples. The learners can tick, circle or grade their responses.

Closed questions

a. Were the resources useful?   Yes/no
b. I thought the resources were useful.   Agree/disagree
c. The resources were useful:

Strongly agree   Strongly disagree

1   2   3   4   5

When using closed questions, questionnaires are an effective way of gathering *quantitative* data. This means that responses can easily be counted. It is good practice to include some open-ended questions, which creates the opportunity for learners to make suggestions for improvement. These *qualitative* data are a little more difficult to manage but they give the learners more scope to write about their personal opinions than closed questions do.

Here are some examples. The learners can either write their answers or produce them electronically.

Open-ended questions

❱ How could the use of resources be improved?
❱ If you were going to do the course again, which resources would you like to see included?
❱ List the resources you think should be used on the course.
❱ What were the most effective resources used on the course?

Other methods include one-to-one interviews with the learners. If you use this method, try to record the discussion (with the learner's permission) so that you don't forget any of the information. A group interview can also be used. Many learning programmes have course representatives, whose role it is to act as a spokesperson on behalf of the group, so feedback can be given via this person.

If a course is relatively short, evaluation usually takes place at the end. However, if you are teaching a long programme, it is advisable to integrate an evaluation at a midway point as well as at the end; if there are any problems, you won't have time to address them if you wait until the end. Once the results of your evaluation have been collated, you may have some issues that need to be addressed and these will form the basis of an action plan. The process of evaluation is a continual one, so when you have delivered the course again and evaluated it again, you may find that you have a different set of actions to address. Don't worry about this. It simply means that learning events are different for different groups of learners and should develop according to the students' needs.

In Chapter 6, we looked at the importance of quality assurance. Evaluation is also part of that process. In all likelihood, your organisation or workplace will want to know how viable your course is; 'viability' basically answers the question, 'Shall we run it again?' If your course is evaluated positively by your learners, and your retention (how many learners stay on the course) and achievement (how many learners pass it) figures are high, then it is highly likely the course will run again. The external verifier from your awarding body may want to see evidence of evaluation too, so make sure your responses are stored and easily accessible. Learning providers maintain a SAR (Self-Assessment Report) or SED (Self-Evaluation Document) to review and evaluate the effectiveness of course provision across all curriculum areas. This is used by the organisation to monitor progress and to identify strengths and areas of development, and will be informed by staff evaluations. It is also used by Ofsted who will assess for themselves the accuracy of the provider's quality statements.

The main thing to remember about evaluation is that you must do something with the results. Your actions must inform future course planning. This is important because creating valuable learning experiences for our students is at the heart of everything we do.

TALKING POINT

How effectively do you think questionnaires can capture the quality of a learner's experience on a course? Can you see any problems? How will you get feedback from your learners during or at the end of your course?

THE PROCESS OF REFLECTION

Underpinning self-evaluation is *reflection*; this is the act of looking back on an event and considering it from a different viewpoint. It is an 'important human activity in which people recapture their experience, think about it, mull it over and evaluate it' (Wallace, 2010, p. 69).

TASK 7.2

How easy is it to reflect on an event or situation?

Although self-reflection is critical to improving our teaching, it can be a difficult process to engage with. One of the reasons for this is because it can make us feel vulnerable and open to self-doubt. Sometimes, it is a challenge to be objective about a situation if we have invested a lot of time and energy in it. For example, you might have spent a long time looking for a particular resource only to find that your learners thought it was boring – as you can imagine, this can be a little disheartening and might lead you to ask 'What's the point?' In this situation, it is more productive to ask ourselves 'Why did they find it boring?' or 'What could I use next time that will interest them more?' Reflection requires us to experience a range of emotions and feelings, which may make us feel uncomfortable. On a practical level, reflecting on a lesson can seem like an unnecessary extra burden at the end of a hard day's teaching and this can render it meaningless. Finally, reflection doesn't necessarily come easily; it requires a particular skill set that enables us to move from the purely descriptive to a place where we can bring about real change to our teaching practice. Once we have accepted that reflection has the potential to bring about transformative change, we can engage with it more openly and honestly.

Look at the extracts below which come from different trainee teachers' learning journals. They are each reviewing a lesson they have taught. Do you think they are reflective? Why? Why not?

✔ **TASK 7.3**

Ruby

"My interpersonal skills were clear at most times. But at the back of my mind I was cautious about giving too many instructions at the same time – so I decided to break these down. I was very attentive as to what group was on what page by observing each group. This helped as it gave the students the confidence to ask questions. My teaching techniques were good and I felt I provided learners with a range of ways for learning. For example, mix and match cards, rank in order, comprehension questions, gap fill, etc. I also found it necessary to move learners around. This avoids learners talking in their own language and makes them feel energised."

Rebeka

"My main strength as a teacher is the ability to create fun and productive resources for my students, which in turn helps them learn as well as stimulate and motivate their willingness to participate in the lesson with each other. A further strength I have gained and improved greatly upon is the use of checking questions in my lessons. These should be incorporated into every lesson to make sure students have learnt what has been taught, and also to give them confidence that they have learnt something too. The impact this has had on my teaching is that it has allowed my lessons to be more coherent and relevant to the students' needs."

What did you think about the Ruby and Rebeka's extracts? Do you think they are reflective? Why? Why not? The points below might help you focus your thoughts.

Ruby understands:

❯ that teaching is a real-time event which requires quick decisions to be made ('…at the back of my mind I was cautious about giving too many instructions at the same time – so I decided to break these down');

❯ the positive impact her actions can have on learners' responses ('I was very attentive as to what group was on what page by observing each group. This helped as it gave the students the confidence to ask questions'); and

❯ her strengths and the ways in which she can connect with her learners ('My teaching techniques were good and I felt I provided learners with a range of ways for learning').

Rebeka understands:

⟩ how to elicit positive responses from her learners ('My main strength as a teacher is the ability to create fun and productive resources for my students, which in turn helps them to learn as well as stimulate and motivate their willingness to participate in the lesson with each other');
⟩ that mastering a teaching strategy takes continual practice ('A further strength I have gained and improved greatly upon is the use of checking questions in my lessons');
⟩ that teaching and learning is a two-way event – the reactions she gets from her learners can influence the way she teaches ('These should be incorporated into every lesson to make sure students have learnt what has been taught, and also to give them confidence that they have learnt something too. The impact this has had on my teaching is that it has allowed my lessons to be more coherent and relevant to the students' needs').

Overall, both Ruby and Rebeka engage openly with the process of refection and are able to step back from simply describing events to reflecting on them and thinking about their impact on teaching.

TALKING POINT

From reading the above, to what extent do you agree about the benefits of reflection? Use the scale to answer the questions below.

Strongly agree				Strongly disagree
1	2	3	4	5

⟩ It can help us become better teachers.
⟩ It can improve our critical thinking skills.
⟩ We can learn from reflecting on our teaching.
⟩ We can learn better from taking our own advice.
⟩ It improves our decision-making skills.
⟩ It improves our problem-solving skills.

MODELS OF REFLECTION

In order to understand the nature of reflection, it is useful for you to know about some different theoretical perspectives. The section below outlines some well-regarded models of reflection.

✔ TASK 7.4

Read the scenario below. Can you identify why Esther's approaches worked successfully for her?

Esther teaches an NVQ Level 2 Hairdressing course. The learners she teaches are generally good when they are doing practical work but she experiences problems managing them when they have to do their classroom-based theory work. They are rather noisy and don't listen to her or each other; they are also constantly using their mobile phones when they should be concentrating. She decides to discuss the problem with her colleague, Kemi. Kemi is sympathetic and offers to come and sit in on the class. Esther finds this really useful because in the discussion they have afterwards, Kemi tells her that she thinks the problems start when the learners have to do written work. They struggle with this because quite a few of them have weak literacy skills. She also thinks that problems occur when certain members of the group sit together at the same table. Kemi advises her to move them around to change the dynamic. In the next lesson, Esther does exactly this and, to her surprise, there is an improvement in behaviour. She also decides to do some research into how to support her learners with writing and discovers some interesting techniques in a book she finds in the library. She decides to try these out and is pleased to find that they seem to be working; the learners' behaviour begins to improve as does their writing. Esther thinks she needs to know more about classroom management and speaks to her manager about doing some training.

Compare your ideas with the models of reflection below.

Brookfield's four lenses

Some of these behaviours are fairly typical of learners in classrooms and workplaces up and down the country. Without addressing the issues, we run the risk of becoming extremely stressed and anxious. It is clear that an important aspect of Esther's approach is that instead of giving up on her learners, she decides to dig deeper to see why the problems are occurring. In other words, she separates the behaviours her learners are displaying from the learners themselves. As we saw in Chapter 2, this is key to managing behaviour. This worked effectively for her because she was able to get an objective opinion on the situation by asking her colleague, who offered her a perspective that she hadn't considered before. Doing her own research enabled her to gain insights from the 'experts', i.e. the approaches she read about in the library books. She used her new knowledge to try out strategies which helped transform her learners' behaviour. One other thing she might also have done is ask her learners the reasons for their behaviour. Brookfield (1995) suggests that we use four lenses to review and reflect upon our professional practice. In this model, the lenses are:

❭ those of our students
❭ those of our colleagues

❭ our own view(s)
❭ the theoretical perspectives to be found in educational literature

If we apply this model to Esther's situation, we can see the benefits it brings.

David Kolb's experiential learning cycle

We can use David Kolb's (1984) experiential cycle, an influential and well-regarded theory of learning, to explain the role that reflection has to play in learning and teaching. We can use it to explain the role that reflection has to play in learning. The cycle is made up of four distinct stages as set out below:

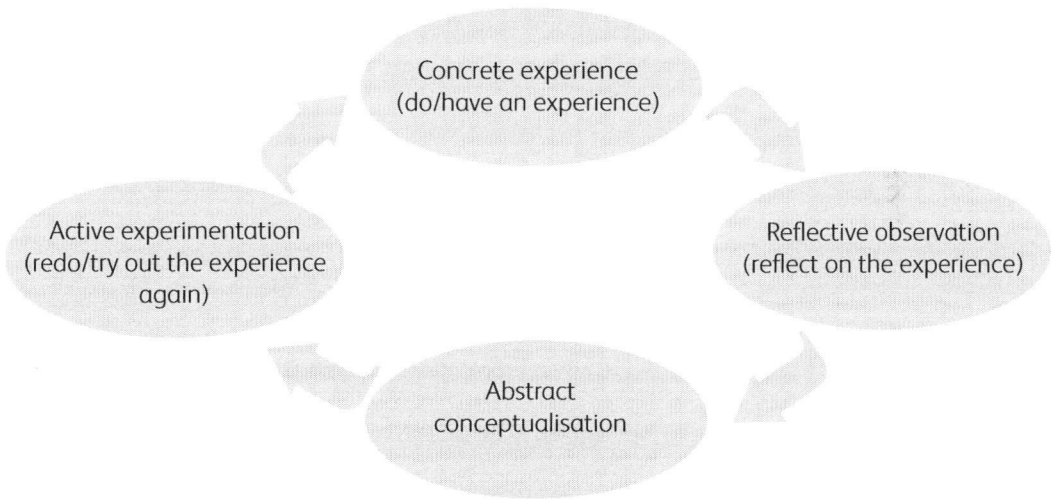

Concrete experience
(do/have an experience)

Reflective observation
(reflect on the experience)

Abstract
conceptualisation

Active experimentation
(redo/try out the experience
again)

Concrete experience. At this stage, you do something, have an experience or engage in a task (the *doing* it stage).
Reflective observation. At this stage, you step back, think about the experience and create meaning as you do so (the *reflecting* on it stage).
Abstract conceptualization. At this stage, you think about your experience in the light of theory, which leads to new ways of thinking and new ways of thinking about how things could be done differently next time (the *researching* it stage).
Active experimentation. At this stage, you put your new knowledge into practice and see what happens. The cycle then starts all over again (the *doing it again* stage).

Let's take a simple everyday example. Sue decides to make a cheese sauce (*concrete experience*) but finds that it won't thicken. She thinks back to the last time she made a cheese sauce and remembers that she used different proportions of the ingredients (*reflective observation*). She checks her cookery book for the quantity of flour to butter and milk, and realises that she needs to add some more flour (*abstract conceptualisation*). The sauce begins to thicken and she makes a mental note to herself to use the right amounts of ingredients the next time she makes a sauce (*active experimentation*).

✔ TASK 7.5

Match the teaching activity on the left with a stage of Kolb's cycle on the right.

1. You set your learners a test; most fail the question on climate change.	a. Active experimentation
	b. Abstract conceptualisation
2. You realise you covered the topic at the beginning of term but didn't revise it before the test.	c. Concrete experience
	d. Reflective observation
3. You do some internet research and find some different ways to present the topic, which you think will appeal to your learners.	
4. You go over the topic again the next time you teach the learners and find their test scores improve.	

How did you do? The correct answers are 1c (this is what happened – the *doing* stage), 2d (this is thinking about the event after it happened – the *reflecting* stage), 3b (this is how you sought alternative ways to do the event again – the *researching* stage) and 4a (this is re-enacting the event in a different way to see what happens – the *doing it again* stage).

The cycle can be started at any point but in order for learning to happen, it needs to be completed.

Donald Schön (Reflection-in-action and Reflection-on-action)

Think for a moment about the nature of teaching. We could say that it is an 'in-the-moment' activity. What do we mean by this? Generally speaking, it means that it is most often an unconscious act, something that we do in present and real time without really thinking about it. Let's take an example. Remember when you learned to drive? The individual actions of switching on the engine, putting the car into gear, looking in the mirror before moving, driving away – once you developed your confidence, these individual 'mechanical' actions became one fluid movement. The same analogy can be applied to teaching. However, to really begin to think more critically about our teaching and why we act in the ways we do, it is useful to break it down in into parts so we can understand how the parts work as a 'whole'. According to Schön, reflection can be one of two things:

❭ Reflection-in-action
❭ Reflection-on-action

Reflection-in-action happens in the moment and applies to a person who is 'thinking on their feet'. It refers to reflecting in the situation, assessing it in the light of unexpected responses and then reacting by making some alteration in an attempt to improve. For example, you have planned for your learners to do a group presentation in class; however, during the lesson, things don't go according to plan. They are reluctant to participate. You cannot get them to work together and they won't do any of the preparation. What do you do? You still need to meet the lesson outcomes so you make a spur-of-the-moment decision to do things in a different way. You might, for example, allow them to write an essay or do a role play.

After the lesson, when you are back in the staffroom, you may continue the process of reflection by thinking about the situation more. You might find yourself asking, 'Why didn't they want to do the presentation?' 'Is it because they don't feel confident speaking in front of their classmates?' 'Is it because they needed more preparation time than I planned for?' 'Is it because they are bored of doing presentations?' In other words, you are thinking about the situation and reflecting on it from a more removed perspective. This is called *reflection-on-action*. It is important for us to engage with both processes if we are to understand our professional practice on a deeper level.

TALKING POINT

If you are already teaching, think about a time when you reflected-in-action. What happened? What decisions did you make? If you aren't teaching, think about which models of reflection might be useful in other areas of your life.

SUMMARY

In this chapter, you have considered the role of evaluation in improving course provision and some different ways that you can engage with this process. You also explored what reflection is and its value in developing your professional teaching practice. You then examined three different theoretical models of reflection: Brookfield, Kolb and Schön.

REFERENCES AND FURTHER READING

Duckworth, V., Wood, J. Dickinson, J. and Bostock, J. (2010) *Successful Teaching Practice in the Lifelong Learning Sector*. Exeter: Learning Matters.

Gravells, A. (2008) *Preparing to Teach in the Lifelong Learning Sector*. Exeter: Learning Matters.

Roffey-Barentsen, J. and Malthouse, R. (2009) *Reflective Practice in the Lifelong Learning Sector*. Exeter. Learning Matters.

Wallace, S. (ed.) (2010) *The Lifelong Learning Sector Reflective Reader*. Exeter: Learning Matters.

Websites

http://infed.org/mobi/donald-schon-learning-reflection-change/ (further information about reflection-in-action and reflection-on-action)

www.simplypsychology.org/learning-kolb.html (further information about Kolb's experiential learning cycle and learning styles)

www.brainboxx.co.uk/a3_aspects/pages/ReflectionModels.htm (summaries of models of reflective practice)

Microteaching

PLANNING AND PREPARATION

One of the most nerve-wracking but exciting aspects of the Level 3 Award is the practical element: microteaching. This is a short, scaled-down teaching session, ranging from five to 30 minutes in duration, which aims to give new and experienced teachers the opportunity to develop their teaching skills within a secure and supportive environment. Microteaching sessions can be used to hone a particular skill. For example, you might want to improve your classroom management skills or use a greater variety of assessment methods, or they may be mini-lessons with a beginning, middle and end. The process of microteaching is essentially the same as what goes on any teaching situation, just on a smaller scale. You will have to plan, devise or select materials, locate appropriate resources, decide how to assess learning and then evaluate your lesson. It is based on a model of *prepare* (plan, find materials and resources, set up the learning environment), *teach* (facilitate and assess learning) and *feedback*. The comments from the feedback will influence the future planning of microteaching or full teaching sessions (see the model opposite).

Prepare

Feedback

Teach

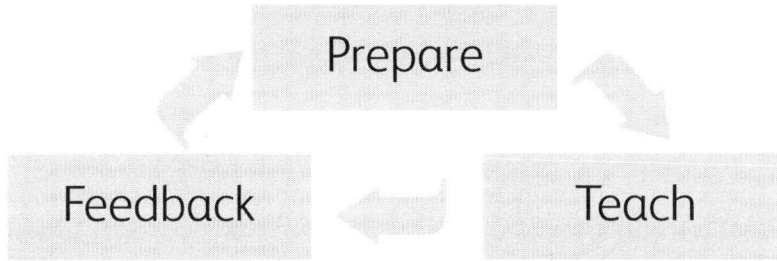

Feedback is a very important part of the microteaching process. The session is usually followed by these stages:

1. Teacher reflects on how the lesson went
2. Peers evaluate lesson
3. Observer gives verbal and written feedback

The comments made should be constructive and hopefully will make you more aware of your personal strengths and areas for development. Observing teaching is also a very useful exercise as you can see examples of good practice and examples of when something didn't go to plan. Delivering feedback is a skill in itself and observing a microteaching session gives you the opportunity to develop this.

Brookfield (2006, p. 8) likens teaching to 'white-water rafting' as 'periods of apparent calm are interspersed with sudden frenetic turbulence.' Generally speaking, however, microteaching is not considered to be a 'turbulent' exercise. Usually it is a positive experience as we can see from these comments made by a novice and by an experienced teacher:

"I felt really nervous about microteaching. I didn't sleep for about four weeks before I had to do it! I think there was so much to think about – the planning, making sure everyone was included, what you are going to do if something doesn't work out on the day. What do you do to back it up? But in the end, it was a real eye-opener. I never realised how much a teacher had to do."

"Personally, I found it a really positive experience; I learned from it. It reinforced that I was doing the right thing. It worked in two ways: I found out my teaching was OK and I learned from other people. Watching other people do their microteaching was really useful because I could pick up ideas and useful hints to help with my teaching."

As part of the assessment for this course, you will have to plan and deliver a lesson for a minimum of 15 minutes. If you are already teaching, you may prefer to be observed delivering a session to your own class. For assessment of Unit 302, you will need to participate in and show evidence of one hour's microteaching. This does not mean you are teaching for one hour; you can demonstrate your commitment to the process through observation of your peers doing microteaching or provide other suitable evidence.

☑ TASK 8.1

Preparing for your microteaching session is essential: 'Preparation pays off. Thinking through and preparing properly matter even more than enthusiasm and giving a good performance' Minton (1997, p. 27). What do you need to consider when planning for your microteaching session? Make a list of ideas.

You may have referred to the checklist on lesson planning in Chapter 4 (p. 79) as a guide. Here are some key factors to consider.

The topic/skill

It makes sense to choose a topic or skill related to the subject you are currently teaching or want to teach. You will need to be familiar with the topic so that you can deal with questions and make the process as stress-free as possible. It is important that you think of your colleagues as real learners rather than their roleplaying being students. You need to treat them as themselves, with real needs and personalities. If you pitch your lesson at the wrong level, it will be difficult to determine whether there is any real learning taking place. For example, as an ESOL teacher it would be better to review use of apostrophes with a group of peers rather than looking at the Roman alphabet. You can presume your colleagues are familiar with the latter.

Your learners' previous knowledge

Finding out what your peers know about the topic or skill will help you to plan accordingly and deliver a session which has the right level of challenge. It is useful to devise a short questionnaire to distribute to your peers a few weeks before you are to teach to gain some understanding of their prior knowledge. You will also need to consider whether any of your peers require specialist support and adapt the learning environment, your delivery and use of materials and resources accordingly.

Aims and objectives

Think about what you want your 'learners' to be able to do by the end of the session. Given the time constraints, you should not be too ambitious and consider what can be realistically achieved within the short timeframe. It is very useful to write SMART objectives (see Chapter 4).

Teaching and learning strategies

It is important to include a variety of activities and involve all your peers in the learning process. You will also need to consider whether there is scope for developing functional skills (see Chapter 10).

Learning environment

You will need to consider whether it is practical to deliver your session in your current learning environment. For example, if you are planning to deliver a session on art and design to your peers, it would be difficult to locate and transport 12 easels to a training classroom. If you are to deliver an ICT session, you may need to book a room with a computer suite.

Resources

As above, you need to decide which resources are feasible. You will also have to think about health and safety. For example, if you decide to deliver a session on different knives used in cooking (see the lesson plan below) and bring in the objects, you will obviously have to be careful that these are handled with extreme care.

Assessment methods

Consider how you will check that learning is taking place. We shall look at possible ways of assessing understanding later on in this chapter.

Contingency/back-up plan

Finally, as with any lesson, make sure you have a back-up plan. What will you do if the PowerPoint isn't working? How will you amend your lesson if an activity takes longer than expected?

☑ TASK 8.2

Look at the lesson plan below for a microteaching session devised by a cookery teacher. Why do you think the teacher may have selected this topic?

Course/topic: KNIFE SKILLS **Time:** 12.45–1.15 **Duration:** 30 MINS
Aim: To raise awareness of different knives and their uses in the professional kitchen
Objectives/outcomes:
1. **To name the six main knives used in a professional kitchen**
2. **To sharpen a knife correctly and safely**
3. **To classify the different uses of the knives**

Timing	Resources	Teacher activities	Learner activities	Assessment
12.45 (5 mins)	Learners	Starter activity Introduction of the topic: elicit job role (from uniform and hat) Clarification of learning objectives	Using pictures of dishes, participants put them into 2 columns: likes and dislikes (extension task: participants discuss how easy they are to cook)	Monitoring and feedback (no right answer!)
12.50 (5 mins)	Flipchart paper and pens.	Facilitate group discussions – do not feed in too much	Discussion in groups on knives used in a domestic and	Monitoring progress

		information here as want to see how much the participants know about the topic	professional kitchen: divide groups into two (three knives each)	
12.55 (5 mins)	Mini-presentations via flipchart	Lead feedback on what groups have discussed. Feed in correct terminology if necessary	Feedback to group on what they have discussed	Ask for peer correction
1.00 (5 mins)	Knife set	Explanation and demonstration of knife set Point out health and safety rules Q&A, e.g. 'What is this knife called?' 'Which knife is the sharpest?' 'Why?'	Participants try out knife sharpening under my supervision	Careful supervision – ask participants to modify what they are doing if necessary – explain why
1.10	Closing activity Cards: dominoes	Facilitate knife-matching game	In groups complete the knife-matching dominoes game: matching visuals to uses	Successful completion of activity

As part of microteaching, you will need to produce a rationale, outlining why you chose the topic, the teaching and learning strategies, materials and resources, and assessment methods for your peers (see Appendix E for a form you can use for this). You should write this before you teach. In her rationale, the teacher explained that she had selected this topic for its simplicity and because it is one of the first things chefs have to learn in the professional kitchen. She had originally thought of asking the participants to prepare some kind of culinary dish but realised this was impractical. She would have had to bring in a lot of ingredients and she was concerned the lesson might have become chaotic and, therefore, difficult to manage.

TALKING POINT

How do you feel about microteaching? Does it fill you with trepidation or are you looking forward to the process? If you are keeping a reflective journal, you might want to record some of your thoughts now and revisit these after the session has been delivered. It is useful to start thinking about the session as soon as you can. You can use the handout (Appendix D) to help you prepare your ideas and consider which materials and assessment methods you are going to include in the session.

ENABLING LEARNING

As we have seen, microteaching allows you to practise the skills needed for effective teaching, such as the following:

❱ Devising interesting 'starter' activities
❱ Leading into activities
❱ Giving instructions
❱ Delivering feedback
❱ Setting up different classroom interaction patterns
❱ Managing behaviour
❱ Assessing understanding
❱ Summarising learning

It takes time to develop these techniques and the more practice you can get in a secure environment, the better. As you gain more experience, you will need to do less preparatory work and will be able to adopt a more flexible approach to your teaching.

When you first start teaching, it is easy and understandable to get bogged down with your own performance in the classroom. For example, if there is a technological hitch it can feel like the end of the world when, in fact, your learners may not even be aware of anything untoward as long as you remain calm and unflustered. It is always worth remembering that your role is primarily to facilitate inclusive learning. Your learners may appreciate having an enthusiastic and dynamic teacher but they should be given as many opportunities as possible to be involved in the learning process. Microteaching is a good place to start.

In Chapter 5, we looked at different ways of enabling inclusive learning such as role plays, discussions, demonstrations, student presentations and quizzes. Given the time constraints involved with microteaching, you cannot spend too long warming up your class. Nevertheless, a lively lead-in will engage your learners from the outset, set the tone of the lesson and create a relaxed and learner-friendly classroom. The 'starter' or warmer should ideally take no longer than five minutes in a 30-minute microteaching session.

✔ TASK 8.3

Kidd and Czerniawski (2010, p. 2) mention that it is important to make yourself and the subject 'sparkle'. Make a list of all the engaging activities that you could use in your session.

Here are a few ideas from some of the microteaching sessions we have observed:

Childcare	Create mindmaps on different aspects of play
Art and design	Match names of artists to facts
ICT	Show different hardware; cover objects and ask learners to remember as many objects as possible
Employment skills	Learners stand on an imaginary line to rank to what extent they are a team player
Science	Learners sit back to back. One describes a picture; the other draws it
Additional learning needs	Quiz to assess prior knowledge of a topic
ESOL	Errors in punctuation displayed around the room. Participants move around the room and correct them

Following the starter activity, the subsequent task or tasks that learners carry out will depend on the topic or skill you are teaching. For example, if the SMART objective is for learners to be able to wire a plug by the end of the lesson, a suitable activity would be to demonstrate how to perform the action and then learners could be asked to do it, working with a partner for support. You will also need to consider the learning environment, needs and personalities of your learners. What do you think they would enjoy doing? Is there room for a 'mingling' activity, a task where the learners have to move around the learning environment and talk to each other? How will the activity enable learning?

Time management is one of the most difficult aspects of microteaching. When setting activities for your target group, consider:

❫ the length of your activities: keep these short. In a microteaching session, there might only be time for one or two activities. Avoid lengthy explanations to keep your spoken contribution to a minimum;
❫ variety to maintain interest;
❫ activities with appropriate challenge; and
❫ setting time limits to keep the participants on task.

Resources

Finally, you will need to decide which resources will help to enable learning in your session. Wallace (2011) maintains that there are three main aspects to consider when selecting resources: interest, variety and suitability.

☑ TASK 8.4

Consider the effectiveness of the following resources: PowerPoint, flipchart, real objects, handouts/worksheets and the whiteboard (and interactive whiteboard). What will you need to think about if you use any of these resources in your microteaching session?

Again, the choices you make will depend on the topic or skill being taught, the learning environment and availability of resources. Some points for consideration are outlined below.

PowerPoint

You might decide to use a PowerPoint presentation to help structure your microteaching session and convey key information. However, be mindful of that dreaded phrase: 'death by PowerPoint'! It is easy to be too reliant on this tool to help you teach rather than use it to facilitate learning. There is a danger of boring learners if there is a lot of information for the learners to digest. It is also questionable whether learning is taking place as the learners are not doing anything with the material. Consider these points:

> Don't put too much text on each slide. Use relevant visuals to help engage your learners and elicit key information.
> Don't read the information verbatim; learners are capable of reading it themselves. Instead, summarise points.
> Reveal information gradually to 'tease' the learners and draw out points.
> Don't make it too jazzy just for the sake of it. Some learners may become irritated and distracted by lots of visual and sound gimmicks.
> Don't be too dependent on the slides; don't use PowerPoint as a 'crutch' to help you structure your teaching. Rehearse your delivery without looking at them and you will feel far more relaxed and confident in dealing with queries should they arise.

Flipchart

If it is not possible to use PowerPoint (perhaps if there is no access to technology in the classroom or if you do not feel confident using it) you could use a flipchart to structure your presentation. It is a good idea to plan this in advance unless you want to use the flipchart as a way of recording learner responses spontaneously. For her microteaching session, the catering teacher used flipchart paper as a resource. Learners shared ideas as a group and recorded them on the paper; they then presented their ideas to each other. This is a good way of encouraging collaboration and communication. However, it is important that during the feedback stage, you ask the participants to clarify responses and you fill in gaps in their knowledge. Some learners may not have made a note of the group's responses so, if you have a mobile device, take a photo of the information and email it to the group later. Of course, you will need to check your institution's policy on use of phones in the classroom beforehand.

Realia (real objects)

Realia means using real objects in the classroom to bring your subject to life and, possibly, to give learners practice using these tools in activities. You will need to decide whether the effort of finding and transporting these objects equates to the effort the learners will make in using them. You can also use objects to present information such as mathematical concepts, for example percentages and fractions.

Handouts/worksheets

Handouts have a variety of functions: to provide information on a topic, to function as a worksheet and to summarise points. They can be very useful learning tools but be careful of making your lessons too paper-based. We looked earlier at how it was important to integrate variety into lessons. Instead of always preparing handouts, consider how you could also introduce different resources and activities in your lessons such as cards, objects, role plays, demonstrations and experiments to enable learning.

To produce effective handouts, ensure they:

- have a clear aim;
- are visually-appealing, with headings, bullet points and pictures;
- are written in an appropriate font;
- do not use too much jargon or complicated vocabulary;
- allow sufficient space for learners to write answers or take notes (if they are worksheets);
- include accurate information (self-explanatory, we know!) and they do not contain any spelling, punctuation or grammar mistakes; and
- correctly acknowledge any copyrighted materials, if relevant.

Whiteboards

Whiteboards, especially interactive whiteboards (IWBs), can be a useful way of conveying information. Sometimes a simple whiteboard is more effective than using a PowerPoint as you can clarify difficulties as they arise rather than preparing everything in advance and being wary of deviating from a safe structure. With the whiteboard, it is important not to spend too long writing up points for learners. For a start, the board is not usually large enough to accommodate a lot of information and what are the learners doing when you are writing? Are they really involved in the learning process? We shall look at some of the merits of the interactive whiteboard in Chapter 11 but bear in mind that, if you use this in your microteaching session, ensure the participants are involved. If you can get them up at the board, for example to move information around, so much the better.

TALKING POINT

"The sessions I liked most were those when I was involved. I particularly enjoyed one when we had to make cards. The teacher had brought in loads of different resources: stickers, coloured pens, greeting labels in different languages to appeal to different cultures. It was really inclusive. It didn't matter if you couldn't draw, like me, because you could just stick something."
(Comment from a participant in a microteaching session)

Consider the above. How are you going to ensure that your session is inclusive? Are your activities and resources accessible for all participants? Have you included tasks which require cooperation and collaboration?

ASSESSING AND EVALUATING THE MICROTEACHING SESSION

The concepts of assessment and evaluation were discussed in detail in Chapters 6 and 7. These, of course, do not mean the same thing. Assessment is to do with observing and measuring the effectiveness of learning in a lesson; we are looking here at learner achievement. With evaluation, we are interested in the strengths and weaknesses of a particular lesson or course: aspects of our own performance, how the learners reacted to the material and tasks, whether the lesson plan 'worked' in practice and so on. Nevertheless, assessment and evaluation are connected and this is the reason why we have grouped them together in this section. We can say that assessment provides the building blocks for evaluation, as 'an indicator of the quality of learning' (Wallace, 2011, p. 119).

One of the limitations of microteaching is that it is not always easy to ascertain whether learning has really taken place. The lesson is decontextualised. To a certain extent, we are guessing what the 'learners' already know about the topic or skill as there are no links to prior learning. The lesson is delivered within a very short and unnatural time frame, offering limited opportunities for real student engagement. Just because the learners are able to do something by the end of the lesson, can we really say that this is down to our teaching? Perhaps they already had a good grasp of the topic or skill and were trying hard to support the teacher.

Nevertheless, assessment is an essential component of the microteaching process. Throughout your lesson, you will be assessing whether the learning outcomes clarified at the beginning of the session have been met. A good teacher is able to observe behaviour and make judgements about what action should be taken. In other words, assessment has an immediate impact on your actions. For example, if you notice that one of the participants looks confused or has not answered a question correctly, you, or another learner, will need to provide clarification. This is, as we saw in Chapter 7, reflection-in-action (Schön, 1983). Teachers need to observe what is going on in their lessons and use their intuition to make any necessary changes to enable learning. In other words, you need to be able to think on your feet.

✔ TASK 8.5

Assessment carried out to monitor learners' understanding and progress during a session is called formative assessment. In Chapter 6, we looked at different assessment methods. Write down which ones you might use in your microteaching session.

There are many ways of carrying out formative assessment but here are a few techniques that might be appropriate for checking learning in your session:

- Oral questions (see Chapter 5): targeting questions to individuals
- Writing definitions of key terms: snowballing technique (see Chapter 5)
- Case studies: excellent for encouraging learners to collaborate and discuss issues
- Quizzes (the feedback will help guide the lesson)
- Using mini whiteboards for learners to record responses: these provide immediate feedback
- Mini-presentations: for learners to feedback what they have learned about a topic or skill to each other
- Using traffic lights (coloured cards or cups) (see Chapter 6)
- Observation (for example when the participants are doing a problem-solving task or discussion)
- Designing a poster
- Peer explanations
- Peer assessment
- Self-assessment

Finally, at the end of the session, you will need to summarise the learning process. Here, you will gain an understanding of how many of the participants achieved the learning outcomes. You will probably only have a few minutes for this. For example, you could assess learning by asking questions, setting a short quiz or asking the learners to write, create or draw something to summarise their learning. If you feel confident and brave, you could ask them to assess their own understanding of what was covered in the microteaching session. Be prepared for honest answers! You might want to leave the room immediately after your microteaching session but ensure you have brought the session to an official close and cleared away any equipment or resources you have used in the session.

Evaluating microteaching

As was mentioned at the beginning of this chapter, after microteaching has taken place, your peers and observer will comment on your lesson, outlining what went well and some points for development. Feedback should be timely so that the experience is fresh in everyone's mind.

It is useful to recognise the different criteria against which you will be assessed. These include:

- the lesson plan (its structure and clear aims and objectives);
- the teacher's delivery (clarity and voice pitch, eye contact, body language, and variations in tone to signal a change in activity. More information is provided in Chapter 2);

❭ use of resources (relevance, variety and accessibility);
❭ materials and activities (level of student involvement, variety);
❭ assessments (inclusiveness, variety, validity and fairness); and
❭ feedback to learners (variety, inclusivity).

You will also need to look back on your lesson and describe its strengths and weaknesses; this is reflection-on-action (Schön, 1983). As we noted earlier, it is easy to obsess about your own performance rather than comment on the effectiveness of learning. Although your peers and tutor may mention some aspects of your delivery, such as your ability to give clear instructions or the clarity and pitch of your voice, it is a good idea to look at the lesson from a more holistic point of view and form a reasoned judgement about whether there was evidence of learner achievement. Comment on your strengths as well as what didn't go so well. You need to be able to capitalise on your strengths in future sessions as well as identify areas for further development.

✓ TASK 8.6

It is useful to ask yourself questions to reflect on your microteaching session. What kinds of questions can you think of?

Your list may look something like the following:

❭ Did everything go to plan?
❭ Did all the participants know what was expected of them?
❭ Was everyone involved?
❭ Did you cater to everyone's needs?
❭ How appropriate and effective were the learning methods and resources used?
❭ Was there sufficient variety of activity and resources?
❭ Were the learners engaged at each stage of the lesson?
❭ How effectively did you deal with difficulties? Could you have anticipated these in the planning process?
❭ Was the learning environment conducive to learning?
❭ Were the timings of each stage appropriate?
❭ Was there an appropriate learning pace?
❭ Were the lesson objectives achieved? How do you know?
❭ What would you do differently next time?

Videoing your lesson

You may find it useful to record your microteaching session via an audio or video recording device. There is a danger that this might only add to your nerves and make the participants feel more self-conscious, behaving in a different way than they usually would. However, generally, people forget they are being recorded once the lesson is in full flow. It is a non-threatening way of assessing different aspects of your teaching and, unless otherwise instructed, you can view it in private. You will probably find there are elements about your teaching which surprise you. For example, you might not be aware of how effective your classroom management strategies are or how you have a tendency to say 'yeah?' as a means of checking understanding.

Receiving feedback

Once you have received oral and written feedback from the observer, there should be an opportunity to negotiate your action plan, outlining points for development. It is important to take feedback in the spirit in which it is given; to provide constructive comments to help you progress rather than criticise. We all have different capacities for receiving feedback. Even if we think we are incredibly receptive to accepting advice, it can still be demoralising to receive 'negative' feedback after you have spent hours planning a session.

Can you recognise yourself from the list below?

> **Buckets**. They are predisposed to receiving feedback. They welcome comments and may ask for feedback on specific aspects of their teaching. However, there is a cautionary note here: beware of a bucket with a hole in it (Russell, 1994). This means that individuals can accept feedback but not act upon it.

> **Tumblers**. They are able to absorb a certain amount of information, perhaps three or four points in total, before they lose interest. In fact, most of us respond better when we have a balance of positive and negative comments (see Chapter 7).

> **Thimbles**. They are likely to be sensitive, and possibly prickly. This may be down to negative experiences of receiving feedback in the past and need a lot of encouragement to keep them motivated.

When delivering feedback to your peers after their microteaching sessions, it is important to value their different personalities. Note their body language and their general reaction to the comments made. If you feel they are wobbling a bit, be gentle and find something positive about the lesson. Always make your comments constructive rather than personal. Rather than 'You should have written more neatly', think of a more tactful way of saying it, commenting on the effect it had on the group; for example, 'It was difficult to read the writing on the board so we weren't sure what to do next. If you write more clearly, the learners will have a clearer idea of what is expected.' Nobody wants to hear a string of negative comments but, alternatively, developmental feedback is an essential part of the teaching process so everyone should expect to receive some points for consideration. The recipient of feedback may not always agree with everything that is said but it is important that all comments are at least considered.

TALKING POINT

Take a minute to reflect on what you have just read. How do you feel about receiving constructive feedback? Do you tend to get bogged down with your own performance and only focus on the negatives? We would both agree that we have been guilty of doing this in the past. Do you welcome comments to improve your teaching or have you been 'scarred' from previous attempts, where you felt the process was not constructive and did not move the learning forward?

TIPS FOR EFFECTIVE MICROTEACHING

We will end this chapter by providing some tips for effective microteaching. The advice comes from our own observations of microteaching and comments made by previous trainees.

- Stay calm and relaxed. Take a minute to compose yourself before you address the class. Bear in mind it really is not the end of the world if something goes awry. The important thing is not to become too flustered and to deal with any difficulties that arise.
- Be prepared. Set up the learning environment in the way you want it. You may need to move tables and chairs around, set up your PowerPoint and prepare resources.
- Think about the needs and interests of your audience and pitch the session accordingly.
- Don't pack too much in. This is very easy to do but it is not a race. If you need to miss something out, then so be it. Don't start something if there is not sufficient time for the participants to engage with the activity.
- Start on a lively note. Ensure there is a middle part of the lesson and an end where you summarise learning.
- Use a variety of activities and resources.
- Set tasks with an appropriate level of challenge.
- Have contingency plans; hardly any lesson will go 100% to plan.
- Stick to time limits where possible.
- Give positive feedback to your participants to show how they are progressing and to keep them motivated.
- Don't be afraid to stop an activity if you realise further clarification is needed.
- Relax and enjoy the experience!

SUMMARY

In this chapter, you have looked at what is meant by microteaching: how it presents a snapshot of your teaching and allows you to hone your skills and techniques. The importance of effective preparation: choosing a straightforward topic or skill, stating clear objectives and devising appropriate and inclusive methods of learning was highlighted. You also looked at how resources used in an appropriate way can enable learning, and how it is important to continually assess progress throughout the session. Finally, the importance of evaluation was outlined along with a willingness to accept constructive feedback to aid development.

REFERENCES AND FURTHER READING

Bee, R. and Bee, F. (1998) *Constructive Feedback*. Guernsey: Chartered Institute of Personnel and Development.

Brookfield, S. (2006) *The Skillful Teacher on Technique, Trust, and Responsiveness in the Classroom*. San Francisco: Jossey-Bass.

Corder, N. (2007) *Learning to Teach Adults: An Introduction*. London and New York: Routledge Farmer.

Francis, M. and Gould, J. (2012) *Achieving your PTLLS Award: A Practical Guide to Teaching in* the Lifelong Learning Sector. London: Sage.

Kidd. W. and Czerniawski. G. (2010) Successful Teaching 14–19: Theory, Practice and Reflection. London: Sage.

Minton, D. (1997) Teaching Skills in Further and Adult Education (2nd edn). London: City & Guilds.

Richards, J. C. and Farrell, S. C. (2011) Practice Teaching: A Reflective Approach. New York: Cambridge University Press.

Russell, T. (1994) Feedback Skills. London: Kogan Page.

Schön, D. (1983) The Reflective Practitioner. How Professionals Think in Action. London: Temple Smith.

Wallace, S. (2011) Teaching, Tutoring and Training in the Lifelong Learning Sector. Exeter: Learning Matters.

Websites

www.tes.co.uk (For a range of useful starter, activities and assessment for teaching and learning ideas)

Supporting learners

LEARNING AIMS

By the end of this chapter, the reader will have a better understanding of:

❭ the importance of supporting learners

❭ the value of tutorials

❭ how to support learners with additional learning needs

❭ working with learners on a one-to-one basis

THE VALUE OF SUPPORT SYSTEMS

Before we think about how to support our learners, let's remind ourselves about the context of the further education and skills sector. Who are the learners? At some point or other, we may find ourselves teaching groups of hard-to-reach individuals who are not in education, employment or training (NEETs). These individuals may be in a post-16 learning environment not because they want to be but because they have no other or limited options. We may have learners who speak two or three community languages fluently but have a limited command of English. Think how frustrating this must feel. We may have a learner who suffers from Attention Deficit Hyperactivity Disorder (ADHD) and has a limited concentration span. Sadly, it is too easy for a learner with this condition to be labelled as badly behaved. We may have a devout Muslim student who needs to pray five times a day but studies in a secular college and there is no dedicated prayer room. Consider the potential disruption to his studies. We may have a teenage mum who has childcare responsibilities and has to leave class early. Think about the learning materials she misses when she does.

What this snapshot of our learner demographic should tell us is that our students' individual backgrounds and personal circumstances vary enormously. As we saw in Chapter 3, in a truly inclusive learning environment, these differences need to be not only recognised but also celebrated. It also demonstrates that an individual's needs have to be supported in different ways and we have a part to play in this.

Support for learners in the further education and skills sector is crucial. We lose far too many learners through lack of diagnosis of additional needs, early intervention and targeted support. One of the reasons for this may be that we feel we lack the necessary specialist skills or that support is someone else's responsibility. We need to recognise that support for learners comes at all stages of a learning programme, whether this is before it begins (pre-entry), while students are engaged with learning (on-course) or after they finish (exit). In Chapter 1, we looked at points of referral. If you discover that one of your learners has a need for support over and above what you are able to do within your teaching role, then you will need to seek guidance from other professionals in your organisation who can advise. We will explore the concept of support in more detail in the following sections.

Pre-entry

Learners may be uncertain about which course of study they want to pursue and will need help in selecting the right programme. Information, advice and guidance measures should aim to establish their existing skill set, whether the course in question can develop them and to what extent it will help them achieve their ambitions. They may have questions about career progression routes and/or further education and training opportunities. They may also have queries about the logistics of the programme, including where it will take place, the costs and the timetable. This stage will involve an initial assessment of literacy and numeracy skills, which might indicate an additional learning need such as dyslexia. At this point, learners can be referred for specialist support. Although you may not be directly involved at the pre-entry stage, you will need to have access to the information in order to help you start to build a picture of the learners who are enrolled onto your course.

On-course

Support for learners once they are on the course is an ongoing feature of your teaching and should be demonstrated in your planning, delivery and assessment. Early signs that learners may be struggling with its demands could be non-submission of homework or other course work tasks, non-attendance or lateness. Learn to pick up on non-verbal signals in class: lack of concentration, fidgeting, persistent talking and generally being off-task can be a request for help disguised as bravado. Try to act quickly before problems are compounded. A one-to-one meeting with the learner is an ideal opportunity for you to raise concerns you have and implement a support plan. Make sure your discussion is recorded so that there is a clear record of your communication. Negotiate targets the learner can manage and set a date to review progress.

Post-course

Once the learner has completed the course, there may be a period of uncertainty about what the next steps are. They may have questions such as 'How do I progress from here?' or 'What can I do now?' We can support them by helping them to explore employment, further education or training options. If there is a need to retake the course, or aspects of it, they will need to understand the implications of this in terms of time and money. For many, transition to this stage is an important step in the direction of independence. It is our responsibility to help them achieve this by ensuring they get access to the best advice and guidance.

TUTORIALS

In educational contexts, a tutorial can refer to tutor-led teaching that happens with small groups of students; this is particularly true of university settings. Alternatively, it can mean a confidential meeting that takes place between a teacher and a learner. In this context, a tutorial is a really useful time for you to meet with your learner to discuss progress they are making with the course, in addition to any challenges they are facing. You may find that your learner is willing to discuss issues with you more openly than they would be in the classroom or workplace. You may also find that they have some pastoral (non-academic) issues that they want to bring your attention to. The time for the tutorial may be limited so try to make sure that there is some kind of 'agenda', which may be topics you want to discuss. It is important to record the conversation that you have with your learner so that it can be revisited the next time you meet. Teachers often use tutorial time to set learning targets using the student's Individual Learning Plan. As mentioned in Chapter 3, the most effective targets are often those which have been agreed with the learner rather than imposed by you. If time is short, then you can organise a group tutorial. Here is an example of a template that you could use to record your discussion.

Tutorial record form

Name:

Course:

Level:

Summary of progress made:

Work to be completed:

Obstacles to progress:

Action plan:

Date of meeting:

Date of next meeting:

Tutor's signature:

Learner's signature:

Unless your organisation has a standard template that you must use, you could produce your own. Remember to store the information securely so that confidentiality is maintained.

Many providers now have a designated tutor system so that every student is allocated a tutor from the start of their course who oversees their whole programme.

SPECIFIC LEARNING DISABILITIES

At some point, you may find that you have a learner with a specific learning disability. You will need to know how to manage this. Complete the quiz below to see how much you know about some common learning disabilities.

✔ TASK 9.1

Read the definitions of specific learning disabilities taken from the Oxford English Dictionary. Match the names of the conditions they describe from the list below.

1. .... is a general term for disorders that involve difficulties in learning to read or interpreting words, letters, and other symbols, but which do not affect intelligence.

2. .... is any of a range of behavioural disorders occurring primarily in children, including such symptoms as poor concentration, hyperactivity and learning difficulties.

3. .... is a mental condition, present from early childhood, characterised by great difficulty in communicating and forming relationships with other people and in using language and abstract concepts.

4. .... is a developmental disorder related to autism and characterised by awkwardness in social interaction, pedantry in speech, and preoccupation with very narrow interests.

Asperger's syndrome   Dyslexia   Autism   ADHD

How did you do? How much did you know? Number 1 refers to dyslexia, number 2 to ADHD, number 3 to autism and, finally, number 4 refers to Asperger's syndrome. We shall now look at these learning disabilities in turn and outline some useful strategies to help you plan and deliver your lessons and ways in which you can support yoiur learners. Bear in mind that your organisation should have structured support systems in place so you will not have to do this alone.

Supporting learners with dyslexia

Dyslexia is not only about literacy, although frequently weaknesses in literacy (reading and writing) are often the most visible sign. It also affects the way in which information is processed, stored and retrieved, with problems of memory, speed of processing, time perception, organisation and sequencing. Learners with dyslexia may feel self-conscious about their condition and may not want attention drawn to it. If you have a dyslexic learner, talk to them about the ways in which they can be supported so that your interventions are focused and specific.

In-class support can include using a multi-sensory approach to presenting materials, which can help learners to absorb information. This is good for learners whether they have dyslexia or not. For example the use of quizzes, puzzles, visuals and audio input work well. Repeated practice and learning rules from lots of examples are also effective strategies. Dyslexic learners tend to not be sensitive to everyday conventions of written English so make these explicit. When engaging in group work tasks, it may be sensible for you to select who does the writing and feeding back so as not to 'put them on the spot'. Above all, remember that dyslexic learners need more time to complete coursework-related tasks. In order to support them with reading and writing, you may find the following support strategies useful. Note that they are good practice for all learners.

Writing	Reading
Provide handouts using 12 point Comic Sans or Arial typeface, or larger	Allow extra time for reading
	Avoid asking learners to read out aloud in class
Allow time for copying from the board	Break text down into manageable chunks using bullet points and/or sub-headings
Avoid having large amounts of text on the board to copy	Encourage the use of coloured highlighters to identify key points
Read words that are written on the board or on handouts	Highlight and explain specialist jargon
Allow the use of equipment such as Dictaphones, laptops or specialist reading pens	Present information in different ways such as diagrams, mind maps and graphs
Use different coloured paper to present information	Use visuals and other non-text-based clues to establish context
Give clear guidance about what is expected in terms of written work; provide exemplars	Provide texts to be used in class in advance
Don't correct every spelling and grammar error	

If you find that your dyslexic learner has problems with memory or organisation, it may be helpful to:

❱ teach them useful study skills such as note-taking and maintaining a course work folder;
❱ give regular reminders about course work deadlines;
❱ use memory techniques such as mnemonics or word association; and
❱ provide a timetable including information about course work submission.

For more information visit The British Dyslexia Association website: www.bda.org

Supporting learners with ADHD

ADHD is a brain disorder, the exact cause of which is not known. It is believed to be a mix of genetic and environmental factors. ADHD tends to run in families so an individual can inherit it from a parent. Boys are more commonly diagnosed with the condition than girls. Symptoms of the condition include hyperactivity, inability to focus, lack of concentration, demands for attention, inability to control behaviours and inattentiveness. Learners with these behaviours can be easily labelled as 'naughty', a term which, if repeated often enough, can damage confidence and self-esteem. What skills do teachers need? Mainly, a good deal of patience, creativity and consistency. The most important thing is to develop strategies to prevent the learner's behaviour from disrupting others and to find strategies to maximise the potential for learning. You may find the following ideas helpful.

Seating

Having the learner seated in a group around a table presents multiple distractions so try to ensure they are sitting at a desk straight in front of you to encourage maximum focus. Try to make sure they are not near a door or window as these are also sources of distraction. Don't remove them from the group – just make sure they are seated in the group in a position where you and they can see each other.

Delivery

Deliver information in short, sharp bursts and avoid lengthy explanations. Keep instructions short and repeat them if necessary. Always make eye contact with the learner. Support verbal instructions with a written handout. Use visual charts, graphs and diagrams where possible. Try to deal with difficult material early on as concentration spans will wane as the lesson progresses.

Work

Make sure there is a quiet area in your classroom, which can be used for study purposes or a 'time-out' area. Long-term project work could be broken up into manageable chunks with different submission dates for segments of completed work. When assessing, create worksheets with reduced items and test areas in small chunks. Give the learner the opportunity to say which assessment method will best suit their learning style.

Study skills

Developing a good set of study skills with an awareness of the importance of time management will set the learner with ADHD in good stead. To that end, encourage the use of files to organise work with different modules being colour coded for ease of access. Make sure the learner knows assessment and course work submission dates; tell them to make a note of them in their files.

Teaching

Use cues the learner recognises (such as a clock to time activities, a bell to start the lesson, a clap to signal transitions). Write out which activities will be covered in the lesson and approximate timings for each. Avoid letting activities go on for too long; change them frequently and vary the pace by using games and competitions. Allow the learner to channel their physical behaviours with a Koosh ball (a soft squeezy ball) or similar object. Develop an unobtrusive sign with the learner that you both recognise, such as a tap on the shoulder as a signal to remain focused and on task. Pick your battles – let small things go if they are not disrupting others. Allow the learner breaks. At the end of the lesson, summarise the learning.

For more information visit the ADHD Foundation website: www.adhdfoundation.org.uk

Supporting learners with autism

Autism is a lifelong developmental disability for which there is no cure. It is sometimes referred to as a 'hidden' disability as it is not immediately obvious if someone has it. Autism affects individuals in different ways but common indicators of the condition include difficulties with processing language, communicating and interacting with others, and developing social relationships. Broadly speaking, those with autism find understanding the world around them difficult. Autism is called a spectrum condition because although people share some common difficulties, the condition affects them in different ways. A person can be mildly or severely autistic. If you have a learner with autism, you will need to know exactly how their condition affects them so that you can adapt your teaching to accommodate this. You may find the following support strategies useful.

Structure

Autistic learners learn most effectively in an environment which is structured. In order to achieve this, establish and define routines clearly. Always greet your learner in the same way using the same language; explain the order of the lesson in steps ('First we'll … then we'll … and finally, we'll…..'). Stick to the routine so that it becomes habitualised and the learner knows what to expect.

Material

Use visuals to teach as these help to maintain focus and interest and help learners make sense of the material to be learned. Long verbal explanations can cause the learner to lose concentration, so keep these short and concise. With printed material, highlight text for emphasis.

Distractions

Background noise can cause an autistic learner to become upset and anxious so try to ensure your classroom is calm. Try to avoid having too many visual stimuli as some learners can have a tendency to over-focus on detail; for example, too many wall charts and posters may be distracting. Tidy the room at the end of the lesson and put things away in boxes and cupboards.

Language

Always use concrete language and keep it simple. Avoid the use of metaphor ('I had a broken heart.') because an autistic learner will translate it literally. Communicate your instructions concisely ('Close your books, put your pens down, look at me.'). If your words are met with blank stares or confusion, find a different way to say the same thing. Don't use sarcasm. If your learner drops their books on the floor, don't say 'Well done' as this may to lead to repeated behaviour. Allow more time for the learners to process what you say to them. It can take an autistic learner longer to understand what you mean when you speak. The use of closed questions ('Do you want to do some reading?') is more effective than open-ended ones ('What do you want to do now?').

Transition

Learners with autism feel secure when things are constant and changing an activity can lead to anxiety because of fear of the unknown. Try to give a warning that you are going to move on to something different in advance. For example, you can say 'In five minutes' time, you'll be working with your partner'. It is also helpful to repeat this ('In three minutes' time….').

Interests

Learners with autism often have specific interests so use these in your teaching. Whether it's football or knitting, personalise the lesson themes. Be creative in your teaching. Think outside the box!

Supporting learners with Asperger's syndrome

People with Asperger's syndrome share similar difficulties as those on the autistic spectrum but tend not to experience speech difficulties and are often of average or above average intelligence. As with autistic learners, those with Asperger's interpret the world differently and have a perspective on life which may be contrary to what would normally be expected. Learners with Asperger's syndrome may have related conditions such as dyspraxia, dyscalculia or ADHD. Problems can include difficulties with:

❯ social communication: interpreting body language or facial expressions; understanding jokes or sarcasm; not fully understanding complex language; not knowing when to start or end conversations or selecting topics to talk about;
❯ social interaction: struggling to make friends; behaving in what can be interpreted as an inappropriate manner; seeming withdrawn or uninterested in other people; not being able to read social rules; finding other people unpredictable or confusing; and
❯ social imagination: understanding or interpreting other people's thoughts or words; being unable to predict alternative outcomes to situations; preferring concrete/logical activities to imaginary ones; fixating on particular areas of interest and pursing them repetitively.

You may find the following support strategies helpful.

Language

Use very specific language, which is free from metaphor and other non-literal nuances. When teaching, provide alternative means of conveying the information, for example the use of visual, kinaesthetic and auditory stimuli. Learners with Asperger's feel reassured by detailed information as they know what to expect so ensure information is set out really clearly. Some learners prefer to have information given to them from one source rather than multiple sources so that clarity and direction is enhanced.

Assessment

Taking an assessment can be stressful as it indicates a change in routine. Provide plenty of warning about the test date and arrange a separate room if necessary. Ensure the language in the assessment task is clear and any unknown language is clarified before the assessment starts. Bear in mind that extra time may be needed, so ensure that the awarding body for your course is notified in advance. Tell the learner which teacher will be invigilating and provide a seating plan in advance if you can.

Environment

Learners with Asperger's syndrome need to have as stable an environment as possible which is ideally free from variation. In practice, this means giving ample warning if the normal classroom routine is to be disrupted. If your lesson is to be covered by a colleague for example, tell the class in advance and the reason why. Try to ensure that timetables do not change and that learners always know which room they should go to for lessons. The almost obsessional compulsion for sameness and routine can indicate inflexibility but when things are mapped out clearly, learners function very well.

Group work

Learners may find working in a group difficult because of problems relating to social interaction. Be flexible in your approach and allow the learner to work alone if that's preferable.

For more information on autism and Asperger's syndrome visit The National Autistic Society website: www.autism.org.uk

As mentioned earlier, you will hopefully be able to work with other professionals in your organisation who have specialist knowledge in supporting learners with the range of conditions above. Talk to your colleagues to see what you can do to ensure that your learners experience high quality learning opportunities in an inclusive environment.

TALKING POINT

Given what you know about dyslexia, autism, Asperger's syndrome and ADHD, think about how you can support learners with these conditions. What adaptions could you make to your teaching and resources?

FURTHER SUPPORT NEEDS

As well as the specific learning disabilities outlined above, there are many others. Familiarising yourself with more and finding out what support is available in addition to what you can do yourself, will put you in a better position to manage your classes and create equal access to learning opportunities for all.

☑ TASK 9.2

What adjustments do you need to make for learners who:

❭ use a wheelchair?
❭ suffer from depression?
❭ wear a hearing aid?
❭ have a sight impairment?

Do you have a mobility issue yourself or know of someone who does? How might you accommodate this most effectively?

Mobility issues

An individual can have a mild, moderate or severe mobility issue. Whatever the extent of the disability, they will have to negotiate physical space to move around. Sometimes, individuals with mobility issues have other physical disabilities as well. In terms of the adjustments we can make to our teaching and learning environments, there are a variety of issues that should be considered. We saw this in Chapter 1. Firstly, classrooms need to be wheelchair accessible and a ramp and/or stair lift may be needed to get to them. Learners may need a height-adjusted table, so check this in advance. Secondly, learners may need access to assistive technology such as a dictaphone, laptop, communication board or speech-to-text software to facilitate the learning process. If there is an exam to take, notify the awarding body of arrangements well in advance of the exam date. Extra time may be needed, so this is another consideration. If the room has to be arranged to accommodate a wheelchair, this will need to be done in advance so as not to waste time. It is advisable to check whether the learner requires a support worker to assist them.

Mental health conditions

Mental health problems affect the ways in which people behave, think and feel, and can affect an individual irrespective of gender, social class or ethnic background. Those who experience issues of this nature can experience stigmatisation (being negatively labelled by others), which in turn can lead to a lack of self-confidence and esteem. There may be potential barriers to learning which the individual needs support for. The following may be helpful.

Emotional support	Practical support
Encouraging the learner to focus on the positive and rewarding them for successes immediately	Negotiating programmes of work and setting learning targets in manageable chunks
Encouraging fair self-reflection	Having regular meetings to review progress and set targets
Helping the learner to recognise achievement	Providing an alternative to group assessments
Finding out what worries, anxieties and stresses the learner feels	Arranging note-takers or recording equipment in exam situations
Being approachable, friendly and non-judgemental	Maintaining regular contact with the learner
Being easily contactable and knowing how to refer on for further support if necessary	Being in regular communication with other agencies with whom the learner may be involved

Try to make sure you know how you can refer the learner for further specialist support from other provisions such as counselling or community-based organisations. You will find regular one-to-one pastoral tutorials helpful as a way of maintaining contact with the learner. You may find it useful to organise a peer support system in your class. Make sure the learner knows who they can contact for external specialist support if they need to.

For more information visit The Mental Health Foundation's website: www.mentalhealth.org.uk

Hearing loss

There are different ways of communicating with learners who have hearing loss, which means that there are different ways of supporting them. Learners may have been born deaf or lost their hearing at a later stage in their lives. It is important to familiarise yourself with the individual's circumstances. Those who suffer from hearing impairments communicate in a variety of ways, either by lip reading or using a signing language such as British Sign Language. You may find the following strategies helpful if you have learner with hearing loss.

- Reduce background noise.
- Emphasise your message using gesture and body language.
- If your learner communicates through a signer, make sure you address the learner rather than the signer so that the learner feels included.
- Make sure the room is well lit so that the learner can see the signing and facial expressions.
- Avoid wandering around between the signer and the learner.
- Make use of assistive technologies where necessary and available.
- When directly communicating with the learner, keep sentences short and reword if necessary.

❱ Provide handouts and a lesson summary before the lesson starts.

For more information, visit www.bbc.co.uk/skillswise/tutors/inclusive-learning/tutors-article-hearing-impairments

Sight impairment

A person can be born blind or experience sight loss later on in life. There are different reasons for this. As with individuals who are hearing impaired, those with sight problems rely on other senses to help them. You may find the following strategies helpful if you have a learner with sight loss.

❱ Use assistive technologies such as screen reading software or a familiar laptop where available and if necessary.
❱ Speak clearly and directly to the learner.
❱ Ensure the learning environment is safe and easy to walk around.
❱ Use the learner's name before asking a question so that they are alert to what is coming.

For more information, visit www.soas.ac.uk/studentadviceandwellbeing/information-for-staff/disabledstudents/visual

Whether your learner has a specific learning difficulty or disability or not, it is very important for you to know about their individual circumstances so that you are able to support them in their learning. Be mindful of and alert to unexplained changes in behaviour. The learner may be experiencing difficulties at home or in other areas of their lives which may begin to affect their studies. Trust your instincts if you feel that something is not right and try to tackle it. Seek support from others as necessary. Individuals tend to know if they want support so try not to assume that they do. If you are in any doubt, ask them.

TALKING POINT

Who is responsible for providing specialist support in your organisation? Have you ever used these systems? How effective are they?

WORKING ONE TO ONE

For various reasons you may, at some point, find yourself working with a learner on a one-to-one basis. This is different to the tutorial scenario outlined earlier on. Working one to one refers to planning for, teaching and assessing an individual learner which may be for the whole course. One-to-one teaching is different to whole-group teaching so you will need to adapt your approaches to reflect this.

☑ TASK 9.3

What are the advantages of working with a learner on a one-to-one basis? Are there any disadvantages?

Working on an individual basis with a learner is an excellent opportunity to give them your undivided attention. It provides an appropriate forum for you to focus on areas of their course work that they are finding difficult and to provide support on a highly personalised level. This type of support may be referred to as a 'professional discussion' (see Chapter 6) if the main focus is on the learner's progress with course work. The discussion should be recorded on an appropriate template such as an Individual or Personal Learning Plan or Action Plan so that there is an audit trail of your discussions which can be revisited at a later date. Individual targets can be set at this meeting with time to agree on a review date meeting to check progress. One-to-one tutorials benefit the learner because they can be geared toward them and you don't need to adapt your teaching to cater for many different ways of learning.

We need to be careful that the boundaries of the meeting are clear and agreed in advance. You will need to remain professional at all times and avoid getting too close to the learner. The purpose of the meeting needs to be clear and the agenda agreed at the outset. If the learner has a pastoral issue which you cannot help with, you will need to refer them on to someone who can assist. This might be a counselling team or an adviser who works with financial or housing issues. Working individually with a learner can be intensive and, therefore, tiring for you and the student. Try to take regular breaks.

💬 TALKING POINT

Think about your teaching specialism. Are there any areas from which a learner would benefit from being taught individually?

SUMMARY

In this chapter, you explored the value of support systems and why they are essential in the further education and skills sector. You learned about a range of specific learning disabilities including autism, Asperger's syndrome, dyslexia and ADHD. You then explored how to support learners with those conditions in a classroom or workplace environment; this included how to arrange the learning space and how to adapt resources and approaches. You also examined how to support those with mental health conditions, those who are visually or hearing impaired, and those who have mobility issues. Finally, you looked at the benefits of working with learners on an individual basis.

REFERENCES AND FURTHER READING

Petty, G. (2009) *Teaching Today: A practical guide* (4th edn). Cheltenham: Nelson Thornes.

Websites

http://kendrik2.wordpress.com/2007/10/10/12-tips-to-setting-up-an-autism-classroom/ (further information about organising a classroom for learners with autism)

www.nhs.uk/Conditions/Attention-deficit-hyperactivity-disorder/Pages/Causes.aspx (information about the possible causes of ADHD)

www.helpguide.org/mental/teaching_tips_add_adhd.htm (further information about teaching learners with ADHD)

www.autism.org.uk/about-autism/autism-and-asperger-syndrome-an-introduction/what-is-asperger-syndrome.aspx (further information about Asperger's syndrome)

Functional skills

⊙ **LEARNING AIMS**

By the end of this chapter, the reader will have a better understanding of:

❯ the importance of providing opportunities for learners to develop their English, mathematics and ICT skills and wider skills

❯ different approaches to delivering functional skills

❯ strategies to help embed English, mathematics and ICT and wider skills within their subject and/or vocational area

THE BACKGROUND TO FUNCTIONAL SKILLS

Learners on vocational and academic learning programmes will use a variety of skills as they process and relay information, and develop their knowledge of the subject. For example, they might have to search for key information on the internet, interpret data from a graph, discuss their findings with somebody else, and then produce a report. These skills in English, maths and ICT (information and communications technology) are also known as functional skills. According to a Department for Education and Skills report in 2006, these skills 'allow individuals to operate confidently, effectively and independently in life and work'. It is not enough to be able to solve a mathematical equation. Individuals need to be able to apply this knowledge to practical contexts in their work and everyday lives.

Functional skills were originally identified in the 2004 Tomlinson Report, *The Final Report of the Working Group on 14-19 reform*, which stated that there needed to be a return to basics. English, maths and ICT were considered to be the foundation of young people's education. The Leitch Review, published in 2006, developed this idea. It revealed that radical reforms were needed to improve the low levels of literacy and numeracy among adults in the UK in order to boost employment and enable the UK to be a key competitor in the global economy.

☑ **TASK 10.1**

A study carried out by the Organisation for Economic Cooperation and Development (OECD) in 2013 revealed that out of 24 countries, England was placed 22nd for literacy and 23rd for numeracy. What might be some of the reasons for poor attainment in these skills?

Socio-economic factors are key to explaining why some individuals have difficulties with literacy and numeracy. They may have struggled at school and now feel disaffected with learning. Educational needs may not have been diagnosed and programmes designed to support them with literacy and numeracy can seem uninviting and forbidding. Some people may feel ashamed that they have difficulties with reading and working out simple calculations and have a real fear of returning to education. However, good literacy and numeracy skills will not only increase employability opportunities but are also likely to boost an individual's self-esteem and personal happiness.

The Leitch Review led to a real drive to develop learners' functional skills in the further education and skills sector. Alison Wolf's report (Wolf, 2011) of pre-19 vocational education highlighted the fact that many young people were enrolled on programmes which did not help them to find work or gain access to higher education. One reason for this was poor performance in English and maths GCSEs (at grades A*–C). One of the report's recommendations was to improve the language and mathematics skills of vocational learners studying in post-16 education.

New standalone qualifications in English, maths and ICT were launched in 2010 as well as being embedded into existing qualifications such as GCSEs, Foundation Learning and Apprenticeships. In order for learners to progress to other courses, they may need to have achieved qualifications in functional skills first. For example, to gain access on to a Level 2 Apprenticeship programme in painting and decorating, a common requirement is to have a Level 1 Functional Skills qualification in English or maths or a GSCE equivalent (see below).

Below is an overview of some of the different standalone qualifications available in English, maths and ICT from Entry Level up to Level 3.

Level	Type of qualification
Entry	Entry Level *Skills for Life* qualifications in ESOL, Numeracy and ICT
1	GCSEs graded D–G Functional Skills in English, maths and ICT *Skills for Life* qualifications in Adult Literacy, Numeracy, ICT and ESOL
2	GCSEs graded A*–C *Skills for Life* qualifications in Adult Literacy, Numeracy, ICT and ESOL Functional Skills in English, maths and ICT at Level 2
3	AS/A Levels in English, maths and ICT.

(Source: www.ofqual.gov.uk)

PLANNING THE DELIVERY OF FUNCTIONAL SKILLS

Educational providers have different approaches towards teaching functional skills. In the planning process, it is important to consider the following questions.

1. What approach towards functional skills should be taken?

There are two main approaches to the delivery of functional skills.

❯ A *discrete* model, whereby functional skills are the responsibility of functional skills or core subject teachers (teachers of English, maths and ICT) and are taught separately from the main curriculum and/or subject area. The advantage of this approach is that learners receive specialist support in these areas. However, if this model is adopted, it is important that teachers delivering vocational learning consider how to support learners in the development of these core skills.

❯ An *embedded* model. Learners develop their English, maths and ICT skills alongside their vocational programme. One of the difficulties with adopting this approach is that learners may not have as many opportunities to develop their functional skills as they should because of the teacher's lack of expertise and/or confidence. Teachers are likely to feel more confident embedding functional skills in their curriculum or vocational area if they know they can consult or liaise with a specialist in English, maths or ICT for support and guidance. The advantage of this approach is that functional skills are not seen as separate skills to acquire which have no relationship with practical contexts:

"Encouraging the learners to recognise their skill development in the context of their specialism can also be an empowering process whereby they learn to value the literacies they bring to the classroom and use in many aspects of their life." (Duckworth and Tummons, 2010, p. 54)

2. Who will deliver functional skills? Will specialist tutors in maths, English and ICT be brought in to support vocational tutors, or will teachers be expected to embed them within their subject area?

The Wolf Report (2011) raised concerns about the ability of vocational teachers to teach functional skills.

"Vocational teachers know about vocational subjects. They are not maths or English teachers."

It is true that unless you are teaching English, maths or ICT, you are not expected to be an expert in these areas. However, whatever the curriculum or vocational area, you will need to be confident that you can, for example, spot errors in learners' writing and speech, help learners interpret basic information from charts and graphs and support learners in ICT. All teachers have to have competent language and literacy, numeracy and ICT skills as part of their job role. This is called the minimum core (see the website referenced at the end of the chapter for more information). If you are not confident in any of these areas, it is important that you recognise this and find out if any training is available to you.

3. How will functional skills be assessed?

In order for functional skills to be delivered effectively, it is necessary to assess the learners' skills in English, maths and ICT throughout the programme, starting at the point of entry. Providers may devise their own initial assessments to determine learners' knowledge of English, maths and ICT or use a paper-based or online assessment tool. However, it is important to recognise that some learners may be reluctant to study maths, English or ICT because they associate them with school. They may have negative experiences of studying one or all of these subjects and are likely to have very different needs.

From the outset, it is essential that functional skills are promoted in a positive light: they should not be seen as an optional component of the learning programme. Individuals on day release from work, for example, may find it difficult to develop their skills in English, maths and ICT as well as learning about their vocational area. However, if they can see how the assessment of functional skills relates to their vocational area, they should be more motivated to study. For instance, learners on a hospitality course should be made aware of how excellent communication and literacy skills will better equip them for work. Below is an example of how one teacher in a further education college assesses English, maths and ICT in her hospitality lessons. The importance of developing wider skills such as being professional and dealing with problems at work is also highlighted.

> "I teach a Level 1 Hospitality group. As part of the course programme, they work as a Counter Service in the college restaurant. They have to dress appropriately, speak to customers and know the prices of the food they are selling. They are assessed on their overall professionalism via an observation: they need to ensure they are welcoming and friendly and use appropriate language. They have to deal with large amounts of people at one time and need to be able to remain calm and unflustered. The learners also operate a trolley service. They go around the college and sell tea, coffee and food they have prepared themselves. They need to be able to promote the service, communicate effectively and handle money transactions. They are responsible for managing a cash float and are assessed on their ability to deal with any problems that might occur. They also assess their own performance, commenting on their strengths and any areas for improvement. Finally, using ICT, they also write a menu including prices. Here, I encourage peers to assess how realistic the prices are and the variety of food on offer."

Functional skills qualifications are available at all levels, from Entry Levels up to Level 2. Entry Level qualifications are concerned with acquiring basic knowledge and skills while a Level 2 qualification requires learners to demonstrate a deeper knowledge of their subject area and be able to apply this to practical contexts.

4. What materials and resources will be used in the delivery of functional skills? What are the implications for teaching and learning?

The purpose of teaching functional skills is to equip individuals with the necessary tools to function in society. In practical terms, this means the integration of problem-solving tasks in lessons to encourage learners to work things out for themselves, analyse information and to work collaboratively. Duckworth and Tummons (2010) highlight the importance of encouraging learners to develop and share their own resources such as producing a recipe book or sharing tips on how to improve their presentation skills (see below) using an online collaborative tool such as Padlet (www.padlet.com):

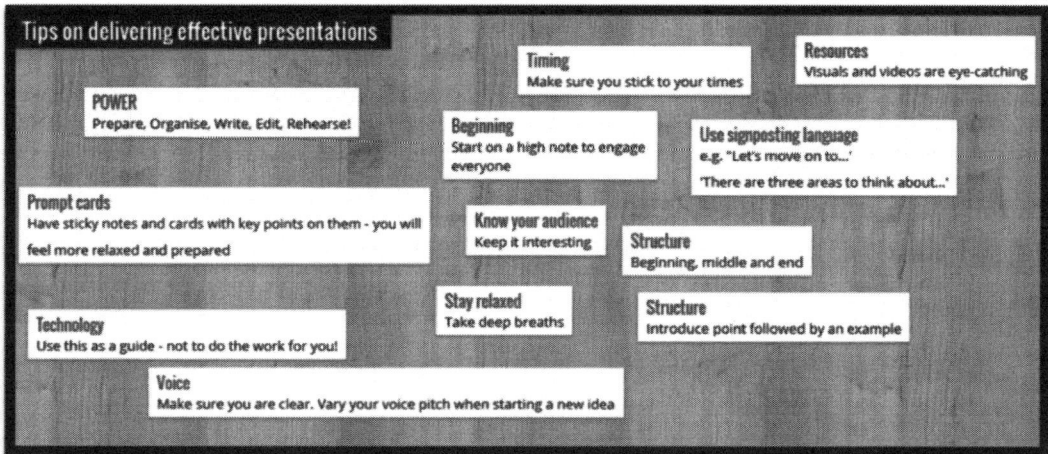

Tips on delivering effective presentations

POWER
Prepare, Organise, Write, Edit, Rehearse!

Timing
Make sure you stick to your times

Resources
Visuals and videos are eye-catching

Beginning
Start on a high note to engage everyone

Use signposting language
e.g. "Let's move on to..."
'There are three areas to think about...'

Prompt cards
Have sticky notes and cards with key points on them - you will feel more relaxed and prepared

Know your audience
Keep it interesting

Structure
Beginning, middle and end

Stay relaxed
Take deep breaths

Structure
Introduce point followed by an example

Technology
Use this as a guide - not to do the work for you!

Voice
Make sure you are clear. Vary your voice pitch when starting a new idea

✔ TASK 10.2

An example is provided below of how one further education college has decided to manage its functional skills provision for the new academic year. How would you describe the model?

CASE STUDY

The college has a wide range of vocational areas including Hair and Beauty, Construction and Engineering, Catering and Hospitality, and Business, among others. There is also an academic curriculum which currently offers GCSE and A Level provision including English and maths. The college's strategic plan for the delivery of English and maths is managed by individual curriculum areas.

In this model, the subject specialist teachers deliver the vocational curriculum, while the specialist English and maths tutors deliver functional skills lessons which are contextualised for the course the learner is studying on. For example, a learner on an NVQ Level 2 Hairdressing course may learn about ratios for mixing hair colouring solutions and costing up customers' bills in their maths lessons. Additionally, a learner on an NVQ Level 2 Motor Vehicle Maintenance course may develop their English skills through learning how to spell the technical jargon relating to the subject. The vocational tutors work alongside the English and maths tutors in planning the content to ensure there is a strong link between the development of the learner's subject specialist knowledge, and their English and maths skills.

Learners attend their functional skills lessons for 1.5 hours a week with additional supported independent study time factored into their timetables.

☑ TASK 10.3

Think of your curriculum and/or vocational area. What skills do you think your learners might need to develop? Consider the following:

❱ English (speaking, listening and communication, reading, writing)
❱ Maths (for example, working out basic calculations)
❱ ICT (for example, finding and sharing information via the web)

It is important to find out whether your learners are taking standalone qualifications in functional skills and then check the assessment criteria corresponding to the appropriate level. However, the range of skills that learners would be expected to develop is likely to be similar to the following.

You will probably have deduced that the model is a discrete one. However, although the learners are taught English, maths and ICT away from the vocational area, the skills and vocational specialists work closely together so that the content of the delivery is closely related to the vocational curriculum.

As we saw in Chapter 1, there are many different types of learners studying in the further education and skills sector and what works for one organisation will not necessarily be appropriate for another.

WHAT SKILLS DO LEARNERS NEED TO DEVELOP?

When delivering functional skills, it is essential that learners can demonstrate their language, maths and ICT skills in practical contexts. They need to recognise that they will need to apply these skills at work and in their everyday lives. Learners on an Electrical Installations course, for example, will need to develop their language and numeracy skills because, in a work context, they will be conversing with clients on a regular basis and designing, inspecting and testing electrical installations. Being able to do these things will increase their confidence and build their independence.

English		
Speaking, listening and communication	Reading	Writing
• Participate in discussions and recognise speakers' intentions • Express statements in a clear and coherent way • Present information clearly and persuasively	• Recognise the purpose of different text types • Relay key information • Summarise and compare texts • Recognise and sort data into alphabetical order • Summarise and compare texts • Read for inference	• Construct sentences using appropriate punctuation • Use correct spelling in written work • Plan, draft and organise writing • Use grammar dependent on the level appropriately • Monitor and proofread work

Mathematics
• Use addition, subtraction, multiplication and division in practical contexts
• Estimate and calculate length, capacity, temperature and weight
• Recognise and use fractions and decimals in practical contexts
• Complete calculations involving money and measures
• Calculate areas and perimeters in practical contexts
• Use metric units in practical contexts
• Understand and use simple formulae and equations
• Extract, use and compare statistical information from graphs, lists and charts
• Collate and record items of data

ICT
• Find and select information from the internet using search engines
• Insert graphics, images, tables, numbers and graphs into documents
• Edit and format documents
• Receive and send emails
• Recognise the need and adhere to e-safety procedures
• Use different software applications
• Store and label information
• Recognise the need for copyright when selecting and reproducing information
• Process, analyse and display numerical data

(Adapted from the Edexcel syllabus)

In practical terms, there should be opportunities to embed all functional skills within a lesson. Examples of how these different skills can be contextualised in vocational contexts can be found by visiting www.excellencegateway.org.uk/node/2745

☑ TASK 10.4

The future of functional skills is uncertain. The Lingfield Review (2012) did not mention functional skills explicitly but recommended there should be less provision for 'remedial literacy and numeracy' in the further education and skills sector. Although it was reported that learners would always probably need some support in these 'foundation skills', this should not be the sector's primary focus:

"It is timely for FE to re-affirm its primary mission to offer practical learning which leads to the availability of a technically-skilled workforce to power high economic performance." (Lingfield, 2012)

For many providers, it has proven difficult to deliver functional skills in the further education and skills sector. Why do you think this might be the case?

First of all, the delivery of functional skills places huge demands on institutions in terms of staffing, resources and costs. Institutions which need to deal with large numbers of learners on vocational courses and a shortage of funding of functional skills has meant that provision is not necessarily cost-effective. There is a concern over the qualifications of vocational trainers and teachers to deliver functional skills. Do they have the knowledge and experience to be able to deliver functional skills in English and maths at Level 2? Do teachers of these core skills also have appropriate qualifications (see Chapter 12)? The value of functional skills has also been questioned. In theory, a Level 2 functional skills qualification in English should be equivalent to an A–C grade GCSE but is that the case in reality? For example, individuals wishing to do new Level 3 Early Years Education (EYE) qualifications need to have an A–C grade in GCSE maths and English; a functional skills qualification is not accepted as an equivalent qualification.

Finally, the assessment of the functional skills qualification is more robust and complicated than its predecessor, key skills. The assessment is not in a multiple choice format or portfolio based, which makes it difficult to manage. This explains why some providers are looking for alternatives to delivering functional skills.

Nevertheless, whatever the future of functional skills holds, learners are likely to always need support with language and literacy, numeracy and ICT. In addition, bear in mind that there are also likely to be learners in your classes who do not have English as a first language. They may be doing additional ESOL classes to improve their language skills but you will still need to be mindful of your delivery, activities and resources to ensure that these learners are provided with equal opportunities to learn.

TIPS FOR SUPPORTING LEARNERS WITH LANGUAGE, LITERACY, NUMERACY AND ICT IN LESSONS

We shall end this chapter by highlighting a few strategies that you might want to use to support your learners with language and literacy (English), numeracy (maths) and ICT. If you are teaching on vocational courses, relate activities as much as possible to work-related contexts. It is useful to refer to the ESOL, literacy and numeracy core curricula (www.excellence gateway.org.uk/sflcurriculum). These outline the skills that adults are advised to have to function effectively in society and in the workplace. They were developed as part of the *Skills for Life* programme, designed to provide support for adults who have difficulty with literacy, numeracy and ESOL. There is no adult curriculum for ICT but individuals will still need support in this area. This should be linked to the course module or syllabus the learners are working from. You need to consider if and how technology can enhance learning (see Chapter 11).

Language and literacy (English)

> Ensure your own delivery is clear. ESOL learners may need help understanding idiomatic language (such as 'It's up to you') and phrasal verbs (*put up* and *get on with*, for example)
> Draw attention to key terminology by keeping a vocabulary or jargon box (see Chapter 13: teaching ideas) and providing learners with a glossary of terms. Providing visuals of difficult concepts is also advisable.
> Clarify strategies needed for skills development. Some examples are provided below.

Speaking

> In group discussions, encourage learners to recognise the importance of non-linguistic features (gestures and body language), taking turns and responding appropriately to other people's opinions.

Writing

> Encourage learners to make notes via flowcharts, mindmaps or any other useful method before writing.
> Provide learners with models to scaffold the writing process.
> Use a correction code (see below) to encourage learners to correct their work.

^	Missing word or letter
[ ]	Unnecessary word or letter
T	Tense
Gr	Grammar
P	Punctuation
WW	Wrong word
WO	Word order
Sp	Spelling
?	I don't understand this

Listening

> Encourage learners to take notes of key points. ESOL learners, in particular, should recognise that they do not need to understand every word to make sense of the message. Providing contextual clues and activating the learners' schemata (knowledge of the world) before they listen can help here.

> Make learners aware of the importance of intonation (the rise and fall of our voice) and pitch. Changes in pitch and intonation can affect meaning.

> Remind learners to ask for clarification if they are unsure of anything. Encourage them to use language such as, 'Could you repeat that, please?' and 'So, what you mean here is…?'

Reading

> Use a jigsaw activity to break down large texts (see Chapter 5). Learners read different sections and then explain what they have read to somebody else.

> Focus attention on different sub-skills used in the reading process such as *skimming* to gain an overall impression of what they have read and *scanning* to locate specific information.

> Encourage learners to deduce the meaning of unknown words from context by looking forwards and backwards in the text and looking at the part of speech (noun, verb and so on)

Numeracy (maths)

> Draw attention to the language of numeracy. ESOL learners, in particular, will need help with this. For example, they may need help with the pronunciation of large numbers.

> Encourage learners to make sense of information shown in graphs, table or charts. They may need support in understanding specific vocabulary (such as rows, columns, axis and sector) and how to access information.

> Integrate ordering activities such as 'Reorder the temperatures from lowest to highest'.

> Use investigational approaches to encourage learners to problem solve (a key aspect of functional skills). An example of this is for learners to carry out a survey and report on their findings: 'One in three learners…', '40% of us feels…'.

> Integrate numeracy games appropriate to the level. An example of a numeracy game is Countdown (see http://nrich.maths.org/6499 for details).

ICT

> Learners, particularly ESOL learners, will need to help with the language of ICT. Words and phrases such as browser, search engine, or navigate the web could all cause difficulties.

> Encourage learners to use ICT as part of a research project to give them pratice searching the web. Webquests (see Chapter 13: teaching ideas) can also be created for learners to complete.

> Learners can showcase their work using PowerPoint or by using camcorders to produce videos. For example, students on a catering course can be filmed carrying out different cooking techniques. However, if you are teaching young adults, make sure you are adhering to safeguarding legislation (see Chapter 1).

❭ Record roleplays and make podcasts (see Chapter 11). Again, be mindful of safeguarding legislation.

❭ Create online interactive wordsearches and crosswords to engage your learners as soon as they walk through the door.

❭ Use discussion forums via blogs and the VLE (see Chapter 11) to encourage learners to share ideas and respond to and post questions.

TALKING POINT

After reading this chapter, how confident do you feel about your own skills in literacy, language, numeracy and ICT? Do you feel you have the necessary skills to support learners' development of these skills? If you have identified any areas which you think you need to develop, record these in your action plan (see Appendix F).

SUMMARY

In this chapter, you have read about what is meant by functional skills and the importance of relating these skills to practical contexts. You looked at different models of functional skills and the importance of working alongside subject specialists. You also considered which skills in English, maths and ICT would be important for learners to develop in the subject or vocational area you are teaching or wish to teach. Finally, some strategies were provided to help you think about how to support learners with language, literacy, numeracy and ICT.

REFERENCES AND FURTHER READING

Duckworth, V. and Tummons, J. (2010) *Contemporary Issues in Lifelong Learning*. Maidenhead: Open University Press.

Francis, M. and Gould, J. (2012) *Achieving Your PTLLS Award: A Practical Guide to Teaching in the Lifelong Learning Sector*. London: Sage.

Huddleston, P. and Unwin, L. (2013) *Teaching and Learning in Further Education: Diversity and Change* (4th edn). Abingdon: Routledge.

Learning and Skills Network (2009) *Functional Skills for Adults: Preparing to Coordinate and Manage Functional Skills*. London: Learning and Skills Network.

Lingfield, R. (2012) *Professionalism in Further Education: Final Report of the Independent Review Panel. Established by the Minister of State for Further Education, Skills and Lifelong Learning*. October 2012, pp. 27–8.

OECD (2013) *OECD Skills Outlook 2013*. See http://skill.oecd.org/OECD_skills_outlook_2013.pdf

Wallace, S. (2013). *Understanding the Further Education Sector: A Critical Guide to Policies and Practices*. St Albans: Critical Publishing.

Wolf, A. (2011) *Review of Vocational Education – The Wolf Report*. London: Department for Education.

Websites

www.bbc.co.uk/skillswise (For materials on functional skills)

www.excellencegateway.co.uk/node/20280 (For guidance on functional skills)

www.excellencegateway.org.uk/sflcurriculum (Curricula in numeracy, literacy, ESOL)

www.excellencegateway.org.uk/node/12019 (More information on the minimum core: the minimum level of knowledge of language, literacy, numeracy and ICT required of all teachers)

www.feweek.co.uk (To keep up to date with current policy)

www.rwp.quia.oxi.net/embeddedlearning (For advice on how to embed English, maths and ICT in vocational areas)

Teaching with technology

LEARNING AIMS

By the end of this chapter, the reader will have a better understanding of:

> the advantages and limitations of e-learning

> common terminology used in e-learning

> the rationale for adopting a Bring Your Own Device policy

> the importance of accessibility in e-learning

> appropriate behaviour in the use of online resources and interacting with others

COMMON TERMINOLOGY USED IN E-LEARNING

When you see or hear the acronym ICT (Information and Communications Technology), how does it makes you feel? Do you embrace the idea of using ICT in the learning environment or are you afraid that you have been left behind and are not up to speed with current technological trends? Do you feel it can have a positive impact on learning or do you consider it an irritating 'extra'? ICT is being increasingly used in education as a medium of instruction, as a way of storing and retrieving information and as a means of collaboration. We are likely to be faced with learners who think nothing of sending text messages, surfing the internet for information and communicating via social media. However, even if you are not fully confident using digital technologies, it is never too late to learn. In this section, we shall consider how using only a few digital tools can provide a positive learning experience for your learners.

WHAT IS E-LEARNING?

In essence, e-learning means learning online. Courses can be fully online such as distance learning programmes, or a mixture of traditional face-to-face learning and using web-based resources to complement delivery. The latter is known as mixed, hybrid or, perhaps most commonly, blended learning (see figure on p. 176).

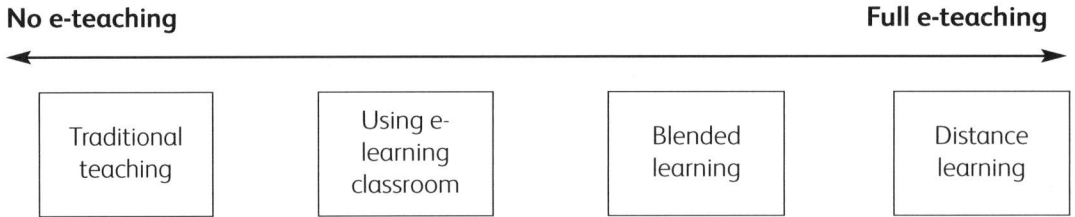

No e-teaching   **Full e-teaching**

| Traditional teaching | Using e-learning classroom | Blended learning | Distance learning |

Continuum of e-learning, based on a model by Bates and Poole (2003, p. 127).

E-learning can include:

❯ using computers, both desktops and laptops
❯ software (including assistive software)
❯ interactive whiteboards
❯ digital cameras
❯ mobile devices
❯ electronic communication tools such as email and discussion boards
❯ Virtual Learning Environments (VLEs)

(JISC, 2004)

 **TASK 11.1**

What do you consider to be the benefits of e-learning?

Some key benefits are highlighted below.

❯ There is greater flexibility for learners as they can access materials anywhere. Their work and family responsibilities are less affected and they also have more flexibility as to when they contribute to online discussion forums and chat to colleagues. Asynchronous delivery (the tutor(s) and learners do not have to be online at the same time) gives learners more opportunities to reflect rather than having to respond immediately to something they have read, calculated or written (Lynch, 2004).
❯ There is an argument that e-learning adds variety to a lesson owing to its multimodality. Learners can access images and sound files and watch videos, all as part of the learning process. Learning can also be delivered in a number of ways which, if done effectively, will be stimulating and motivating for the participants.
❯ If learners are doing a distance learning programme, they can study at their own pace, requesting support when needed. This may not, however, suit all learners, as some individuals need more of a push to keep them motivated and on task.
❯ E-learning resources can be highly interactive. As we saw in Chapter 3, collaboration is key to an inclusive learning environment and through study groups, contributions to discussion

boards, participation in quizzes and the dissemination of resources, there is a real sense of a community of practice.

❯ For some individuals, traditional classrooms bring back horrific memories of learning. E-learning can help break down barriers, increase participation and make all learners feel included.

❯ Finally, knowledge of web-based resources is useful for individuals in their social and professional lives. By being more exposed to a variety of online pedagogic tools, individuals will hopefully become more confident in using them.

Of course, there are some limitations to e-learning. Some learners may find it hard to adjust to a less traditional way of learning and prefer a more structured approach. They may feel out of their depth and worry about falling behind the other members of the group. Sometimes, however, it just takes a little time for learners to get used to a blended way of learning and, over time, to see how powerful and influential e-learning tools can be. It is worth bearing in mind that in the 2014 Professional Standards (see Chapter 1) it is stated that professional teachers or trainers should 'promote the benefits of technology and support learners in its use'. Nevertheless, we should not use technology for the sake of it. We need to consider how it can enhance learning.

WHAT DO WE NEED TO CONSIDER WHEN SELECTING E-LEARNING RESOURCES FOR OUR LEARNERS?

It is important to consider:

❯ the aim of the resource: how it links to curriculum and session objectives and which skills and knowledge are being acquired;
❯ how it encourages collaboration and interaction, and critical thinking skills;
❯ how the material will be assessed;
❯ any issues of accessibility and e-safety (we shall look at these points later on in this chapter);
❯ ease of use; and
❯ your role as a teacher. Is the resource being used as a means of instruction or are the learners going to be using it more independently?

We shall now look at some common terminology used in e-teaching and the pedagogical implications of a few tools.

☑ **TASK 11.2**

Quiz

How many of the questions can you answer below?

1. What is a VLE?
2. What is flipped learning?
3. What is the purpose of an interactive whiteboard?
4. What do we mean by cloud-based presentation tools?
5. What is the difference between a blog and a wiki?
6. What is meant by Web 2.0 technologies?

Hopefully, you were able to answer some of the questions.

1. VLE

VLE stands for Virtual Learning Environment. It is a way of supporting teaching and learning online. An example of an e-learning platform is Moodle (Modular Object-Oriented Dynamic Learning Environment). Tutors can create courses and upload assessments and learning materials to the platform for learners to view and access remotely. Teachers and learners can also communicate with each other using the VLE. One way of doing this is via an online forum.

2. Flipped learning

Flipped learning is a phrase you are likely to come across as it is becoming more widespread in education. It is not a new method of instruction but is now being used with a greater variety of subject and vocational areas. It is a blended learning model which reverses the concept of a traditional classroom. Course input no longer needs to be delivered in the learning environment. Instead, learners can watch lecturers at home via vodcasts (podcasts containing video content) and come to their sessions with any queries they might have. This allows there to be more opportunities for hands-on activities in the learning environment rather than learners having to be reliant on the teacher for key content. Homework can be done during the session to ensure that learners are engaging with the work and aspects with which individuals are struggling can be reviewed in more depth.

In theory, this is a very inclusive approach as the facilitator is able to devote more attention to each learner. The course content has still been determined by the teacher but has been presented in a way which is hopefully more meaningful for the learners. Some individuals, however, may find the transition from a traditional to a flipped classroom problematic.

3. Interactive whiteboards

Interaction is key to successful e-learning and there are many ways in which we can ensure our learners are actively participating using technology. One way is to use the interactive whiteboard (IWB). This is a large display panel which links to a computer and projector. The computer image can be controlled by using a special pen to write on the panel or by touching the screen. It is important not to use this tool as a glorified whiteboard: it is called interactive for a reason. Teachers can use it to integrate a variety of multimedia into their sessions such as visuals, graphs, videos and links to websites. They can annotate directly onto the board and encourage learners do the same. For example, in a science lesson, learners could label different parts of the body. They can also manipulate objects around the screen, participate in interactive activities such as quizzes, crosswords and wordsearches, and use voting devices as a means of assessment and feedback. IWBs work better with smaller groups as it can be difficult to include everyone if teaching a larger class. As with all tools, the IWB needs to be used in conjunction with effective classroom practice.

4. Cloud-based presentation tools

In Chapter 8 we looked at some of the pitfalls of using PowerPoint as a presentation tool. If you want to adopt a different, more visually-striking, less linear approach, it is worth finding out what other presentation tools are out there. So, what do we mean by the cloud? Put simply, cloud computing means displaying or sharing information over the internet instead of using your computer's hard drive.

There are a number of cloud presentation tools. You may have heard of Blendspace, Glogster, Prezi, SlideRocket or Powtoon. Below is an example of how Prezi can be used in the classroom. The learners are encouraged to be active participants throughout the presentation. Using a flipped learning approach, they could also view the material at home in advance of the session.

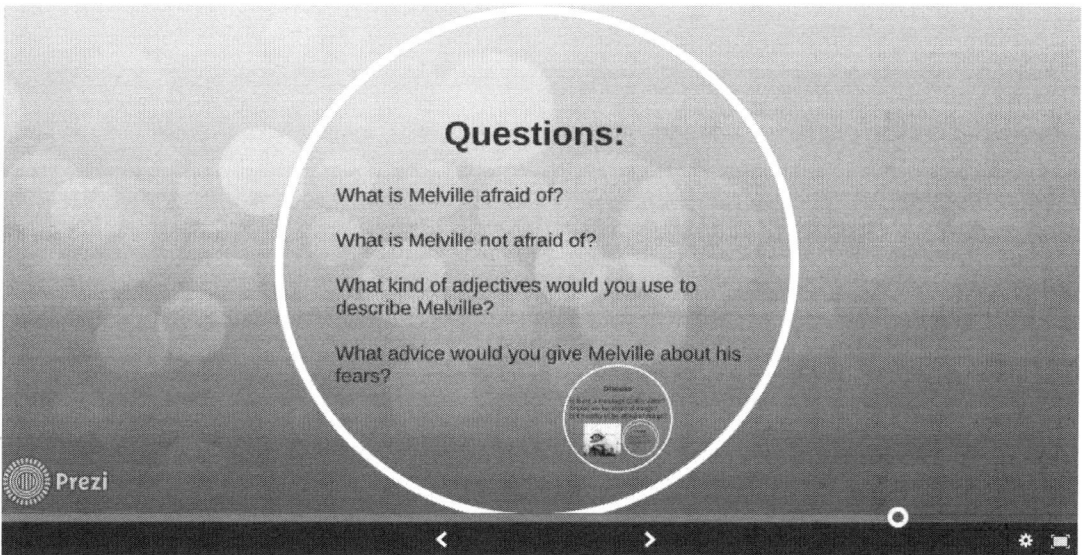

Questions:

What is Melville afraid of?

What is Melville not afraid of?

What kind of adjectives would you use to describe Melville?

What advice would you give Melville about his fears?

Prezi

(Used with permission from Prezi Inc. and Rebeka Rangelov.)

5. The difference between a blog and a wiki

A blog is a combination of the words web and log. It is a kind of online diary where you can record your comments, thoughts and opinions. Images, graphics, sound files, videos and interactive exercises can be integrated into blogs. Blogs can easily be shared with learners by providing them with the URL or website address. They can be used in a number of ways:

❭ As a reflective tool for learners to record their thoughts.
❭ Learners can be asked to work collaboratively on a project. Their work can then be displayed on the blog.
❭ Individuals can post comments on topics.

❭ Teachers can summarise sessions and provide learners with points for consideration. They can record the information in different ways (see below).

Monday, 17 February 2014

Tips on lesson planning

I hope that now you have had the session on lesson planning, you feel more confident preparing your first lessons for teaching practice. If you don't fancy reading all the information below, you can listen to my three-minute summary here:

Below are a few tips.

👍 Like   🐦 Tweet

▶ clareyt
Tips on lesson planning

0:00 ●━━━━━━━━━━━━━━━━━━━━━━━━━ 2:30   audioBoo

1. Think about the lesson objectives of your session, It is a good idea to make these **SMART** (Specific, Measurable, Achievable, Relevant and Time-led). Consider what you want the learners to be able to do by the end of the lesson and go from there. Avoid using words such as 'understand' and 'know' in your lesson objectives as it is difficult to assess whether the learners are actually learning something. Remember as well that you want the learners to put some cognitive effort into the lesson, i.e. there should be some evidence of deeper learning going on. All learners should be 'stretched' and 'challenged' to some degree. A useful resource is Bloom's taxonomy. This provides some useful language which you can use when writing your lesson objectives. The video clip focuses on the cognitive components of Bloom's taxonomy.

It is worth remembering that blogs can be viewed by anyone unless you create a private blog with your learners as multi-users.

Wikipedia is the most commonly known wiki. Wikis tend to be more informative, text-based and factual than blogs. Blogs are more personal accounts depicting the views of the user, while wikis are often used to provide information on a learning programme, for example.

Wikis are generally more collaborative as, provided users are given permission, they can amend content. Information via blogs is usually presented chronologically in reverse order; with wikis, it is easier to archive information. Both tools are useful ways of encouraging learners to interact with each other and course material.

6. Web 2.0 technologies

Web 2.0 technologies are applications and websites which enable users to create and share information. Wikis and blogs are both examples of Web 2.0 technology alongside Youtube, Pinterest and social networking sites such as Facebook and Twitter.

Can and should social networking sites be used in education? They allow learners to interact with each other and there can be a real sense of group learning albeit in a 'virtual' context. For example, learners can join a private group on Facebook to catch up on class notes, organise events, chat online and create study groups. Twitter encourages learners to view trends, developing their awareness of world events. They can also react to something they have read or heard by tweeting.

Not all learners feel comfortable with social networking sites: they suit some personalities more than others. There are also privacy and integrity issues to consider. It is natural to have some concerns over using social networking sites in the learning environment but there are ways of using them without invading individuals' privacy. It is worth considering their potential for facilitating collaboration and interaction and whether they are likely to contribute to a positive learning experience for your students.

TALKING POINT

In Chapter 10 we mentioned that all teachers were expected to have a minimum core in English, Maths and ICT. However, Giles and Yellend (2010, p. 11) maintain that 'the emphasis was more on the development of the personal skills of the 'apprentice' teachers in relation to their own abilities in English, maths and ICT rather than embedding these within their own teaching.' Bearing this in mind, comment on how confident you feel integrating the ICT skills below in your teaching. You may want to make a note of any area for development and link this to your action plan (see Appendix F).

Skill	✔
1. Create PowerPoint presentations for educational use	
2. Use search engines such as Google to find information on the internet	
3. Use the interactive whiteboard effectively	
4. Create online quizzes	
5. Use cloud-based presentation tools	
6. Set up a blog or wiki	
7. Create a mini podcast	
8. Contribute to online discussion forums	
9. Access a virtual learning environment	
10. Upload videos so they are available for a wider audience	

BRING YOUR OWN DEVICE

BYOD – does this acronym sound familiar? Despite some concerns about how the strategy can be used effectively, bring your own device is becoming more and more popular in the schools and the further education and skills sectors. It includes the terms: BYOT (bring your own technology) and BYOP (bring your own phone). The idea behind it is for learners to bring in their own devices such as laptops, notebooks, smartphones and tablets and use them to aid the learning process.

✔ TASK 11.3

What do you think might be the benefits of BYOD?

There are several advantages of adopting a BYOD strategy. First of all, it is more cost-effective. Educational providers need to find ways of saving money; it is expensive to keep and maintain computers, laptops and tablets for learners. Individuals are more likely to take care of their own devices, they are familiar with their in-built technology, which saves on training, and hopefully will be motivated and inspired to carry on learning outside the classroom environment.

Adopting a BYOD strategy

Planning is key to implementing an effective BYOD strategy. It is important to be aware of your educational provider's policy on BYOD and what safety and privacy rules and guidelines are in place to protect your learners. This is particularly important if you are teaching or supporting younger learners. Students need to know the purpose of using these devices, i.e. how they are contributing to their learning. We have to ensure that individuals under our supervision are using them appropriately, for educational reasons. Mobile phones, in particular, can be a source of distraction, used for texting or to access social networking sites. If you are going to get the best of BYOD, you need to consider how these devices can really develop learning.

A potential difficulty is ensuring that all learners have access to a mobile device. Some individuals will bring in the latest gadgets, others may be embarrassed by their old-fashioned, clunky phone and some learners will not have a phone or laptop at all. In Chapter 1, we looked at equality in the learning process. We have a duty to ensure that all learners have access to technology, perhaps by having a spare set of mobile devices available or encouraging learners to share one. It is also important to consider the learners' needs, interests and abilities: how they feel about using these devices and their competence in accessing relevant information.

We shall now look at how mobile phones or smartphones can be used in the classroom.

☑ TASK 11.4

Do you have a mobile phone? If you do, have a look at it now and its features. Can you think of how you could use the device in enabling learning in your subject area?

Mobile phones are now a way of life, almost like an extra limb for some people, something they would find difficult to live without. If you have a mobile phone, you are likely to be able to do some, and perhaps all, of the following.

❯ Send text messages
❯ Take photos and record videos
❯ Record audio
❯ Connect to the internet
❯ Use applications (apps)

With a little imagination, you can build tasks around these features to enable learners to use their phones in the learning environment. Handing over learning to students provides real possibilities for differentiation to occur (see Chapter 3) as individuals can work at their own pace and personalise their learning. Here are a few ideas to get you started.

Taking photos

This is one of the easiest and most satisfying ways of using mobile devices. Examples of good practice can be captured and posted to a blog or college website for everyone to see. Learners can take photos as a stimulus for discussion or language (the latter being particularly useful in ESOL and modern language classes). Learners can also take a series of photos, for example, to show events in a sequence. This works well in vocational areas, displaying processes, and showing science experiments.

Photos can also be made into comic strips (Chapter 13). For example, in a childcare lesson, different theorists' ideas about how children learn can be summarised through a dialogue and learners identify which theorist is being described. Encouraging learners to produce their own comic strips is a good way of assessing understanding and embedding literacy (Cowley, 2013).

Recording videos

Learners can record roleplays and interviews and feedback on each other's performance. This feature can also be used to record field trips; individuals comment on their observations to other learners (see www.pontydysgu.org/2009/11/25-practical-ideas-for-using-mobile-phones-in-the-classroom for more on this).

Audio

Learners can make mini podcasts, recording their thoughts and describing processes or key terminology in their subject area.

Text messaging

This is perhaps the most controversial area but if learners do it anyway, even if they think you cannot notice them texting under the table, then we should at least consider whether it can be applied to the learning process. Learners can send text messages to each other as a way of sharing information and collaborating on tasks. This will be of considerable benefit for learners who have limited access to face-to-face interaction, perhaps those who are working in vocational contexts and attend sessions one day a week. Teachers can text the group to remind everyone of assignment deadlines, homework and other updates; individuals may respond better to texts than emails because they always have their phone with them. It is possible to send messages via email so that your personal mobile number is not revealed or you may have access to a separate work device.

Learners need to be made aware of any additional costs involved so that there are no unpleasant surprises on their phone bills. It is also worth clarifying the language to be used in 'textspeak'. There is a concern that the language used when sending texts, such as 'gr8', may also be reflected in learners' academic written work and you might not want to be seen as enforcing bad habits.

Access to the internet and apps

Learners can carry out research quickly by searching on their phone. This saves time and avoids the teachers having to book a computer suite. Learners can bookmark sites which are important for their course, contribute to blogs and use simple apps such as a calculator or access online maps in a geography class.

Using QR codes

QR (Quick Response) codes are essentially barcodes which contain key information; when they are scanned by a smartphone via an application tool, they link to display pictures, websites, contact details, photos, and so on.

One trainee teacher explains why he decided to use QR codes with his class:

"Basically, I wanted to use an infographic I'd found on the net to show the class but the image was too big to print off and even when pulled up on the computer screen/projector there was still lots of scrolling involved to look at all of it, so I tried giving it to the class as a URL and QR code, then they could get it on their phones and look through it at their own pace in the lesson and also refer back to it in class if I wanted to move the projector on to something else.

In the first class I tried it with, only about half of them had smart phones (or were willing to get them out) and not all of those had a barcode scanner; having a tinyURL to give out was a good back-up and those without a capable phone could just work in pairs with those who did. The class responded tentatively to it at first; I think for a few the idea of tarnishing their fun, personal item with a not-so-fun educational experience put them off! But just the novelty of being able to use their device did still capture the attention of most. The only other minor issues were that some students seemed keen to try it all out but reluctant to share their phone when working in a pair, but after a bit of encouragement they didn't mind, and on some phones with smaller screens it was tricky to read, even when zooming in.

The second class I tried it with had far more smart phones and more barcode scanners, and they really jumped at the chance to use their phones. This time I gave QR codes a bit more of an introduction, rather than just sticking it up on the board and asking for phones out, and many more students wanted it to try it then."

QR codes, despite some limitations, are relatively easy to use in the classroom and can be used in all sort of innovative ways. For example, a scavenger hunt – placing QR codes around the classroom which all lead to particular websites – is a great opportunity to liven up a group and encourage the learners to be responsible for their own learning.

Encouraging learners to use their own devices is great way of boosting motivation, encouraging interaction and collaboration, opening up opportunities for differentiation and adding variety to your lessons. It is worth reiterating, however, that technology is not a substitute for good teaching. Its use must be underpinned by pedagogy and it is the teacher who decides how it can best be used to facilitate learning.

TALKING POINT

'Please turn off your mobile phone!' How often have you seen or heard that? It is often included in a course code of conduct (see Chapter 1) that phones must be switched off during class time. They are seen as a distraction and there are doubts whether they really enhance learning. What is your view? Can you see any benefits to adopting a BYOD strategy?

ACCESSIBILITY OF ONLINE RESOURCES

In Chapter 3 we looked at the importance of inclusion and how it should be integrated into all aspects of our working practice. In order to ensure we are providing an inclusive environment for all our learners, we need to adhere to the principles of accessibility and usability.

✔ TASK 11.5

What do you consider to be the difference between usability and accessibility?

Usability refers to how easily an online resource can be used; whether it is clear and caters for different needs and interests. E-learning resources such as websites and apps are accessible if it is possible for everyone to use them irrespective of ability, including individuals with learning difficulties and the elderly. Resources should be customised to accommodate learners' particular needs; for example, the tool 'Podcastomatic' converts podcasts into speech for learners who are visually-impaired or struggle with reading. Other learners may welcome the opportunity to have resources sent to them in advance of the session so they do not feel left behind in the session. Another way of making 'reasonable adjustments' (see Chapter 1) to e-learning resources is to provide subtitles to videos to assist deaf or hard-of-hearing students and to ensure that the learning environment is not too noisy. Some learners may struggle to use a mouse and will need to navigate websites via a keyboard only. You will need to check whether it is possible for these individuals to interact with the resource by clicking on links or using drop-down menus. The needs of your learners need to be given special consideration when devising and selecting e-resources.

✔ TASK 11.6

What do you consider to be the difference between usability and accessibility?

You may have come up with a list similar to the following.

1. Some learners may lack the necessary skills to use ICT effectively. These learners will need access to training to allow them to locate and use resources effectively; a tutor presence is essential. Those in charge of delivering a distance or blended learning programme need to be fully confident and aware of their role in supporting learning. You cannot simply give learners access to ICT and expect them to get on with it. In line with a Vygotskian (1978) view of learning, teachers need to provide scaffolding to help learners with tasks and prevent them from becoming demotivated: 'good support can negate accessibility issues while poor support can add to them' (www.jisctechdis.ac.uk).

2. The language of the online resource. If it contains difficult language or a lot of jargon, it will be off-putting for some learners, particularly for second English language speakers. In addition, documents may be formatted in a way which makes them difficult for learners to navigate. Some VLEs are overly complex and cumbersome to use. It is necessary to ensure that all websites are up to date, content is categorised under clear headings and learners know how to access resources. The example opposite shows how resources are organised according to topic area, accessed via a simple click of the mouse.

Select a course topic by clicking on the icons below:

COURSE OVERVIEW	VOCABULARY	CLASSROOM MANAGEMENT	REFLECTIVE PRACTITIONER	RECEPTIVE SKILLS	LESSON PLANNING	STRESS
DRILLING	TEACHING GRAMMAR	CHECKING AND CLARIFYING MEANING	PHONEMIC SCRIPT	EMBEDDED ICT	LANGUAGE CLARIFICATION	CONNECTED SPEECH
DIFFERENTIATION	ROLE OF THE TEACHER IN PCET	ACTIVE LEARNING METHODS	ASSESSMENT PROCEDURES	ESOL AND CORE CURRICULUM	FUNCTIONAL SKILLS	SPEAKING
STYLE AND REGISTER	TEACHING LITERACY	SCHEMES OF WORK	WRITING	INTONATION	JOBS IN ESOL	PRACTICE ACTIVITIES

(With thanks to Newham College of Further Education for permission to reproduce here.)

3. The content of the online resource. You need to check this is appropriate and culturally-sensitive, including graphics and images, use of language, clarity of voice and accents. Lynch (2004, p, 42) argues that e-learning can be liberating for some learners and can 'promote a sense of equality by granting each participant an equal voice. Some learners may feel more at ease contributing to a discussion forum rather than responding to a teacher's questions under the scrutiny of their peers. However, learners have to be careful of the written word. The tone of a response is crucial to conveying an effective message; there are no non-verbal cues or paralinguistic features to help clarify a point. We are sure you have heard of individuals who have sent and posted derogatory texts and messages via social media. It is easy to hide behind the written word and for contributions to be misinterpreted.

4. Availability and performance of the technology. Learners will become very frustrated if it takes a long time to connect to a particular website. If they are using their own devices, there may be issues regarding bandwidth and connectively. It is always important to have a contingency plan rather than relying solely on technology.

5. Finally, be careful of presuming that learners will automatically know how to carry out a task. For example, some learners may not know how to do a crossword or navigate the web. Always check understanding first.

When designing and choosing online resources, it is essential to check potential barriers to accessibility. We all need to adhere to the principles of the Equality Act (see Chapter 1) and provide an inclusive learning environment for all learners; we want everyone to benefit from the learning experience.

TALKING POINT

If you are currently working in the further education and skills sector and have access to a VLE, it is worth checking out what tools it offers and how easy it is to circumnavigate. Check what support is available for those with learning disabilities and whether learners can contribute to blogs, forums or wikis.

ETHICS AND E-SAFETY

All kinds of people use ICT and it is not always easy to ensure that individuals interact with each other in an appropriate way. This not be intentional; for example, some people may get carried away with their own views when contributing to discussion forums and come across as confrontational. Others may lack the necessary language skills to convey their message effectively or they may simply disregard other people's viewpoints as they are incompatible with their own (Lynch, 2004). It is essential that learners value each other's opinions and abide by certain rules known as 'netiquette' to ensure that individuals are free to express themselves in a supportive environment without fear of reproach or recrimination.

✔ TASK 11.7

What ground rules can be set to ensure that learners interact with each other in an appropriate manner?

If you are currently working in the further education and skills sector, your institution may have a set of netiquette guidelines to which everyone should adhere so as to facilitate appropriate use of the internet. The following principles are based on those outlined in Virginia Shea's book, *Netiquette* (2004) (www.albion.com/netiquette/corerules.html).

1. Remember the human. We all need to bear in mind that we are conversing with individuals even if we can't see them. We need to be sensitive to each other's point of view. Messages can be misinterpreted and cause offence.

2. Adhere to the same standards of behaviour that you follow in real life. In other words, we should not act any differently in online interaction than when chatting face-to-face.

3. Know where you are in cyberspace. Rules may be different in different domains of cyberspace. For example, we will probably use different language on a social networking site when conversing with friends than when we send emails to other professionals in the sector.

4. Respect each other people's time and bandwidth. Sometimes learners expect immediate responses from the teacher but it is important to establish when you are likely to respond to messages. You are not at the beck and call of anybody!

5. Make yourself look good online. It is important to ensure that the content of what we write is clear and makes sense.

6. Share expert knowledge. Some learners are reluctant to express themselves because they fear they have nothing to say of any importance but need your support to be confident that their views are valuable.

7. Help keep flame wars under control. 'Flaming' means strongly held opinions, likely to provoke heated debates. This may not be a bad thing, but if individuals continually court controversy, the group dynamic may be jeopardised and it is not fair to those who are not involved and wish to engage in more friendly debates.

8. Respect each other people's privacy. Emails are private and should remain so.

9. Don't abuse your power. Everyone should be treated fairly regardless of status or ICT ability.

10. Be forgiving of other people's mistakes. If someone makes a factual, spelling or punctuation mistake, it is important that we do not act in a superior manner and correct the error in an insensitive way.

Individuals may make some social faux pas when interacting online but having a set of core rules will make learners aware of boundaries which should not be overstepped. They may be negotiated with learners and included in a code of conduct to formalise the process.

Plagiarism

As part of the assessment process, learners are often encouraged to research information online. However, it is important that if they refer to information from an online source, they need to reference it rather than passing it off as their own. Failure to acknowledge the source is known as plagiarism. Learners should also remember to cite the source if they have used images, graphs, diagrams and other third-party materials in their work. They should be made aware that there will be serious repercussions if they are found to be guilty of plagiarism. There are various plagiarism detection tools such as Turnitin which tutors can use if they suspect inconsistencies in learners' work. There is also no guarantee that the information on a website is correct; learners need to be wary of the quality of the information and consider how reliable it is likely to be (Hill, 2003).

Copyright

In Chapter 1 we looked at key legislation. One act to which all those working in the further education and skills sector must adhere is the Copyright, Designs and Patents Act, 1988: 'Everything on the Internet is copyrighted at the moment of its creation. Even if it doesn't carry a copyright symbol or statement, it is still the property of the creator and needs to be properly cited.' (Lynch, 2004, p. 181). In practice, this means reading the small print and seeing whether it is possible to make adjustments to a web page, make copies and share it with your learners without the permission of whoever created it. Learners should also be made aware of copyright policies. They are usually allowed to download material from a website under the concept of 'fair dealing' as long as this is for study purposes only and they acknowledge the source. For further guidance on copyright issues, refer to www.jisclegal/LegalAreas/CopyrightIPR.aspx

E-safety

One of the most important aspects to consider when integrating ICT in your teaching is e-safety; this is using technology in a safe and responsible way. More and more young adults are studying in the further education and skills sector and we have a responsibility to safeguard these learners as best we can.

✔ TASK 11.8

What are the potential risks and threats to learners' safety online?

It is important you are aware of your institution's policies on e-safety so that you can provide appropriate guidance for learners and enable them to develop strategies to protect themselves online. So what are the risks? These are sometimes labelled the four C's (Becta, 2009).

Content

Inappropriate or illegal content may be pornographic images or materials which could incite racial hatred, for example. In the past, organisations have blocked access to specific sites to try to minimise risks to individuals. However, this has not generally been found to be a successful strategy:

> "Organisations are finding that a blocking and banning approach, which merely limits exposure to risk, is not sustainable. Organisations need to focus on a model of empowerment; equipping learners with the skills and knowledge they need to use technology safely and responsibly and managing the risks, whenever and wherever they go online; and to promote safe and responsible behaviours in using technology at college, in the workplace, in the home and beyond." (Becta, 2009)

Learners need to recognise the need to keep their passwords secure, tighten up their privacy settings (Hockly et al., 2013) and be mindful of what they share online. If they post inappropriate photos of themselves online, for example, they may be putting themselves in jeopardy. They should also be aware of the fact that employers may search for information about prospective employees online (Clarke, 2011).

Contact

Again, learners need to be aware of safety guidelines. They may interact with people they don't know and it is important they are on the alert so that they recognise unwelcome or inappropriate contact such as online predators. As we saw in Chapter 1, young adults should follow the safeguarding procedures put in place in their institution if they feel uncomfortable with any online contact.

Conduct

As was mentioned in the previous sector on ethics, learners should follow an online code of conduct so that they can behave appropriately. However, some individuals may be victims of cyberbullies. Cyberbullying is using email, the web, mobile phones or other technological devices to intimidate, harass or threaten somebody. Institutions may have a 'panic button' on the intranet or VLE which learners press if they feel they are being bullied.

Commerce

Under no circumstances should learners reveal any financial details online to protect themselves from identity theft. They need to be wary of 'phishing' scams, carried out to fraudulently extract personal information, usually by email.

There are, of course, risks involved with using online technology but there should be strategies put in place to educate learners so that they can equip themselves with the skills to protect their digital selves.

TALKING POINT

Find out what your organisation's policies are in respect of e-safety. Are you aware of your own role in the process?

SUMMARY

In this chapter you have looked at the growing phenomenon of e-learning: how it can enhance learning and its limitations. Some common terminology used in e-teaching and the growing trend of learners using their own devices in the learning environment were mentioned. You examined the challenges of ensuring that e-learning resources are fit for purpose and accessible for all learners. Finally, you looked at the concept of ethics in e-learning: the need to adopt an ethical approach to using online resources and interacting online, adhering to safeguarding, copyright and data protection legislation. We need to ensure that the online environment is a safe and responsible place to learn.

REFERENCES AND FURTHER READING

Atwell, G. and Hughes, J. (2010) *Pedagogical Approaches to Using Technology for Learning*. London: Lifelong Learning UK.

Bates, A. W. (2005) *Technology, E-learning and Distance Education* (2nd edn). Abingdon: Routledge.

Bates, A. W. and Poole, G. (2003) *Effective Teaching with Technology in Higher Education: Foundations for Success*. San Francisco: Jossey-Bass.

Becta (2009) *Harnessing Technology, Safeguarding-Further Education and Skills Learners in a Digital World*. www.e-learningcentre.co.uk/wp-content/uploads/ht_safeguarding.pdf [accessed 4 July 2014].

Clarke, A. (2011) *How to Use Technology Effectively in Post-Compulsory Education*. Abingdon: Routledge.

Cowley, S. (2013) *The Seven Ts of Practical Differentiation*. Bristol: Sue Cowley Books Ltd.

Giles, J. and Yelland, A. (2010) *A Minimal Approach to the Minimum Core? An Investigation into How Well New Teachers are Supported to Integrate English, Maths and ICT into Their Teaching*. London: London Centre for Excellence in Teacher Training. www.loncett.org.uk/uploads/documents/doc_383.pdf [accessed 4 July 2014].

Hill, C. (2003) *Teaching Using Information and Learning Technology in Further Education*. Exeter: Learning Matters.

Hockly, N., Dudeney, G. and Pegrum, M. (2013) *Digital Literacies*. Harlow: Pearson.

JISC (2004) *Effective Practice with e-Learning: A Good Practice Guide in Designing for Learning*. Bristol: Higher Education Funding Council. www.jisc.ac.uk/media/documents/publications/effectivepracticeelearning.pdf [accessed 4 July 2014].

Lynch, M. M. (2004) Learning Online: A Guide to Success in the Virtual Classroom. Abingdon: Routledge.

Vgotsky, L. (1978) *Mind in Society: The Development of Highly Psychological Processes*. Cambridge, MA: Harvard University Press.

Websites

E-learning and using mobile devices
www.pontydysgu.org
www.shaunwilden.com

Flipped learning
www.edudemic.com/guides/flipped-classrooms-guide/
www.flippedlearning.org

Blogging
http://blogbasics.com/what-is-a-blog
www.blogger.com

Accessibility
www.bbc.co.uk/accessibility/best_practice/what_is.shtml

E-safety
www.e-language.wikispaces.com/digital-safety
http://archive.excellencegateway.org.uk/page.aspx?o=281841

Professionalism and continuing professional development

By the end of this chapter, the reader will have a better understanding of:

❯ aspects of professionalism

❯ continuing professional development (CPD)

PROFESSIONALISM

As we have seen, developing our professional skills then reflecting on how effective they are is important. In this sense, reflection and professionalism go hand in hand. We saw in Chapter 1 that the further education and skills sector is separate from the compulsory school one. Practitioners in our sector come from a vast range of different backgrounds. More often than not, they come with technical expertise, and knowledge and understanding of their particular vocational area such as hospitality and catering, plumbing or travel and tourism. Others have more traditional backgrounds and may teach on academic programmes such as GCSE and A Level courses. This is what makes it such a hugely rich and interesting source of learning. What we all have in common, though, is a desire to make a difference to the lives and aspirations of young people. Being experts in our subject specialist area in addition to holding a teaching qualification enables us to achieve this. This is called *dual professionalism*. Consider for a moment the notion of 'being a professional'. What does this mean to you?

✔ TASK 12.1

Read through the scenarios below. Do the teachers act professionally? What advice would you give them?

1. Shanaz's lesson starts at 4pm. When she arrives at 4.10, the learners are waiting for her at the door.
2. One of Amir's learners asks him a question he doesn't know the answer to. Amir says he will find out for the next lesson.
3. It's raining so Steve offers his 15-year-old female student a lift home.

4. Sarah feels she needs to brush up on her IT skills so seeks advice from her manager about training courses offered at her workplace.
5. George is an art and design teacher and regularly wears jeans to work.
6. Amal adds one of her students as a friend on Facebook.
7. Jestin tells the learners that the reason they haven't had their assessment back is because her colleague, Tom, hasn't marked them.

These are fairly thought-provoking scenarios. What's your personal opinion about each of them?

Scenario 1

You would be right to think that arriving late is unprofessional; Shanaz needs to set her learners a good example by being punctual.

Scenario 2

Sometimes, despite the best preparation, you may not know the answer to a question a learner asks. The main thing is not to panic – or to pretend that you do know. Amir does the right thing to say that he will find out for next time. A word of warning, though; if this happens to you, make sure you do the research and tell the learner the next time you see him/her. You can also suggest the learner does the research too and then you can compare notes next time.

Scenario 3

This is a tricky one. Steve obviously thinks he is helping the learner out. However, given the fact that he is the older male teacher of a younger female learner who is under the age of 18, he should not take the learner home. If he did, he may be open to any accusations the learner chose to throw at him.

Scenario 4

Sarah acts entirely appropriately in seeking advice and guidance about training opportunities from her manager. Hopefully, there is a course available at her workplace that she can attend.

Scenario 5

In the main, teachers should dress smartly and this means not wearing casual clothes in the classroom. However, given the subject matter that George teaches, his manager may agree that jeans are acceptable. If you find yourself in this situation and are not sure about the dress code, check with your manager or human resources department.

Scenario 6

Social networking is a part of most students' lives. Amal may think that accepting a friend request from her learner is perfectly innocent. However, in teaching there must be clear boundaries between the teacher and learners both in the classroom and beyond.

Scenario 7

This is not a good idea. Although it may not be your fault that the learners' work is late, it is not respectful to openly blame another colleague in front of the same students he or she will later have to teach. A better course of action is for Jestin and Tom to agree the deadlines so that they present a united front to the learners.

Being professional can mean different things to different people and it is for this reason that it is a hotly contested issue. To some, 'professional' means working in a field such as the medical or legal sectors – doctors and solicitors are examples of these. In each case, there is a body of knowledge and particular codes of practice. Professionalism also equally relates to those who work in the technical and vocational industries, whose practice is underpinned by shared skills and expertise, and ways of working. Within education, teachers have a code of professional practice and broadly similar value systems. We must remember that it is not only subject knowledge that learners gain from us. Every time we enter a classroom and engage with them, they are sensitive to the way in which we dress, the language we use and beliefs we hold. This is sometimes called the *hidden curriculum*. For this reason we must remember at all times that we are role models for our students.

What is appropriate behaviour for a professional teacher? Consider the following list:

⟩ Dress appropriately. Depending on your subject area, casual wear may be permitted. Ask your manager if you are not sure.
⟩ Be punctual. If you turn up late for your lessons, your students will learn that this behaviour is acceptable and copy it.
⟩ Maintain boundaries. Don't offer or accept lifts from students, exchange phone numbers or engage in social networking activities with them. This can send the wrong signals and behaviours can be easily misinterpreted.
⟩ Stay up to date with your subject specialism. Knowledge and ideas are not static. In order to teach what is current, you need to ensure you undertake professional development and training.
⟩ Work as part of a team. Your colleague may hold different beliefs to you but you need to respect these. If there is a problem, speak to your manager or another colleague about how to manage it.
⟩ Being professional is also closely linked to notions of good teaching and the routines of a good teacher. The following 'golden rules' will help you develop your professional identity.

Planning

⟩ Have a lesson plan with clear objectives
⟩ Factor in opportunities for functional skills development
⟩ Plan a variety of activities and skills work
⟩ Have a contingency plan in case things go wrong
⟩ Ensure each stage has an aim
⟩ Make sure that each stage follows on from the one before and is linked to the one after

Enabling

❱ Make the best use of the time you have available
❱ Use a mix of pair and group work along with individual and teacher-led work
❱ Personalise the learning so it is meaningful
❱ Communicate clearly and use language learners understand
❱ Praise appropriately
❱ Experiment with different teaching ideas

Assessing

❱ Link assessment methods appropriately to learning outcomes
❱ Build in recapping opportunities for different stages of the lesson
❱ Allow time for a plenary stage to recap on what the students have learned
❱ Ensure the assessment methods are varied
❱ Return work in a timely manner
❱ Ensure learners understand the feedback you provide

Evaluating

❱ Reflect on your lesson once it's finished
❱ Try to keep a log of what works well with your learners
❱ Ask your students how they like to learn
❱ Evaluate in different ways
❱ Action the areas that need improving
❱ Keep a record of your evaluations

Sticking to the menu above will ensure you develop good relationships with your learners, which are built on mutual trust and respect. The benefits you will reap from this are unquantifiable.

TALKING POINT

Think about your professional identity. What will be the key elements of this? For example, what kind of image will you project to your learners? What will you wear? How would you like to be perceived?

CONTINUING PROFESSIONAL DEVELOPMENT

What does continuing professional development (CPD) mean and why is it important? As teaching professionals we should maintain our CPD in two aspects: teaching and learning, and subject knowledge. As teachers, it is important for us to demonstrate our engagement with professional development so that we can stay abreast of developments in terms of what and how we teach, and keep up to date with teaching methodology.

✔ TASK 12.2

What CPD activities would you suggest for the practitioners below?

Imran has worked in a college of further education as a key skills lecturer for a number of years. The syllabus has changed and he is feeling unconfident about what to teach his students.

The learning provider where Sonia works has just changed its IT system and she would like to update her skills.

Njani is teaching a new topic to her Level 2 Accountancy class. She hasn't taught it before.

Ingrid has attended a seminar offered by a national training provider. She would like to share what she learned with her colleagues.

Simon has just started teaching at his local community centre after working for many years in the construction trade.

What activities would the practitioners benefit from? Imran could update his knowledge by liaising with the awarding body and reading through the new syllabus specifications. Sonia could book herself onto an IT training workshop at her institution. Njani could peer observe a colleague teaching the same topic to pick up some ideas. Ingrid could disseminate the information at a team meeting or write an article for her institution's intranet. Finally, Simon could work with a mentor to support him in the early stages of teaching; he could also enrol on to a teacher training course.

Of course, there are no right or wrong answers here. Often, what we do depends on the resources available – usually time and money. It is important, though, to recognise that CPD can be more or less formal. For example, going to a workshop which results in a certificate at the end is classed as 'formal'. On the other hand, discussing a lesson with a colleague in the staffroom is equally as valuable but does not result in a certificate – this is classed as 'informal'. Teachers engage with both.

Some of the ideas listed here will give you a useful starting point in regard to your professional development. Bear in mind that this is only a small sample of ideas – the list is by no means exhaustive.

❯ Enrol on to a teaching qualification. This could be a 'full' qualification such as the Certificate in Education (for those with vocational qualifications), PGCE (for graduates) or Diploma in Education and Training. It might be an induction qualification such as the Award in Education and Training. If you work with groups of learners supporting the learning, you could consider one of the Supporting Learning qualifications with an exam board such as City and Guilds. If you work as an assessor, it might be the Assessor or Verifier awards.

❯ Observe a colleague in the same team. Much can be learned from observing a colleague who teaches the same subject as you or the same learners as you in a different context. You can pick up useful tips and hints that you can 'borrow'. You might witness some practices that don't work; in this case, reflect on why.

❱ Take out a subscription to a professional journal or magazine. This will enable you to stay at the forefront of all the latest developments in your subject area. Ask your department to consider buying in a subscription so that the whole team can benefit.

❱ Do some research into an area of interest. This could be anything at all that you find worthwhile or useful. You might come across something on the internet or in a book that piques your interest. Follow it up as you might be able to use it in a lesson.

❱ Read a book, journal or magazine article and tell your colleagues about it. There can be nothing more relevant for professional development than chatting to a colleague, mentor, peer, manager or other critical friend about it. More often than not, you will benefit from the insights others have.

❱ Go to a team meeting. This is a really useful forum for exchanging ideas and sharing practice. Sometimes it can be the only time you get to engage with your colleagues.

❱ Attend a seminar or workshop. These can be a very useful way of gaining a lot of information on one particular area. You will meet other professionals with whom you can exchange ideas. You can also 'pick the brains' of the person delivering! You may be asked to cascade the information down to your colleagues. This means you will tell them about what you learned.

❱ Visit another learning provider that has the same teaching area as you. This will enable you to see how things are arranged and managed. You will be able to compare and contrast approaches with a view to customising them for your own area.

❱ Experiment with a new teaching idea. It is easy to go 'stale' if you always teach in the same way using the same ideas. Not only will you get bored, but your learners will too. Your new idea isn't guaranteed to work but the important thing is to try it and see. You might surprise yourself!

❱ Do some action research into an area of interest. Carrying out action research enables us to define and research an area of our teaching that we want to improve and develop. For example, if you want to improve your ability to manage your learners' behaviour, you might try different ways of grouping them. Doing this will allow you to see which configurations work best.

❱ Write an article for a trade or teaching journal. As professionals, it is helpful for us to share our practice. This can be on a small or large scale. One way of doing this is to write an article that you could have published on your college's intranet or in a newsletter.

❱ Get a Twitter, LinkedIn or other social network account. All of these are great sources of information and provide an excellent forum for the exchange of ideas.

❱ Team teach. Collaborating with a colleague over a lesson then delivering it is an excellent way of learning about teaching from a different perspective.

❱ Professional development centre. Go along to a session at your institution's professional development centre, if there is one. If there isn't, start one!

In all of the cases above, commitment to CPD will have an impact on our professional practice. Remember to reflect on what works effectively for you and why. It is also important to record the information about your activities somewhere so that they are easy to access should an external verifier or manager want to know about them. We are teachers but we are also learners – be responsive to change and development and you will reap the benefits.

REVISED SPECIALIST QUALIFICATIONS

The Lingfield Review (2012) identified that those teaching 'foundation skills' (see Chapter 10) in ESOL, literacy and numeracy, as well as those teaching students with learning difficulties or disabilities, require specialist teacher training. The reason for this was because these teachers were unlikely to be dual professionals. In other words, unlike chefs, for example, who will have gained experience in a professional kitchen, these practitioners will not have developed their skills in the same way and need to learn how to teach these subjects as 'specialist' activities.

The revised qualifications were launched in 2013. Two options are available. The first is an integrated specialist Diploma at Level 5 in one of the following areas:

- Teaching English (Literacy)
- Teaching English (ESOL)
- Teaching English (Literacy and ESOL)
- Teaching Mathematics (Numeracy)
- Teaching Disabled Learners

This qualification is suitable for those teaching these subjects who wish to gain more specialist knowledge and develop their teaching skills. The other option is to do the Level 5 Diploma in Education and Training, including a specialist pathway in one of the areas mentioned above. This qualification is suitable for those who may be teaching English (literacy and/or ESOL) or mathematics (numeracy) as part of their role or who may interested in learning about how to develop their knowledge of the subject.

TALKING POINT

As you have seen, CPD is a really important part of professional development. Which of the activities listed earlier appeal to you? Which are most useful? Why? Are there any that you don't find useful? Can you add to the list?

SUMMARY

In this chapter, you have looked at what it means to be a professional and how you can demonstrate professionalism. You also reviewed the routines of a good teacher. Finally, you looked at some different ways in which to engage with continuing professional development, taking into account specialist qualifications in ESOL, literacy, numeracy and teaching disabled learners.

REFERENCES AND FURTHER READING

Duckworth, V., Wood, J., Dickinson, J. and Bostock, J. (2010) *Successful Teaching Practice in the Lifelong Learning Sector*. Exeter: Learning Matters.

Roffey-Barentsen, J. and Malthouse, R. (2009) *Reflective Practice in the Lifelong Learning Sector*. Exeter: Learning Matters.

Tummons, J. (2010) *Becoming a Professional Tutor in the Lifelong Learning Sector* (2nd edn). Exeter: Learning Matters.

Wallace, S. (ed.) (2010) *The Lifelong Learning Sector Reflective Reader*. Exeter: Learning Matters.

Websites

www.et-foundation.co.uk (the Education and Training Foundation website: an organisation that leads on teaching and learning in the FE and skills sector)

www.157group.co.uk (the 157Group: an organisation that leads on policy and leadership strategy relating to the FE and skills sector)

www.aoc.co.uk (the Association of Colleges: an organisation that represents the interests of colleges in the FE and skills sector)

www.talent.ac.uk (provides information about employment, training and resources)

Practical teaching ideas and strategies

In this chapter, you will find a wide range of interesting and dynamic ways to motivate and engage your learners. Some of the activities require you to do some pre-lesson materials preparation but many of them don't. We recommend that you preserve the quality of the resources you prepare such as laminating the dominoes (activity 3) and snakes and ladders (activity 5) so that you can use them again with different groups of learners. There are many different uses for the activities and they can be used at various stages of the lesson. We have signposted at which stage we think the activity lends itself to most easily.

GENERAL

1. Pass the parcel

Procedure and purpose	The aim of this activity is to revise key jargon, formulae, calculations and so on. Key words, questions or sums are written on cards and placed in a bag. The learners sit in a circle and pass around the bag; the teacher controls the audio and stops this at regular intervals. When the music stops, the learner who has the bag pulls out a card and asks a question or defines a word. Whoever guesses correctly, keeps the card. The learner with the most cards is the winner.
Strengths	It is a good way of fostering a lively atmosphere and bringing out learners' competitive spirit. Learners have an opportunity to cement their knowledge. It is a useful diagnostic tool; you can assess understanding and deal with any difficulties the learners might have
Points for consideration	This activity can become very noisy so you need to be mindful of other teachers and learners. Some learners may find it childish. Explain the rationale for the activity and consider whether it is appropriate for the needs and interests of your group.
Stage of lesson	Good for reviewing key terms. Can be used at the start or end of a lesson.

2. Half a crossword

Procedure and purpose	Crosswords focusing on key terminology using an online tool are created (for example, www.eclipsecrossword.com); you do not need clues for this activity. The class is divided into two groups, A and B: one group is given half the crossword filled in; the other group has the other half. Without showing each other their papers, a learner from each group takes it in turns to give a definition of their words and the learner from the other group tries to guess it. At the end of the activity, the crossword should be complete.
Strengths	This is a good way of developing learners' functional skills: encouraging individuals to communicate effectively and listen carefully for information.

If learners are unsure of anything, they should ask for clarification. This will encourage learners to modify their output. |
| **Points for consideration** | The instructions for this activity are quite complex so it is a good idea to do a couple of examples with the learners first. Some learners may need support. To boost their confidence, ask learners in group A and in group B to work together first to pool their knowledge and think of definitions before explaining their words to a member of the other group. Give them ample time to prepare. |
| **Stage of lesson** | Good for assessing key terms either at the start or end of a lesson. |

3. Dominoes

Procedure and purpose	This is a useful way of checking learners have understood key concepts. It is essentially a way of matching words or visuals to definitions on cards; it is important not to place these on the same card. The learners are put in groups of three or four and the cards are handed out. One learner puts a card down and the other members of the group take it in turns to see if they can match a picture, word or definition to either side of the card. If they cannot do this, they hand over to the next person in the group. The winner is the person who gets rid of their cards first. You can create your own dominoes or use an online website such as www.toolsforeducators.com/dominoes/
Strengths	Fun.

An excellent way of reviewing previous work. |

Points for consideration	The instructions are quite complex so clear demonstrations are needed. Don't presume that all learners are familiar with dominos. It can be used in a more traditional way: to consolidate understanding of numbers.
Stage of lesson	Good for reviewing key terms. Can be used at the start or end of a lesson.

4. Reflection cubes

Procedure and purpose	Cubes are a great way of assessing learning and reviewing past learning. On each face is written a different prompt to which the learners should respond. Questions are written on each face or just question words such as 'who', 'what', 'when', 'how', 'where' and 'why'. The learners can then ask each other questions using the prompts.
Strengths	Fun and involving. They can be used in a variety of ways. They are a useful self-assessment tool.
Points for consideration	Different cubes can be rolled together to make combinations; this works well in a numeracy session, for example. You can also ask more generic questions such as 'What have you learned from today's session?'
Stage of the lesson	Good for assessing and reflecting on learning. Can be used at the start, middle or end of a lesson. The questions can be easily differentiated to make them simpler or more complex.

5. Snakes and ladders

Procedure and purpose	This is based on the children's board game but on some of the squares, the word 'card' is written. The learners work in groups. Each learner rolls a die and moves the numbers of places shown. If they land on a square with the word 'card', they pick up a card and have to answer the question written on it. If they get it wrong, they have to stay where they are and pick up another card. If they land on a snake's head, they automatically move down the snake. If they land at the bottom of a ladder, they proceed upwards. The person who reaches the 'finish' first is the winner.

Strengths	It is fun and gets the learners talking and thinking.
	It brings out learners' competitive spirit.
Points for consideration	It takes a while to prepare, although if you laminate the board you can use it with different groups.
	Some learners may find it childish. The rationale for the activity needs to be explained.
Stage of lesson	Good for assessing learning at the end of a lesson.

6. Questions in a bag

Procedure and purpose	Questions are written on slips of paper and placed in a bag. The learners stand in a circle and pull out a question. They ask their question to another learner; the other learners agree whether the question has been answered correctly. This is a way of consolidating knowledge.
Strengths	Quick and easy to prepare.
	It allows you to assess understanding.
	It gives learners an opportunity to consolidate their learning.
Points for consideration	Learners can write their own questions to assess each other's understanding.
	You might have to nominate the recipients of the questions to ensure that all learners are included.
Stage of lesson	Good for assessing learning at the end of a lesson.

7. Run for the question

| Procedure and purpose | This is a way of consolidating knowledge. Questions are written on slips of paper and placed at the front of the class. The learners are put in groups. One individual from each group comes up to the front, grabs a slip of paper and brings it back to the group. The learners try to work out the answer, write it down and bring it back to the front. If it is correct, they can take another slip. If not, they need to work out the answer again. The group with the most correct answers is the winner. |
| Strengths | Fun and lively. |

	It can be applied to different subject areas. It consolidates learning.
Points for consideration	Learners may not be able to work out the answer to a question; establish a rule at the beginning of the activity. For example, they can be given three attempts before being given another question to answer. The questions need to be easy to assess: closed questions work best.
Stage of the lesson	Good for increasing pace in the middle and assessing learning at the end of a lesson.

8. Five-point star

Procedure and purpose	This is a quick way of learners recalling key information from the session. They draw a five-point star and at each point they write down something they remember from the session. They then compare with their partner before feeding back to the whole group.
Strengths	Quick and simple to set up. A good way of encouraging learners to share ideas. It can be applied to different subject areas.
Points for consideration	Some of the learners might not be able to think of five key points so may need a little prompting.
Stage of the lesson	Good for assessing learning at the end of the lesson.

9. Back to the board

Procedure and purpose	This is a good way of assessing understanding and rounding off the lesson in a fun way. The class is divided into two groups. Two learners from each group sit on chairs away from the board so it is not visible. The teacher writes a word on the board and the other members of the group define the word without saying it. The person who shouts out the answer first gets a point for their group. The group with the most points wins.
Strengths	Fun and lively.

	It can be used in a variety of subject and vocational areas to revise key terminology.
Points for consideration	It can get quite chaotic and hard to keep score. You need to ensure that the learners in the group define the words rather than just shout out words (this tends to happen when they get excited). To help them, provide some sentence starters relevant to your subject area such as, 'This is a type of person who…' and 'This is something we use to…'.
Stage of the lesson	Good for assessing learning at the end of a lesson.

10. Bingo

Procedure and purpose	This activity does not only need to be used in numeracy lessons; it can be adapted for a variety of subject areas. The learners are provided with grids with images, words or numbers written on them. As they hear one of their items being called, they cross it off. When the learners have deleted all their items, they shout, 'Bingo!' To make this more challenging, learners could be provided with answers and need to listen out for the corresponding questions; for example, 'What is the chemical symbol for potassium?' An alternative is to provide questions and the learners listen out for the corresponding answer.
Strengths	Fun. A quick way to assess understanding.
Points for consideration	This activity takes a little time to prepare although learners can make bingo cards for each other.
Stage of the lesson	Good for reviewing learning during the lesson.

11. Place yourself on the line

Procedure and purpose	This is a way of encouraging learners to assess their understanding of a topic and for the teacher to plan accordingly. The learners stand on an imaginary line (the x axis) ranking their understanding of a topic: the left being poor and the right being excellent.
Strengths	Quick.

	It helps you to gain an overall impression of learners' understanding. It encourages learners to reflect on their learning.
Points for consideration	It is obviously very subjective: some learners are very confident in their ability whilst others find it difficult to identify their strengths.
Stage of the lesson	Good for self-assessment at the start of a lesson.

12. Find the answer

Procedure and purpose	This is a way of ensuring all the learners are included in the session. As the learners come into the lesson, give them an envelope or a slip of paper with something they have to do by the end of the session. This can be a question they need to be able to answer, a task they have to do or a key term they should be able to describe to the rest of the class.
Strengths	Tasks can be set with individual needs in mind. It encourages learner autonomy and participation.
Points for consideration	It is difficult to do this activity with a very large group as you will not be able to elicit feedback from every individual. You can adapt the activity by giving groups different tasks to do by the end of the lesson; this allows the learners to collaborate on mini-projects.
Stage of the lesson	Good for encouraging independent learning. The tasks can be easily differentiated according to individual ability.

13. Jeopardy

Procedure and purpose	This is a good way of assessing learning and encouraging learners to work together collaboratively. Organise the learners into teams and tell them to write context-related questions. Tell them they must know the answers to the questions they write. Set a time limit. Each group then swaps their questions around. Teams score points for correct answers.
Strengths	Fun. An interactive way to assess learning.

Points for consideration	It relies on learners being able to remember information from the previous lesson.
	It can take a long time for the groups to write questions. It is useful to set a time limit or restrict the numbe of questions the learners write.
	Groups work at different paces.
Stage of the lesson	Good for encouraging teamwork and collaborative learning. Can be used effectively at the start or end of a lesson.

14. Reconstruction (based on an idea from https://teachinghow2s.com)

Procedure and purpose	This is a good way of consolidating the learners' knowledge by asking them to produce what they remember from a session in a different format. The learners are split into groups; these can be assigned randomly or according to interest, ability, etc. They choose (or are provided with) different genres, such as a poem, a quiz or a mindmap, and are asked to record what they remember from the session in this format. They then present their ideas to the rest of the group.
Strengths	This activity lends itself to differentiation by task or resource. It can be applied to different subject and vocational areas.
Points for consideration	Some learners may feel uncomfortable writing a poem or song; if this is the case, they can choose a different format.
	Leave sufficient time for this activity: at least 20 minutes.
Stage of lesson	Good for assessing knowledge at the end of or during a lesson.

15. A different corner (based on an idea by Sue Cowley in The Seven T's of Practical Differentiation)

Procedure and purpose	This is a good way of differentiating via choice. The teacher places some topic headers in each corner of the room. The learners are asked to stand under the topic about which they would most like to find out. The learners are then given task sheets to complete on this topic before feeding back as a class.
Strengths	It encourages co-operative learning.
	It encourages learners to become responsible for their own learning.

Points for consideration	You might need to restrict the numbers in each group to avoid all learners moving to the same corner.
	Learners might choose the topic which they find easiest. You will need to make a decision about whether to let the learners choose their own groups or be assigned a group.
Stage of the lesson	Good for encouraging self-assessment and collaborative learning during a lesson.

16. Vocabulary/jargon bag

Procedure and purpose	This is a useful way of revising key vocabulary pertaining to a specific subject area. As the learners are introduced to new terminology, key words are recorded on slips of paper and placed in a bag (the teacher or individual learners can be responsible for doing this). These words can then be revised periodically in a number of ways. For example, the learners can test each other by defining the words orally or in a written exercise, they can categorise them according to how confident they feel using them or they can organise their words into groups, explaining their reasons for the different classifications.
Strengths	It is important to continually review learning.
	The vocabulary can be checked at any stage of the lesson.
	It lends itself to a variety of subject areas.
Points for consideration	If the learners are responsible for recording words, check that that the words have been written down correctly to avoid potential confusion later.
Stage of the lesson	Good for reviewing key terms at the start or end of a lesson.

17. Traffic lights

Procedure and purpose	This is a useful self-assessment tool. Learners are provided with green, red and amber (yellow/orange) cups or visuals of traffic lights, slips of coloured paper, or they simply write the name of the colour to show their understanding of the topic. Green means they have a good understanding of the topic, amber implies they have a solid understanding but may need some more guidance and red means they do not really understand the topic and need a lot more support.

Strengths	It encourages self-assessment.
	It allows the teacher to ascertain the general understanding of the group and to find out who needs more support.
	Learners can assess their understanding at any stage of the lesson: they can assess this at the beginning of the lesson and at the end (hopefully, there will have been some progress made!).
Points for consideration	If the learners are responsible for recording words, check that that the words have been written down correctly to avoid potential confusion later.
Stage of the lesson	Good for self-assessment at the start of a lesson.

18. Pelmanism

Procedure and purpose	This requires the learners to recall key information. It is a memory activity which requires learners to match pairs such as words and their definitions, visuals and their descriptions, beginnings and endings, questions and answers. If they turn over two matching pairs, they keep the cards; if not, they turn them face down and watch the other learners do the activity. They try to recall the information on each card and where it is placed. The individual with the most matching pairs is the winner.
Strengths	The activity encourages cooperative learning.
	Because the learners are likely to see, and possibly say, key information several times, they are more likely to remember it.
Points for consideration	It is repetitive and can become frustrating if the learners cannot remember where the matching pairs are. Ensure there are not too many cards for the learners to remember.
	The activity takes a little preparation time.
Stage of the lesson	Good for assessing learning during a lesson.

19. Pictionary

Procedure and purpose	This is a way of enabling learners to show their understanding of a concept through a visual representation. The learners are put into teams; the learners take it in turns to convey the meaning of a word on a card by drawing a picture. They are not allowed to speak as they draw. The rest of the group have to guess what the pictures represent. Whoever guesses first, gains a point. The team with the most points wins.
Strengths	Fun and lively. Pictorial representations can demonstrate a sound understanding of key terminology. Involving.
Points for consideration	Individuals who do not like drawing may not enjoy this activity. Reassure learners that they only have to produce a sketch rather than an artistic masterpiece.
Stage of the lesson	Good for reviewing learning at the start, middle or end of a lesson.

20. The magic five

Procedure and purpose	Individual learners write down five key points from the session. They compare what they have written with a partner and explain their choices. Together, they write a few sentences, summarising their learning, using the key words as guidance. They then relay this information to the rest of the group.
Strengths	This is a useful study skills activity, encouraging the learners to summarise key information. Learners can support each other.
Points for consideration	Summarising can be difficult for learners. They may find it difficult to condense information, noting the salient points of a session. If the learners' summaries are quite vague, ask individuals to clarify points.
Stage of the lesson	Good for summarising key learning points at the start of end of a lesson.

TEACHING WITH TECHNOLOGY

We would never claim to be experts on using ICT in our teaching but we have found the following websites/ideas useful in enabling and assessing learning.

21. Webquest

Procedure and purpose	A webquest is an activity which encourages learners to search different websites to find and make sense of information related to a specific topic. If the task is devised through Google forms, the teacher can see the learners' responses.
Strengths	Motivating. Clear and easy to follow. Learner-centred. It has a clear focus if the website addresses are provided. Learners can go at their own pace.
Points for consideration	A webquest can take a long time to complete. Avoid setting too many questions to avoid frustrating your learners. Ensure the task is clear so that the learners can see the rationale for the activity.
Stage of the lesson	Good for developing collaborative learning skills. Can be used at any stage of the lesson.

22. Animoto

www.animoto.com

Procedure and purpose	A slideshow tool which produces videos using photos, videoclips and songs.
Strengths	Visually appealing. It is a good way of leading into a topic; you can ask your learners to predict the subject. Learners can make their own videos quickly and easily.

Points for consideration	The free tool only allows you and your learners to use 30 seconds of video so sources need to be selected carefully.
	It is difficult to exploit. We find it works well as a lead-in into topics.
Stage of a lesson	Good for leading into a lesson.

23. Digital storytelling

www.storybird.com
www.toondoo.com
www.storyboardthat.com
www.dfilm.com
www.pixton.com/uk/

Procedure and purpose	This is a way of conveying information in an imaginative and visually appealing way by combining images, voice, videos and narrative.
Strengths	Interesting, engaging and a different way of sharing knowledge.
	It encourages active learning if the learners create their own stories.
	Literacy (reading and writing) is embedded.
Points for consideration	It can be difficult for learners to formulate their ideas succinctly. They are likely to need support.
	Ensure that you and the learners adhere to copyright law when using videos and images to enhance stories.
Stage of the lesson	Good for leading into or ending a lesson.

24. Online quiz

www.quizlet.com
www.classtools.net
www.proprofs.com

Procedure and purpose	Different test types can be created via online quizzes, such as multiple choice questions, true and false, cloze tests and matching exercises.

Strengths	Quizzes are a good way of revising previous weeks' work and closing activities. They add variety and are fun.
	They are an excellent self-study tool. Learners can work through them quickly and receive timely feedback.
	Learners can choose tests which are appropriate for their needs.
Points for consideration	Ensure that learners are familiar with the type of quiz set.
	Be wary of overusing quizzes. They are a simple way of closing a lesson but learning needs to be consolidated in other ways.
Stage of the lesson	Good for assessing learning. Can be used at any stage of the lesson.

25. Using Pinterest

www.pinterest.com

Procedure and purpose	An image-based social website where material is collated from other websites and pinned on an online board. It is a good opportunity for teachers to share resources with each other.
Strengths	You can pin examples of learners' work.
	It is collaborative tool. You can encourage learners to pin interesting material related to the project they're working on in class.
Points for consideration	Learners need to tighten up their privacy settings and be careful not to infringe copyright.
	Ensure that there is a clear rationale for using Pinterest with your learners.
Stage of the lesson	Good for sharing and collaborating with colleagues at any time.

Abbreviations

AfL	Assessment for Learning
APEL	Accreditation of Prior and Experiential Learning
BIS	Department for Business, Innovation and Skills
BTEC	Business and Technology Education Council
BYOD	Bring Your Own Device
BYOP	Bring Your Own Phone
BYOT	Bring Your Own Technology
COSHH	Control of Substances Hazardous to Health
CPD	Continuing Professional Development
DBS	Disclosure and Barring Service
E&D	Equality and Diversity
ESOL	English for Speakers of Other Languages
FE	Further Education
HE	Higher Education
ICT	Information and Communications Technology
IfL	Institute for Learning
ILP	Individual Learning Plan
ITE	Initial Teacher Education
IWB	Interactive Whiteboard
JCP	Jobcentre Plus
JISC	Joint Information Systems Committee
LLN	Literacy, Language and Numeracy
LLUK	Lifelong Learning UK
Moodle	Modular Object-Oriented Dynamic Learning Environment
NIACE	National Institute of Adult Continuing Education
NOCN	National Open College Network
NVQ	National Vocational Qualification
Ofqual	Office of Qualifications and Examination regulations
Ofsted	Office for Standards in Education, Children's Services and Skills
PDP	Personal Development Plan
PLP	Personal Learning Plan
QCF	Qualifications and Credit Framework
QR	Quick Response (Codes)
QTLS	Qualified Teacher Learning and Skills
SFA	Skills Funding Agency
SMART	Specific, Measurable, Achievement, Relevant and Time-bound
T&L	Teaching and Learning
URL	Uniform Resource Locater
VLE	Virtual Learning Environment

Glossary of terms

Accreditation of Prior and Experiential Learning (APEL)
The process of formally recognising skills and previous qualifications and experience which can be used to award credits and allow individuals to gain exemption from course modules.

ADHD
A condition of the brain which leads to hyperactivity and problems with concentration.

Aim
A broad statement of intent, describing a learning goal towards which learners should strive.

Andragogy
A theory of how adults learn.

Asperger's syndrome
A disability related to problems with developing relationships with others and communication.

Assessment for learning
Assessment of a learner's skills, knowledge or understanding which is used to move their learning forward.

Assessment of learning
Assessment of a learner's skills, knowledge or understanding which looks back on what they have achieved.

Asychronous delivery
The process of instruction whereby the facilitator and learners do not engage in the learning process at the same time.

Authenticity
A term used to describe the fact that the work produced by a learner belongs to him/her. Also used to describe the characteristic of a task given to a learner that they might be expected to undertake in a workplace situation.

Autism
A disability related to problems with social communication and language.

Behaviourism
A theory of learning which views learning as measurable changes in behaviour.

Behavioural objectives
These describe a change in behaviour that has resulted from learning taking place.

Blended learning
An approach which uses a combination of face-to-face teaching and learning online.

Blog
A kind of online journal where you can record your thoughts, comments and opinions.

Code of practice
A set of behaviours required of those working in an educational or employment setting, outlining how they should conduct themselves.

Constructivism
A theory of learning which focuses on the connections learners make between old and new information to make meaning.

Continuing professional development
The activities in which teachers and trainers engage to update their knowledge and skills.

Cyberbullying
Using email, the web, mobile phones or other technological devices to intimidate, threaten or harass someone.

Deep learning
Long-term learning that promotes higher-order thinking skills and encourages learners to be actively involved in the quest for meaning.

Diagnostic assessment
Assessment carried out to check the learners' knowledge and abilities and to allow the teacher to plan activities in accordance with the individuals' needs.

Didactic
A term which is used to describe teaching which is teacher-focused.

Differentiation
The process of matching the curriculum, learning and teaching methods and assessment to accommodate the needs of the individual learners.

Diversity
The process of valuing individuals and their differences in age, gender, academic background, sexuality, ethnicity, knowledge, skills and experience.

Dyslexia
A disability related to problems with information processing, memory recall and literacy.

E-learning
Using technology to enable learning.

Equality
The process of treating individuals fairly so they are protected against discrimination and have the same opportunity as everyone else to access education.

Evaluation
The process of reflecting on an event or situation with a view to improving it.

Experiential learning cycle
A cycle of learning that involves having an experience and reflecting on it with a view to doing things differently next time.

External verification
The process by which the elements of a course are checked by someone other than the programme team to ensure its quality.

Extrinsic motivation
Motivation which is external to the individual. This occurs as a result of factors such as promotion or rewards.

Fairness
A term used to describe an assessment which is free from bias of any kind.

Feedback
Information about the quality of a learner's work.

Flipped learning
An approach to learning which reverses the concept of a traditional classroom whereby learners view the presentation of material at home before applying their knowledge in class.

Formative assessment
Assessment which is takes place on an ongoing basis while the learner is on the programme of study.

Functional skills
Skills in English, mathematics and ICT which can be transferred to practical contexts.

Group profile
Information about learners' backgrounds, motivations for studying, ages, previous educational experiences and so on that teachers use to plan learning.

Group work
A teaching method used by the teacher which requires learners to work together in a group.

Ground rules
Rules drawn up by the teacher and/or learners which define acceptable standards of classroom behaviour.

Guided discovery
An approach to teaching which focuses on students discovering information for themselves using clues provided by the teacher.

Humanism
A theory of learner which puts the student's emotional and personal development at the heart of all learning.

Icebreaker
An activity carried out at the beginning of the course to enable learners to get to know each other and the facilitator, and ease them back into learning.

Inclusion
The process of including all learners in education irrespective of their differences, accommodating their needs and valuing their contributions.

Individual learning plan
A document which outlines an individual's learning targets and is reviewed on a regular basis to check progress is being made.

Induction
The settling-in period carried out at the beginning of a learning programme to make learners aware of the course components, introduce them to their peers and give them an opportunity to have their own queries answered.

Initial assessment
Assessment to gauge the starting points of learners and to determine any support needs they might have.

Internal verification
The process by which course work is checked by other members of the same team or department.

Intrinsic motivation
Motivation which is internal to the learner. This occurs because an individual is naturally motivated to learn and/or better themselves.

Ipsative assessment
A process of self-assessment by which a learner can progressively measure the development of their skills, knowledge and understanding.

Learning outcome
A specific statement which describes what a learner will be able to do by the end of a lesson.

Learning style
A student's preferred way of receiving information.

Lesson plan
A working document which describes the framework of a lesson.

Method
A strategy used by teachers to convey information to learners.

Microteaching
A short, scaled-down teaching session, designed for teachers or trainee teachers to develop their skills within a secure and supportive environment.

Mindmap
A diagram used to show ideas and information, and how these are connected to each other and a common theme.

Netiquette
A set of guidelines for interacting online.

Non-behavioural objectives
Broad statements of educational intent.

Peer assessment
Assessment that learners do of each other's work.

Personal development plan (see Individual Learning Plan)

Personal learning plan (see Individual Learning Plan)

Plagiarism
Copying or paraphrasing work without obtaining permission or acknowledging the source.

Podcast
A digital audio file which can be downloaded from the internet.

Quality assurance
The process of ensuring all the elements of a programme of study are up to the required exam board regulations.

Realia
Real-life objects and materials used in teaching, for example using real coins in a shopping scenario.

Reasonable adjustments
The process of making suitable adaptations to your practice to ensure no individual is disadvantaged and has equality of opportunity.

Record-keeping
The process of keeping and storing evidence of a course or a learner's course work.

Reflection
The process of thinking about one's work or performance after it has been completed.

Reliability
A term used to describe the consistency of markers' judgements about a learner's course work.

Risk assessment
A procedure carried out by employers or assessors/placement officers.

Safeguarding
The procedure of protecting and promoting the welfare of children and young people, and adults at risk.

Scheme of work
A document which outlines the prescribed structure and content of a course or learning programme.

S.M.A.R.T
Objectives that are specific, measurable, achievable, relevant and time-bound.

Standardisation
The process of ensuring that different markers' interpretations of a learner's work are to the same standard.

Student-centred approach
An approach to teaching which is led by learners working out information for themselves (compared with a teacher-centred approach)

Study skills
Approaches to help learners develop specific skills to help them become more effective in their learning, for example developing their note-taking skills and how to use academic referencing.

Sufficiency
A term used to describe the amount of evidence needed to make a judgement about a learner's skills, knowledge or understanding.

Summative assessment
Assessment that happens at the end of a programme of study.

Surface learning
Learning which is concerned with more basic aspects such as the recall of information or description of a process; it is unlikely to be retained in the memory for a long period of time.

Synchronous delivery
The process of instruction whereby the facilitator and learners are online at the same time but not in the same place.

Teacher-centred approach
An approach to teaching which is centered on the teacher. It can be compared with a student-centred approach).

Transparency
A term used to describe the fact that learners know the criteria by which they will be assessed.

Validity
A term used to describe the fact that an assessment measures what it is supposed to measure and nothing more.

Virtual learning environment
An online education platform which allows learners to access teaching and learning materials remotely, to upload assessments and to share ideas.

Vocational
Relating specifically to work or employment.

Web 2.0 technologies
Applications and websites which enable users to create and share information.

Wiki
A website which allows collaborators to amend content.

Appendices

APPENDIX A: MAPPING THE CONTENT OF EACH CHAPTER TO THE CRITERIA OF THE LEVEL 3 AWARD IN EDUCATION AND TRAINING

	Assessment criteria	Chapter number
UNIT 301: UNDERSTANDING ROLES, RESPONSIBILITIES AND RELATIONSHIPS IN EDUCATION AND TRAINING		
Learning outcome 1: Understand the teaching role and responsibilities in education and training		
1.1	Explain the teaching role and responsibilities in education and training	1
1.2	Summarise key aspects of legislation, regulatory requirements and codes of practice relating to own role and responsibilities	1
1.3	Explain ways to promote equality and value diversity	1
		3
		11
1.4	Explain why it is important to identify and meet individual learner needs	3
		4
		9
		11
Learning outcome 2: Understand ways to maintain a safe and supportive learning environment		
2.1	Explain ways to maintain a safe and supportive learning environment	1
		2
2.2	Explain why it is important to promote appropriate behaviour and respect for others.	1
		2
Learning outcome 3: Understand the relationships between teachers and other professionals in education and training		
3.1	Explain how the teaching role involves working with other professionals	1
		12
3.2	Explain the boundaries between the teaching role and other professional roles	1
		9
3.3	Describe points of referral to meet the individual needs of learners	1
		9

UNIT 302: UNDERSTANDING AND USING INCLUSIVE TEACHING AND LEARNING APPROACHES IN EDUCATION AND TRAINING		
Learning outcome 1: Understand inclusive teaching and learning approaches in education and training		
1.1	Describe features of inclusive teaching and learning	2
		3
		4
		8
1.2	Compare the strengths and limitations of teaching and learning approaches used in own area of specialism in relation to meeting individual learner needs	5
		6
1.3	Explain why it is important to provide opportunities for learners to develop their English, mathematics, ICT and wider skills	10
Learning outcome 2: Understand ways to create an inclusive teaching and learning environment		
2.1	Explain why it is important to create an inclusive teaching and learning environment	2
		3
		8
		11
2.2	Explain why it is important to select teaching and learning approaches, resources and assessment methods to meet individual learner needs	3
		4
		6
		11
2.3	Explain ways to engage and motivate learners	2
		4
		5
		8
2.4	Summarise ways to establish ground rules with learners	1
		2
		11
Learning outcome 3: Be able to plan inclusive teaching and learning		
3.1	Devise an inclusive teaching and learning plan	4
		8

3.2	Justify own selection of teaching and learning approaches, resources and assessment methods in relation to meeting individual learner needs	4
		6
		8

Learning outcome 4: Be able to deliver inclusive teaching and learning

4.1	Use teaching and learning approaches, resources and assessment methods to meet individual learner needs	3
		6
		8
		11
4.2	Communicate with learners in ways that meet their individual needs	2
		3
		8
4.3	Provide constructive feedback to learners to meet their individual needs	6

Learning outcome 5: Be able to evaluate the delivery of inclusive teaching and learning

5.1	Review the effectiveness of own delivery of inclusive teaching and learning	7
		8
5.2	Identify areas for improvement in own delivery of inclusive teaching and learning	7
		8

UNIT 303: FACILITATE LEARNING AND DEVELOPMENT FOR INDIVIDUALS

Learning outcome 1: Understand principles and practices of one-to- one learning and development

1.1	Explain purposes of one-to-one learning and development	9
1.2	Explain factors to be considered when facilitating learning and development to meet individual needs	3
		4
		9
1.3	Evaluate methods for facilitating learning and development to meet the needs of individuals	3
		7
		8
1.4	Explain how to manage risks and safeguard individuals when facilitating one-to-one learning and development	9
1.5	Explain how to overcome individual barriers to learning	2
		3

1.6	Explain how to monitor individual learner progress	3
		8
1.7	Explain how to adapt delivery to meet individual learner needs	3
		4
		8

Learning outcome 2: Be able to facilitate one-to-one learning and development

2.1	Clarify facilitation methods with individuals to meet their learning and/or development objectives	3
		8
2.2	Implement activities to meet learning and/or development objectives	2
		3
		8
2.3	Manage risks and safeguard learners participating in one-to-one learning and/or development	9
		11

Learning outcome 3: Be able to assist individual learners in applying new knowledge and skills in practical contexts

3.1	Develop opportunities for individuals to apply their new knowledge and learning in practical contexts	4
		8
		10
3.2	Explain benefits to individuals of applying new knowledge and skills	2
		7
		8
		10

Learning outcome 4: Be able to assist individual learners in reflecting on their learning and/or development

4.1	Explain benefits of self-evaluation to individuals	6
		7
		8
4.2	Review individual responses to one-to-one learning and/or development	3
		7
4.3	Assist individual learners to identify their future learning and/or development needs.	3

UNIT 304: FACILITATE LEARNING AND DEVELOPMENT IN GROUPS		
Learning outcome 1: Understand principles and practices of learning and development in groups		
1.1	Explain purposes of group learning and development	5
1.2	Explain why delivery of learning and development must reflect group dynamics	5
1.3	Evaluate methods for facilitating learning and development to meet the needs of groups	7 8 11
1.4	Explain how to manage risks and safeguard individuals when facilitating learning and development in groups	5
1.5	Explain how to overcome barriers to learning in groups	2
1.6	Explain how to monitor individual learner progress within group learning and development activities	3 4 5
1.7	Explain how to adapt delivery based on feedback from learners in groups	2 6
Learning outcome 2: Be able to facilitate learning and development in groups		
2.1	Clarify facilitation methods with group members to meet group and individual learning objectives	8
2.2	Implement learning and development activities to meet learning objectives	4 5 8
2.3	Manage risks to group and individual learning and development	5
Learning outcome 3: Be able to assist groups to apply new knowledge and skills in practical contexts		
3.1	Develop opportunities for individuals to apply new knowledge and skills in practical contexts	8 10
3.2	Provide feedback to improve the application of learning	6
Learning outcome 4: Be able to assist learners to reflect on their learning and development undertaken in groups		
4.1	Support self-evaluation by learners	7

4.2	Review individual responses to learning and development in groups	3
4.3	Assist learners to identify their future learning and development needs	4
		7
		3

UNIT 305: UNDERSTANDING ASSESSMENT IN EDUCATION AND TRAINING

Learning outcome 1: Understand types and methods of assessment used in education and training

1.1	Explain the purposes of types of assessment used in education and training	3
		6
1.2	Describe characteristics of different methods of assessment in education and training	6
		8
1.3	Compare the strengths and limitations of different assessment methods in relation to meeting individual learner needs	6
1.4	Explain how different assessment methods can be adapted to meet individual learner needs	6
		8

Learning outcome 2: Understand how to involve learners and others in the assessment process

2.1	Explain why it is important to involve learners and others in the assessment process	5
		6
		8
		11
2.3	Explain the role and use of peer and self assessment in the assessment process	6
		8
2.3	Identify sources of information that should be made available to learners and others involved in the assessment process	3
		6

Learning outcome 3: Understand the role and use of constructive feedback in the assessment process

3.1	Describe key features of constructive feedback	6
		8
3.2	Explain how constructive feedback contributes to the assessment process	6
3.3	Explain ways to give constructive feedback to learners	6

Learning outcome 4: Understand requirements for keeping records of assessment in education and training		
4.1	Explain the need to keep records of assessment of learning	6
4.2	Summarise the requirements for keeping records of assessment in an organisation	6
UNIT 306: UNDERSTANDING THE PRINCIPLES AND PRACTICES OF ASSESSMENT		
Learning outcome 1: Understand the principles and requirements of assessment		
1.1	Explain the function of assessment in learning and development	6 8
1.2	Define the key concepts and principles of assessment	6 8
1.3	Explain the responsibilities of the assessor	6 8
1.4	Identify the regulations and requirements relevant to assessment in own area of practice	6
Learning outcome 2: Understand different types of assessment method		
2.1	Compare the strengths and limitations of a range of assessment methods with reference to the needs of individual learners	6
Learning outcome 3: Understand how to plan assessment		
3.1	Summarise key factors to consider when planning assessment	6
3.2	Evaluate the benefits of using a holistic approach to assessment	3
3.3	Explain how to plan a holistic approach to assessment	3
3.4	Summarise the types of risks that may be involved in assessment in own area of responsibility	6
3.5	Explain how to minimise risks through the planning process	4
Learning outcome 4: Understand how to involve learners and others in assessment		
4.1	Explain the importance of involving the learner and others in the assessment process	3 6 8
4.2	Summarise types of information that should be made available to learners and others involved in the assessment process	3 6
4.3	Explain how peer and self-assessment can be used effectively to promote learner involvement and personal responsibility in the assessment of learning	3 7 8

4.4	Explain how assessment arrangements can be adapted to meet the needs of individual learners	1 3 6 9
Learning outcome 5: Understand how to make assessment decisions		
5.1	Explain how to judge whether evidence is: • sufficient • authentic • current	6
5.2	Explain how to ensure that assessment decisions are: • made against specified area • valid • reliable • fair	6
Learning outcome 6: Understand quality assurance of the assessment process		
6.1	Evaluate the importance of quality assurance in the assessment process	6
6.2	Summarise quality assurance and standardisation procedures in own area of practice	6
6.3	Summarise the procedures to follow when there are disputes concerning assessment in own area of practice	-
Learning outcome 7: Understand how to manage information relating to assessment		
7.1	Explain the importance of following procedures for the management of information relating to assessment	6
7.2	Explain how feedback and questioning contribute to the assessment process	4 5 6 8
Learning outcome 8: Understand the legal and good practice requirements in relation to assessment		
8.1	Explain the legal issues, policies and procedures relevant to assessment, including those for confidentiality, health, safety and welfare	1 6
8.2	Explain the contribution that technology can make to the assessment process	11
8.3	Evaluate requirements for equality and diversity and, where appropriate, bilingualism in relation to assessment	3 6
8.4	Explain the value of reflective practice and continuing professional development in the assessment process	7

APPENDIX B: THE 2014 PROFESSIONAL STANDARDS

Professional values and attributes
Develop your own judgement of what works and does not work in your teaching and training

1   Reflect on what works best in your teaching and learning to meet the diverse needs of learners
2   Evaluate and challenge your practice, values and beliefs
3   Inspire, motivate and raise aspirations of learners through your enthusiasm and knowledge
4   Be creative and innovative in selecting and adapting strategies to help learners to learn
5   Value and promote social and cultural diversity, equality of opportunity and inclusion
6   Build positive and collaborative relationships with colleagues and learners

Professional knowledge and understanding
Develop deep and critically informed knowledge and understanding in theory and practice

7   Maintain and update knowledge of your subject and/or vocational area
8   Maintain and update your knowledge of educational research to develop evidence-based practice
9   Apply theoretical understanding of effective practice in teaching, learning and assessment drawing on research and other evidence
10 Evaluate your practice with others and assess its impact on learning
11 Manage and promote positive learner behaviour
12 Understand the teaching and professional role and your responsibilities

Professional skills
Develop your expertise and skills to ensure the best outcomes for learners

13 Motivate and inspire learners to promote achievement and develop their skills to enable progression
14 Plan and deliver effective learning programmes for diverse groups or individuals in a safe and inclusive environment
15 Promote the benefits of technology and support learners in its use
16 Address the mathematics and English needs of learners and work creatively to overcome individual barriers to learning
17 Enable learners to share responsibility for their own learning and assessment, setting goals that stretch and challenge
18 Apply appropriate and fair methods of assessment and provide constructive and timely feedback to support progression and achievement
19 Maintain and update your teaching and training expertise and vocational skills through collaboration with employers
20 Contribute to organisational development and quality improvement through collaboration with others

Guidance on how to use these standards can be found at
www.et-foundation.co.uk/supporting/programmes/professional-standards

APPENDIX C: EXAMPLE OF A SESSION PLAN TO BE USED IN MICROTEACHING

This form may be used for Assignment 302.

Teacher: **Location:**   **Date:**

Topic: **Start Time:**   **End Time :**

Aim:

Timing	Learner activities	Teacher activities	Resources	Assessment

Pre-delivery – explain how your choices of teaching and learning approaches, resources and assessment methods meet individual needs.

APPENDIX D: PREPARATORY TASK FOR MICROTEACHING

Topic or skill: you may have more than one at this stage (choose a familiar topic, not too complex and practical if you are presenting a skill)

Learning outcome(s) (What do you want the learners to be able to do by the end of the session?)

Consider what resources and materials you may need to use to support the delivery (Are you going to bring in 'real' objects? Will you need to use a different learning environment to accommodate the materials? How much can be prepared beforehand? Are there any health and safety considerations? What do you think your learners will enjoy doing? How can you include everyone?)

Consider what tasks/activities you will use to ensure that there is evidence of learning. (For example, short questions, sticky note evaluation, sharing ideas and feeding back, self- and peer assessment, mini whiteboards)

APPENDIX E: AN EXAMPLE OF HOW YOU CAN STRUCTURE YOUR RATIONALE

Rationale for the selection of teaching and learning approaches, resources and assessment methods

Training and learning approaches	
Resources	
Assessments	
Communication	
Feedback to learners	

APPENDIX F: SUMMATIVE PROFILE AND ACTION PLAN

My overall development and strengths as a result of attending this programme:

Personal statement: Where I am now, the subject I wish to deliver, and what I wish to do in the future:

Action plan: What I intend to do now to help me gain a teaching/training position or progress with my teaching/training career:

Name: Date:

Signature:

Index